LLEWELLYN'S
2001
MAGICAL
ALMANAC

FEATURING

Ayla, Bernyce Barlow, Elizabeth Barrette, Chas S. Clifton, Estelle Daniels, Lilith Dorsey, Sylvania Dragistur, Nuala Drago, Ellen Dugan, Gerina Dunwich, Marguerite Elsbeth, Breid Foxsong, Mario Furtado, Lily Gardner, Jenny Gibbons, John Michael Greer, Raven Grimassi, David Harrington, Ellen Evert Hopman, Kenneth Johnson, Kirin Lee, Edain McCoy, Ann Moura, M. Macha NightMare, Diana Olsen, Diana L. Paxson, Steven Posch, Silver RavenWolf, deTraci Regula, Janina Renée, Sedwin, Shadow-Cat, Cerridwen Iris Shea, Jami Shoemaker, Maria Kay Simms, Lynne Sturtevant, Paul Tuitéan, Clare Vaughn, Carly Wall, and Jim Weaver

LLEWELLYN'S 2001 MAGICAL ALMANAC

Editor/Designer:	Michael Fallon
Black & White Cover Illustration:	Merle S. Insinga
Color Application to Cover Artwork:	Lisa Novak
Calendar Pages Design:	Andrea Neff
Calendar Pages Illustrations:	Carrie Westfall
Illustrations, pages: 50, 51, 87-8, 91-2, 96-7, 100-1, 106-7, 136, 139-40, 143, 144, 213, 227-9, 231-2, 238-9, 280, 286, 302-3, 310, 311, 314-5, 318-9, 320-1, 333-5, 337-8, 340, 345-7, 349	Carrie Westfall
Clip Art Illustrations:	Dover Publications

Special thanks to Amber Wolfe for the use of daily color and incense correspondences. For more detailed information, please see *Personal Alchemy* by Amber Wolfe.

Moon sign and phase data computed by Astro Communications Services (ACS).

Llewellyn Publications
Dept. 963-6
P.O. Box 64383
St. Paul, MN 55164-0838

ABOUT THE AUTHORS

AYLA is a solitary witch and mom whose interests include crystals, aromatherapy, frame drumming, reading, and scrapbooks. She loves writing poems and "Goddess-cooking," and is a loyal contributor to environmental and animal safety organizations. She has had poems and articles published in *Circle Magazine* and in Llewellyn's *Magical Almanac*. She lives happily and magically in New Hampshire with her family and adopted black cat, Mr. B.

BERNYCE BARLOW is author of Llewellyn's *Sacred Sites of the West* and has been a contributer to Llewellyn's almanacs since 1995. She is a researcher and speaker, and she leads sacred site seminars throughout the U.S. She is most well-known for her magical tools of enlightment that come from the Acme toy company, and she swears that her cartoon totems are real!

ELIZABETH BARRETTE is a regular contributor to *SageWoman, Pan-Gaia, Circle Network News, PagaNet News, LunaSol,* and *Green Egg*. Much of her involvement with the Pagan community takes place online, and she has helped build networking resources such as the Pagan Leaders Mailing List. Visit her website at http://worthlink. net~ysabet/index.html.

CHAS S. CLIFTON edited Llewellyn's *Witchcraft Today* series of books, and he collaborated with Evan John Jones in writing *Sacred Mask, Sacred Dance* (Llewellyn, 1997). He has published several articles in *Fate* magazine over the years. He lives in southern Colorado.

REVEREND ESTELLE DANIELS is a Pagan Minister and member of the Wiccan Church of Minnesota. She is also a professional part-time astrologer since 1972 and author of *Astrologickal Magick* (Weiser, 1995), as well as a regular contributor to the Llewellyn annuals. She is coauthor with Rev. Paul Tuitean of *Pocket Guide to Wicca* (Crossing Press, 1998), and she has been active in the Pagan Community since 1989. She often gives workshops, and is ever eager to talk about astrology or other Wiccan and Pagan topics.

REVEREND LILITH DORSEY comes from many different magical traditions, including Voodoo, Celtic, and Native American spirituality. Her traditional education focused on plant science, anthroplogy, and fine art at the University of Rhode Island, New York University, and the University of London, and her magical training includes empirical research in New Orleans, Brooklyn, and other centers of African-American religious culture. Lilith Dorsey has been practicing magic successfully over the past thirteen years for patrons of her business, Branwen's Pantry, and is editor and publisher of *Oshun African Magickal Quarterly,* as well as a staff writer for the *Rhode Island Minority Times.*

SYLVANIA DRAGISTUR is a solitary Canadian Witch who loves reading, writing, astrology, cycling, camping, playing, and listening to music, dancing, and meeting new people, especially on the internet. She is currently studying environmental policy and sociology, and she plans to use this education to pursue a career in environmental conservation. This is her first publication ever.

NUALA DRAGO is an author, musician, folklorist, and solitary Wiccan. She has been a lifelong student of ancient Celtic culture and speaks Irish Gaelic. She enjoys traditional Celtic music and collects ancient recipes for food and folk remedies. She is also passionate about animal rights.

ELLEN DUGAN is a practicing Witch and a psychic-clairvoyant. She received Master Gardener status in the spring of 2000. Ellen is a garden designer, and she teaches gardening classes in her community. She is currently working on a "Garden Witchery" book.

GERINA DUNWICH is a Wiccan High Priestess, professional astrologer, and author of numerous books, including *Wicca Craft* (Carol, 1991), *The Wicca Spellbook* (Citadel Press, 1994), *Candlelight Spells* (Citadel Press, 1988), *A Wiccan's Guide to Prophecy and Divination* (Carol, 1997), *Everyday Wicca* (Carol, 1997), and *Wicca A to Z* (Carol, 1997).

MARGUERITE ELSBETH (also known as Senihele and Sparrow Hawk) is an hereditary Sicilian strega and part Lenni Lenape (Delaware) Indian. She is a professional tarot reader, astrologer, and practitioner of Nativism (American Indian healing). She has published numerous articles in Llewellyn's annuals, is the author of the Llewellyn books *Crystal Medicine; The Grail Castle: Male Myths and Mysteries in the Celtic Tradition;* and *The Silver Wheel: Women's Myths and Mysteries in the Celtic Tradition* (the latter two with Kenneth Johnson). She currently resides in the Southwest.

BREID FOXSONG is a British Wiccan who has been practicing for more than twenty years. She is the former editor of *Sacred Hart Magazine* and has had articles published in many magazines ranging from *Green Egg* to *Craft/Crafts*. She is active in her community, hosting open circles and introductory classes in Wicca.

MARIO FURTADO has been a practicing Witch for over eight years, and has a passion for herbalism, oils, and crafts. He enjoys being a father and husband and sharing the beauty and magic of the Goddess with his family. He has been published in *Circle Network News, Silver Chalice, Paganet News,* and other periodicals.

LILY GARDNER is a lifelong student of folklore and mythology and a priestess in the Blue Moon coven in Portland, Oregon. She is working on a collection of solstice tales and a book about gratitude.

JENNY GIBBONS has an M.A. in Medieval History and minored in the history of the Witchcraft trials. A solitary Witch, her essays and reviews have appeared in *Pan-Gaia, Reclaiming Quarterly, Green Egg, Enchante,* and the *Pomegranate*.

JOHN MICHAEL GREER has been a student of the Western esoteric tradition since 1975 and teaches Cabalistic magic in the Golden Dawn tradition. He is presently an active member of five fraternal and two magical lodges. He is the author of the Llewellyn books *Inside a Magical Lodge; Earth Divination, Earth Magic; Paths of Wisdom: The Magical Cabala in the Western Tradition;* and *Natural Magic*.

RAVEN GRIMASSI is a hereditary Italian Witch practicing a family tradition of Stregheria. He is also an Initiate of Pictish-Gaelic Wicca, Gardnerian Wicca, and Brittic Witchcraft. Raven is the author of the Llewellyn books *Italian Witchcraft, The Wiccan Mysteries, Wiccan Magick,* and *Hereditary Witchcraft.*

DAVID HARRINGTON has been a chronicler of the magical arts for the past fifteen years. He is also coauthor, with Scott Cunningham, of the Llewellyn books *The Magical Household* and *Spellcrafts.* He is also the coauthor with deTraci Regula of *Whispers of the Moon* (Llewellyn, 1996).

ELLEN EVERT HOPMAN is the author of *Tree Medicine, Tree Magic* (Phoenix, 1991), *A Druid's Herbal for the Sacred Earth Year* (Destiny, 1995), *People of the Earth: New Pagans Speak Out* (Destiny, 1996), and the videos *Gifts from the Healing Earth* and *Pagans* (EFP Services). She can be contacted through her website at: http://www.neopagan.net/WillowsGrove/Index.html.

KENNETH JOHNSON obtained his degree in the study of comparative religions. He has been a practitioner of astrology since 1974 and is the author of six books. Some of them are *Mythic Astrology: Archetypal Powers in the Horoscope* (Llewellyn, 1993); *Jaguar Wisdom: An Introduction to the Mayan Calendar* (Llewellyn, 1967); *Slavic Sorcery* (Llewellyn, 1998); and *Witchcraft and the Shamanic Journey* (Llewellyn, 1998).

KIRIN LEE is a graphic designer and a science fiction writer. She is the managing editor of a rock music magazine and coeditor of the sci-fi fanzine *Starship Earth.* She is present working on a Pagan book and a young adult novel.

EDAIN MCCOY has been a Witch since 1981. She has studied many magical traditions, including Celtic, Appalachian, and Curanderismo. Today she is an elder in the Wittan Irish Pagan Tradition and is a priestess of Brighid. Edain is listed in *Who's Who Among American Authors* and is the author of the Llewellyn books

Witta, A Witch's Guide to Faery Folk, The Sabbats, How to Do Automatic Writing, Celtic Myth and Magick, Mountain Magick, Lady of the Night, Inside a Witch's Coven, Making Magick, Celtic Women's Spirituality, Astral Projection for Beginners, and *Bewitchments.*

ANN MOURA (AOUMIEL) was raised in a family tradition of Green Witchcraft, which she has passed on to her children. She has been a solitary Witch for over thirty-five years, and she holds a bachelor's and master's degree in history. She is the author of the Llewellyn books *Dancing Shadows: The Roots of Western Religious Beliefs; Green Witchcraft; Green Witchcraft II: Balancing Light and Shadow;* and *Green Witchcraft III: The Manual.* She has recently completed a work on the historical roots of Witchcraft.

M. MACHA NIGHTMARE is a writer, Pagan organizer, priestess, and Witch, long active in the San Francisco area. Cocreator with Starhawk of the *Pagan Book of Living and Dying* (HarperSanFrancisco, 1997), she has been moderator, speaker, and presenter at festivals, stores, colleges, and radio and TV stations throughout the U.S. and Canada. Her work has appeared in *Reclaiming Quarterly, PanGaia, Green Egg, The Pomegranate,* and other publications. If you are interested in having Macha teach in your area, contact her at cheiron@earthlink.net.

DIANA OLSEN is a second degree Wiccan priestess in her tradition. She is a recent college graduate who works full time and lives in a rural part of Minnesota with her husband. She is an esoteric generalist who writes, researches, and reads about ways to use ritual to improve quality of life. For more information about her, visit her web page, *Medea's Chariot,* at http://NEXUS. mnic.net~rajchd.

DIANA L. PAXSON is a consecrated priestess of the Fellowship of the Spiral Path in Berkeley, California, and an elder of the Covenant of the Goddess and the Ring of Troth. She currently serves as steerswoman of the Troth, and edits its journal, *Idunna.* She has pioneered the recovery of "high seat" seidh, the oracular tradition

of ancient Scandinavia, and has taught workshops in this around the U.S. and Europe. She is the author of numerous mythic short stories and novels featuring the Old Religion, including, most recently, a four-part Arthurian novel called *The Book of the Sword* (Avon Eos, 1999). She is also a regular contributor to *SageWoman* and *PanGaia magazines.*

STEVEN POSCH read Robert Graves' monumental book *The White Goddess* at thirteen, and it changed his life. More than twenty years ago, he came to the Twin Cities in Minnesota in search of Pagan-istan, and, apart from brief stays in Britain and the Middle East, he has lived there ever since, playing a role in the Midwest's largest Pagan community. A semitist, heortologist, and storyteller, Steve is the founding member of Prodea and of the Covenant of the God-dess' Northern Dawn Council. His writings have appeared in many publications, including: *Green Egg, Mezlim, Circle Network News, The Witchtower,* and *The James White Review.* He is coauthor of several books and has a folktale collection coming out in 2001.

SILVER RAVENWOLF is the author of over thirteen nonfiction how-to and fictional books relating to the application of the magical sci-ences and religion. Silver is the Clan Head of the Black Forest Fam-ily, a Euro-Wiccan organization that currently has eighteen covens in thirteen states. Her primary interests are divinatory tools, astrol-ogy, hypnotherapy, and getting through life in a positive and pro-ductive way. She is also a member of the Divine Circle of the Sacred Grove, a Druid organization based in Arizona. To read about Silver, the Black Forest Clan, her touring schedule, upcoming events, books, and online organization, the Wiccan/Pagan Press Alliance, please visit: http://www.silverravenwolf.com.

DETRACI REGULA is author of the Llewellyn book *The Mysteries of Isis* and coauthor of *Whispers of the Moon,* a biography of Scott Cunningham.

JANINA RENÉE is the author of the Llewellyn books *Tarot Spells* and *Playful Magick.* She lives in farm country, where daily life is full of opportunities to make community with the animal, vegetable,

and mineral worlds. One of Janina's main occupations is creating simple ritual practices that cultivate magical habits of mind.

SEDWIN is an artist and explorer of ancient Goddess spirituality. She has created and teaches a "Speaking the Language of the Goddess" workshop, and writes "The Wheel of the Year" column in *The Light Network Newsletter.* Sedwin enjoys the magic of gardening, cooking, and shamanic work with friends.

SHADOWCAT is a Priestess and Witch in the American Celtic tradition of Lady Sheba, but she prefers solitary work. By day, she spends her time acquiring new manuscripts for Llewellyn. During her free time she fusses over her five feline companions. She is known to her friends and co-workers as the Scary Fondue Lady, and the question of how many fondue sets are in her collection is a great mystery that surrounds her. ShadowCat keeps her secrets.

CERRIDWEN IRIS SHEA is an urban Witch, writer, tarot reader, and theater professional whose plays have been produced throughout the world. When not writing or playing with her cats, she is busy concocting new spells in the kitchen, or attending horse races out at the track.

JAMI SHOEMAKER has been practicing Witchcraft for nearly twenty years, and was initiated as a priestess in the Rowan Tree Church in 1992. She has taught a variety of Craft-related subjects, and worked to help educate her community about the Craft. She has a degree in vocal music, a background in theater and dance, and has always enjoyed writing. She is a publicist for Llewellyn Worldwide, and is pursuing her love of the arts.

MARIA KAY SIMMS, astrologer and Wiccan high priestess, is the author of several books, including *The Witch's Circle* (Llewellyn, 1996) and *Your Magical Child* (ACS, 1994). She is chair of the National Council for Geocosmic Research (NCGR), a professional astrologers' organization, and she holds ministerial credentials from Covenant of the Goddess. She is certified as a professional

consulting astrologer, and for several years she has been listed in *Who's Who in America* and *Who's Who of American Women.*

LYNNE STURTEVANT is a freelance writer specializing in mythology, fairy tales, legends, and folklore. She is also an accomplished craftswoman and an avid collector of folk art. She has a bachelor's degree in philosophy and lives in Virginia with her husband.

REVEREND PAUL TUITÉAN is a Pagan minister and is a founder of the Wiccan Church of Minnesota and the Pagan safety organization the Guardians of the Fourth Face. He has been featured in an article on Pagan safety in the book *People of the Earth: The New Pagans Speak Out* (Destiny, 1996), and is coauthor with Estelle Daniels of the *Pocket Guide to Wicca* and *The Rune Book,* both published by Crossing Press. He also teaches advanced magic, body movement, ballroom dance, and personal safety. He has been active in the Pagan community since 1981 and travels to festivals across the U.S.

CLARE VAUGHN has been studying the Western mystery tradition for more than twenty years. She is also a practitioner of Druidry. Working with elemental beings is her favorite magical activity.

CARLY WALL is the author of *Flower Secrets Revealed: Using Flowers to Heal, Beautify and Energize Your Life!* (ARE Press, 1993), *Naturally Healing Herbs* (Sterling, 1996), and *The Little Encyclopedia of Olde Thyme Home Remedies* (Sterling, 2000). A regular contributor to Llewellyn's annuals for the last seven years, she holds a certificate in aromatherapy and lives on a farm with her husband and cat.

JIM WEAVER is a writer and collector of American folk art. Working in his herb and flower gardens helps him stay close to nature while celebrating the changing seasons.

TABLE OF CONTENTS

Great Father, Great Mother

By Sylvania Dragistur

Great Father,
Bright Sun that shines upon me,
I can feel your warmth, your protection.
When I look at my shadow I know
it is a reminder
that you are behind me always.
From your elements of air and fire
I learn expression and passion.
You teach me the difference between assertion
and domination.

Great Mother,
Bright Moon that shines upon me,
I can feel your comfort and compassion.
When I look at your eye in the sky I know
it is a reminder
that you watch over me even as I sleep.
From your elements of water and earth
I learn love and strength.
You teach me the difference between understanding
and pity.

I honor both my Mother and Father
because I am aware that I am not whole
when one of them is missing.

By the elements of air, fire, water, and earth,
I express my passion, love, and strength
to my Father and my Mother.
To my true parents.

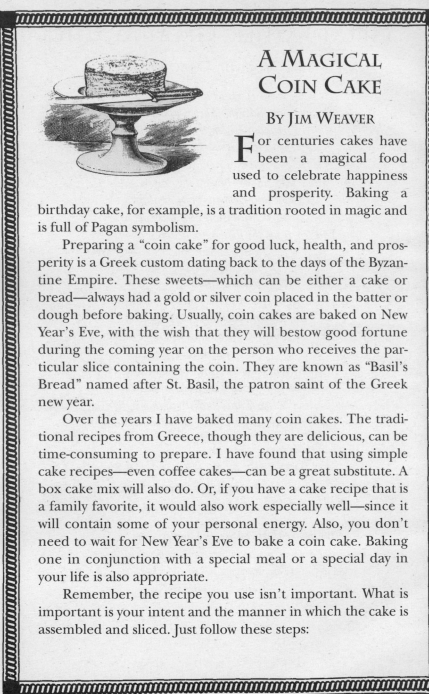

A MAGICAL COIN CAKE

By Jim Weaver

For centuries cakes have been a magical food used to celebrate happiness and prosperity. Baking a birthday cake, for example, is a tradition rooted in magic and is full of Pagan symbolism.

Preparing a "coin cake" for good luck, health, and prosperity is a Greek custom dating back to the days of the Byzantine Empire. These sweets—which can be either a cake or bread—always had a gold or silver coin placed in the batter or dough before baking. Usually, coin cakes are baked on New Year's Eve, with the wish that they will bestow good fortune during the coming year on the person who receives the particular slice containing the coin. They are known as "Basil's Bread" named after St. Basil, the patron saint of the Greek new year.

Over the years I have baked many coin cakes. The traditional recipes from Greece, though they are delicious, can be time-consuming to prepare. I have found that using simple cake recipes—even coffee cakes—can be a great substitute. A box cake mix will also do. Or, if you have a cake recipe that is a family favorite, it would also work especially well—since it will contain some of your personal energy. Also, you don't need to wait for New Year's Eve to bake a coin cake. Baking one in conjunction with a special meal or a special day in your life is also appropriate.

Remember, the recipe you use isn't important. What is important is your intent and the manner in which the cake is assembled and sliced. Just follow these steps:

Once you've decided on a cake recipe, thoroughly blend all ingredients according to the directions. Take a quarter and wash it in warm soapy water, then dry it and wrap it in a small piece of foil. (To prevent accidental swallowing, never use a coin smaller than a quarter and tell those who will be eating it that there is a coin baked into this cake.)

Concentrating on the good things you are wishing for, drop the foil-wrapped coin into the batter and blend well, stirring in a clockwise direction.

After the cake is baked and you are ready to cut it, take a moment to give thanks for the good things in life you that already possess.

The first piece that is cut is important because this slice is set aside for your home.

The next slice is offered to the head of the household. After this, give slices to the other members of the household according to age, starting with the oldest and ending with the youngest.

The person who discovers the coin in their slice should be congratulated; good luck is coming to them. If the coin is in the first slice that has been reserved for the home, the entire household will be blessed with good fortune.

May your coin cake bring you and your family good health and prosperity.

SACRED SABBAT OILS

By Ayla

I have always been intruiged by aromatherapy, herbs, and crystals, but somehow, I never thought of mixing up oils for sabbats—until now. I was inspired by Scott Cunningham's great recipes for oils and incense, but disappointed to discover that he had few, if any, sabbat oils. Though I could always buy ready-made oils through catalogs or magical oriented shops, my feeling was that ones you make with the power of your own hands are infinitely better.

So, using my knowledge of aromatherapy, herbs, and crystals, I spent much time meditating on the special smells and feelings of each of the eight sacred days. I was also influenced by the recipes of other Witches. I kept this, discarded that, and added my own ideas to make the oils that were perfect for me. Here are some guidelines to use before you try out these recipes:

1. Always use clean, dark glass bottles like amber and glass droppers for adding essential oils.

2. Keep oils in a cool, dark spot for storage. A magical cabinet is ideal, of course.

3. Add essential oils first, swirl gently to blend, then pour the base oils (almond, olive, etc.) into the bottle. Put the cover on and roll the bottle between your palms to mix the oils together. Then uncap and add the herbs and crystals.

4. Clean, clear, and charge all crystals and herbs before adding them to the finished oil. You can use any methods that appeal to you for doing this, like salt-water baths to cleanse and clear, then sunlight or moonlight to charge. My favorite method for crystals is to submerge them into a glass bowl of spring water mixed with ½

cup of sea salt and then put the bowl in the sun for the whole day.

5. Label the bottle with the name of the oil, time, date, day, Moon phase, and sign with waterproof, acid-free ink. You may also want to add a colored ribbon around the bottle neck that correlates with the sabbat colors. Another idea is decorating with holiday stickers on the outside of the bottle. Colors and symbols for Imbolc include white, suns, candles, snowflakes, or flames; for Ostara white, pastel colors of pink, yellow, purple, eggs, baskets, or bunnies; for Beltane white, red, hearts, baskets, braids, flowers, or Maypole; for Midsummer red, gold, yellow, green, sunflowers, suns, fairies, or couples; for Lammas yellow, brown, green, leaves, bread, apples, berries, or potatoes; for Mabon red, yellow, orange, brown, corn, wheat, or leaves; for Samhain red, orange, black, pumpkins, skeletons, cats, witches, or besoms; and for Yule red, green, silver, gold, tree, logs, gifts, snow, bells, deer, or candles.

6. If you have trouble finding specific small crystals, then use clear quartz crystals. These work well in all situations—just charge with your intentions. I like to use the small nugget crystals you can get from long gemstone necklaces. They are fairly inexpensive, the perfect size for small bottles, and usually good quality. You could also use small crystal/stone round beads or anything that fits your bottle.

IMBOLC OIL

5   drops frankincense

5   drops rosemary

3   drops cinnamon

2   drops sandalwood

½   ounce almond oil

Add a piece of rowan and a small hematite, garnet, and clear quartz crystal. A spicy, sunny scent for awakening the earth.

Ostara Oil

5   drops lavender

5   drops jasmine

5   drops patchouli

5   drops rose

½   ounce olive oil

Add a lavender bud and small lapis lazuli, rose, and clear quartz crystals. This has the gentle smell of spring beginning to blossom. Very lovely!

Beltane Oil

5   drops frankincense

3   drops rose

3   drops sandalwood

2   drops neroli

2   drops jasmine

½   ounce apricot oil

Add a piece of sweet woodruff and rosebud with rose quartz and garnet crystals. A very sensual, sexy, summer smell!

Midsummer Oil

5   drops lavender

4   drops rosemary

4   drops rose

½   ounce sunflower oil

Add a piece of dried vervain, a small citrine, clear quartz crystal, and a sprinkle of gold glitter. So magical and beautiful!

LAMMAS OIL

5   drops frankincense
5   drops rose
5   drops yarrow
½   ounce grapeseed oil

Add a piece of wheat and a blackberry leaf with a cat's-eye, citrine, and moss agate crystals. A very special oil for annointing the handle of your bread knife and your candles.

MABON OIL

3   drops frankincense
3   drops pine
3   drops juniper
3   drops rosemary
2   drops sandalwood
½   ounce corn, hazelnut, or almond oil

Add a piece of dried oak leaf or small acorn with amber, aventurine, and clear quartz crystals. A warm, calming oil that reminds me of cool, crisp days raking leaves and walking through forests in the fall.

SAMHAIN OIL

3   drops cedarwood
3   drops clove
3   drops frankincense
3   drops patchouli
3   drops rosemary
½   sunflower or grapeseed oil

Add a piece of dried marigold and three dried pumpkin seeds with obsidian, amber, and ruby crystals. This is a light and dark oil that captures all the mystery and ambience of this special night of meditation.

YULE OIL

4 drops pine

3 drops cedarwood

3 drops cinnamon

2 drops frankincense

2 drops juniper

½ ounce almond oil

Add a pinch of dried pine needles from your tree with garnet, green tourmaline, and clear quartz crystals. A great Yule tree smell with the hint of log fires and spicy pomanders!

Enjoy these sacred oils!

BIBLIOGRAPHY

Cabot, Laurie and Jean Mills. *Celebrate the Earth: A Year of Holidays in the Pagan Tradition*. New York, NY: Dell Publishing, 1994.

Cunningham, Scott. *The Complete Book of Incense, Oils and Brews*. St. Paul, MN: Llewellyn Publications, 1989.

Cunningham, Scott. *Magical Aromatherapy*. St. Paul, MN: Llewellyn Publications, 1989.

Worwood, Valerie Ann. *The Complete Book of Essential Oils and Aromatherapy*. San Rafael, CA: New World Library, 1991.

Sabbat Recipes

By Gerina Dunwich

These recipes are perfect for the holiday season. Try them and enjoy!

Covenstead Bread

¾	cup water
½	cup honey
½	cup chopped citron
½	cup sugar
2	tablespoons anise seeds
2½	cups flour
1½	teaspoons baking soda
1	teaspoon nutmeg
1	teaspoon cinnamon
¼	teaspoon allspice

Bring the water to a boil in a saucepan. Add honey, citron, sugar, and anise seeds. Stir until sugar dissolves and then remove from heat. Sift together flour, baking soda, salt, and spices, and fold into the hot honey mixture. Turn batter into a well-greased 9 x 5 x 3-inch pan and bake in a preheated 350°F oven for one hour. Turn out on a wire rack to cool. This recipe yields one loaf of bread, ideal for Lammas and Autumn Equinox sabbats and at coven meetings. The bread improves if allowed to stand for a day.

Cauldron Cookies

¾	cup softened butter
2	cups brown sugar
2	eggs
1	tablespoon lemon juice
2	teaspoons grated lemon rind

| 2 | cups flour |
| 1 | cup finely chopped pecans |

Cream the butter in a large cast-iron cauldron or mixing bowl. Add brown sugar, then eggs, lemon juice, rind, and beat until the mixture is well blended. Stir in the flour and pecans. Cover the cauldron with a lid or aluminum foil and refrigerate overnight. When ready, shape the dough into one-inch balls and place them about three inches apart on greased cookie sheets. Bake in a 375°F preheated oven for approximately eight minutes. Remove from oven and place on wire racks until cool. This recipe yields about 36 cookies which can be served at any of the eight sabbats, as well as at esbats and other gatherings.

CANDLEMAS CRESCENT CAKES

1¼	cups flour
¾	cup sugar
1	cup finely ground almonds
3	drops almond extract
½	cup butter or margarine, softened
1	tablespoon honey
1	egg yolk

In a mixing bowl, combine the first four ingredients. Add butter, honey, and egg yolk, and mix together. Cover with aluminum foil, and chill for 1–2 hours in the refrigerator. When ready, pinch off pieces of dough about the size of plums and shape into crescents. Place the crescents on a well-greased cookie sheet and bake in a 325°F preheated oven for approximately 20 minutes. (This recipe yields about one dozen Candlemas Crescent Cakes.)

HALLOWEEN PUMPKIN MUFFINS

4	cups flour
3	cups sugar
1¾	teaspoons baking soda
1	teaspoon salt
½	teaspoon baking powder

1	tablespoon each ground cloves, cinnamon, nutmeg
½	tablespoon ginger
1½	cups raisins
½	cup walnuts (chopped)
4	eggs
2½	cups cooked pumpkin, mashed
1	cup vegetable oil
1	cup water

In a large mixing bowl, combine the dry ingredients, the raisins, and the walnuts. Make a well in the middle of the mixture. In a separate bowl, beat the eggs and add the pumpkin, vegetable oil, and water, and mix well. Place the egg mixture in the well stir everything until just moistened. Do not overstir! Spoon the batter into paper-lined muffin pans, filling each about two-thirds. Bake for 20 minutes in a preheated 375°F oven and immediately remove the muffins from the pans to prevent them from scorching or drying out. This recipe yields about 3–4 dozen muffins.

MIDSUMMER RITUAL MEAD

2½	gallons water (preferably fresh rainwater blessed by a Wiccan priestess or priest)
1	cup each meadowsweet herb, woodruff sprigs, heather flowers
3	cloves
1	cup honey
½	cup brown sugar
1	cup barley malt
1	ounce brewer's yeast

Pour water into a large cauldron. Bring to a boil and add herbs and cloves. Boil for an hour and add honey, brown sugar, and barley malt. Stir thirteen times in a clockwise direction and remove from heat. Strain through a cheesecloth and allow the mead to cool. Stir in brewer's yeast. Cover with a towel and let stand for one day and night. Strain, bottle, and store in a cool place until ready to serve. This is an ideal drink to serve at Summer Solstice.

JEFFERS PETROGLYPHS: A TRIBUTE TO THE SACRED

BY BERNYCE BARLOW

The native prairies of Minnesota carry a mystical ambiance about them that is hard to deny. They seem to have the ability to hold the imprint of the spirit of the land and those who lived upon it. Although the prairie winters are stark and cold, the late spring and early summer breezes create an inland ocean of high grassy waves. Wildflowers mingle with sages, making the air heady as medicine plants and cactus take root with the thawing of the snow. Color is everywhere. The twilight horizon is clear cut and straight, and the night sky is immense. It is an appropriate setting for the feeling one gets while sailing on the prairie sea.

Occasionally on this sea, island outcroppings are formed of glacial bedrock, often of a coral/red/orange coloring. It is on these stone islands we sometimes find records in the form of petroglyphs and rock art that tell us about the ones who came before us. The Jeffers Petroglyphs in southwestern Minnesota are a good example of this type of sacred space.

The history of the petroglyphs has been dated as far back as 5,000 years. My guess is some of the rock art and recordings are even older than that. About 8000 B.C., hunters used the region for big-game hunting for animals such as mammoths, saber-toothed tigers, ten-foot beavers, and really, really big bison! A large Clovis spearpoint was found nearby in Pipestone County confirming this. Around 5000 B.C. the weather on the prairie had warmed, so more folks moved into the region to take advantage of the abundant food supply of game and plant life. Cultures emerged at different times throughout the territory such as the Fox Lake culture whose pottery dates back to 200 B.C. and who buried their dead in mounds. Later, the Mississippian culture influenced the land with their southern flavored lifestyles. Their descendants became known as the Oyote. The Dakota Sioux arrived rather late in the area, during the 1600s, after being driven out of northern Minnesota by the Ojibwe Nation (Chippewa). By the time the fur traders arrived, the cultural history of the land had already been set in stone. Hundreds of pictures of stories, star charts, and magical hunt symbols had been recorded on a prairie island at Jeffers. Today, those stone outcroppings are the elders that teach us.

There is a certain active magic about Jeffers that stirs the soul. It has to do with imprint and energy. You expect to see an ancient hunter, knife and spear in hand, walking across the prairie. As you examine the rock pictures of buffalo, hunt shaman, turtles, shields, and lightning, you wonder about the authors of the symbols. A six-fingered shaman left his hand print, another a clan mark. Magical signs designed for an abundant hunt sit beside figures carrying spears. Sun, Moon, and stars are represented, along with a cosmos of star charts. There are symbols representing stories about creation, a hunt or a healing, much like a modern-day storyboard.

Walking around the site made me think about the land's ancestors, their customs, and magical ways. Are the magical communities really so different, then and now? Don't we still carry our magic in symbols and spears? Is our reverence any less or our ceremonies so dissimilar? We have not lost touch with our medicine people and shamans. We still drum, dance, and sing. We honor Father Sky and Mother Earth. We can still shed tears of joy or for injustice. We continue to strive for abundance and honor, and to follow the ways of the Spirit. We leave offerings to the Earth. We are not so different from those who came before nor will we be so unlike those who shall follow after us. But being at a site like Jeffers helps to remind us of the higher states of spirituality we seek to achieve and that which has been sought in the past, the mark of a true sacred site.

MAGICAL FESTIVALS OF JAPAN

By deTraci Regula

If someone mentions Japan, you may think of a busy, modern culture filled with fast trains, huge cities, and vast manufacturing plants. And while this is all true in part, there is another, lesser-known side of Japan. This is a nature-revering culture with a rich folklore and many practices that fit in with Wiccan and other Western Pagan celebrations.

Magic and spirituality is common in Japan. In Tokyo, for instance, streetside shrines receive loving attention, and the Buddhist and Shinto temples on every other block emanate an atmosphere of calm spirituality unchanged for hundreds of years. Magic festivals, which take many forms, are common social events in Japan too.

Overall, Japanese magic festivals are anything but serene. Jumbled crowds, smoke from food vendors, and parades of miniature shrines called *mitoshi* trumpet the people's faith. More than anything else, nature dominates the festivals. The blooming of any plant is a reason to call a festival. For instance, millions of Japanese celebrate the Spring Cherry Blossom Festival in spring. Life slows down for this time, and each person contemplates the symbolic meaning of the blossoms—that is, the swift passing of life. In olden days, both the courtesan and samurai saw in the brief flowering and quick fall of cherry blossoms a metaphor for their all-too-brief lives. At the Hirano-jinja shrine in Kyoto, the delicate blossoms are viewed at night by torchlight. All over Japan, the merits of different viewing areas are debated and compared.

In mid-August, Japan's season for commemorating the dead, the mountainsides become the backdrop to the *daimonji okuribi*. At this time, a giant starlike symbol meaning "Great" or "Big" is set on fire, where it burns red against the dark mountains. This light is supposed to be a beacon for the spirits of the dead, bringing light to them as they return to the spirit world.

The Japanese recognize the spiritual force in animals and in things the West defines as "inanimate." Used and discarded brushes have their own memorial service, held in November each year at Shokaku-an, a subtemple of Tofuku-ji Temple. Here old writing brushes and pencils are ceremonially burned and released. A similar festival is held for hair combs.

In November, the Tori-No-Ichi festival is held, persisting almost unchanged, so say the experts, for three hundred years. At this festival, a special rake is used to make a pathway for good fortune. This has the same meaning as modern pagan and Wiccan "money brooms" which sweep away poverty and sweep in wealth. These Japanese rakes, called *kumade,* are decorated with all kinds of good luck charms, including the popular seven gods of good fortune, and with bits of gold paper symbolizing the precious metal itself.

In Oga City on December 31, the Namahage festival echos modern Halloween trick or treating. Small bands of young men dress up in demonic masks and go knocking on doors, demanding to know if there is anyone wicked in the house. Everyone denies that anyone wicked lives in their house, and to prove it they invite the young men to pray at the family altar. The weird visitors are given sake and rice cakes. On New Year's Day, smoky factories are shut down and the supreme sacred mountain of Fuji is worshipped for the day. Until recently, the solstices and equinoxes which are marked in the West were ignored; it wasn't until this century that the government created national holidays on these days.

In the end, the spiritual glories of Japan are much to be admired, even when compared with the rich spiritual festivals of our own Western culture.

What Makes a Sacred Site Sacred?

By Bernyce Barlow

In the beginning there were shaman sites—sacred places for spiritual, creative, practical, and medicinal uses. These sites were chosen for their raw power, which is based on many things—such as physics, imprint, and holy history. These combined influences give a site its "spirit of place." One site may be a place of dreaming, another may enhance creativity, still another site may give you a boost or charge, and some sites can even amplify your own emotions.

Ages ago, there were no scientific instruments to measure the Earth's energies, but shamans knew about the sacred sites without any such equipment. They knew by observation and experience. Today, modern equipment validates what the shaman have been saying all along—that there are places on this Earth that emit energies that cause specific things to happen. Shamans used sites for purification and healing. They used power centers with energy flows that draw one inward. They used vision quest locations and quiet spaces for introspection or meditation.

I was once explaining to a Hopi shaman the scientific mechanics behind the Hopi rain dance and why it works. I went on and on about the hertz rate and energy frequencies of the traditional site as well as how the dance harnesses that energy—blah blah blah. He looked at me like I was crazy. He couldn't have cared less how it worked as long as the ritual brought rain. He accused me of having to scientifically validate my knowledge, which cut me off from my intuition and spirit voice. He went on to add that while he thought science was indeed a good thing, when it becomes the sole authority, other powers and skills, like spirit faith and respect for the inspiration behind the Earth-mysteries, will suffer.

I asked if the Hopi rain dance would work if it was performed at the same site by people who had no spiritual connection to the meaning of the dance or the Hopi people. Though there is more than one dance within Hopi tradition that evokes rain, one dance in particular is performed on a mesa whose energy field emits ten hertz ratings. The dance is performed by thirty-two people for twelve hours nonstop. The shaman replied that since Hopi faith was part of the formula to make it rain, no, not anyone can do the rain dance. Together, faith and physics work to set up and manifest action. Shamans believe one will not work without the other. At sacred sites, the physics of the land may be right, but if one does not tap into the spirit of place the on-site energies might be overlooked or misdirected. Science can identify an energy anomaly at a sacred site, but is often at a loss regarding its purpose or effect.

Negative air ion sites are a good example. Negative air ions are atoms that have gained an electron. Many sacred sites are located where there is an abundance of negative air ions. Science tells that an abundance of negative air ions affects our mood by altering brain neurotransmitters such as serotonin, leaving a person relaxed and in a good mood. Negative air ions are beneficial to the respiratory, nervous, and immune systems. Commonly, negative air ions are created by moving water. Oceans, lakes, waterfalls, and rain showers generate negative ions. Places like Niagara Falls generate large amounts of them, leaving visitors in an altered state.

While science can tell us what a negative air ion is, and even can tell us how they can make us feel, this is where science ends and the shamanistic journey begins. For it is the shaman's sacred site knowledge of the spirit of place that tells us how the site should be used once the Earth energies take effect. This knowledge is the bridge between faith and physics.

There are other kinds of Earth energies that affect us at sacred sites. Ley lines and grid networks carry electromagnetic energies around the globe. Leys and grids can be compared to the acupuncture meridians in our bodies that carry the chi energy that makes us function. Leys and grids act as the Earth's meridian system, crisscrossing at times to form intersection points, just as human meridian paths do. At intersection points certain energies flow out of the ground and finds its way to the surface. These intersection points throw off a lot of energy at certain times of the year or under certain conditions, such as during sunspots or electromagnetic storms. Sacred sites were built on these intersection points in order to harvest their specific power and intent.

Sacred sites can also be established by imprint, an energy we can weakly measure at best. Imprint is left by past events, often repeated, that went on for hundreds of years. For instance, sacrifice temples and sacred ceremonial grounds often hold an imprint. Visitors to these sites report unusual feelings, unexplained music and chanting, or visual sightings of ghostly forms. Some of these events can be rationally explained, others cannot unless you accept the notion certain energies can and do hold imprint from the past, present, and, according to tribes like the Australian aborigines, the future. Author and researcher Dennis Hauck found that many imprint or haunted sites are found in areas whose hertz rate is around 8.5. My research concurs with this, so a hertz rate or Earth harmonic may also be involved at imprint sites.

Another thing that seems to make an imprint stick is intense emotion. Strong emotions appear to act as a cosmic glue when it comes to imprinting sacred sites. The shamans knew this and took the responsibility of emotional imprinting very seriously. Ceremonies and dances were orchestrated to achieve specific ecstasy states that would imprint a site in order to build its energy and power for future use. As a result, we became the modern-day benefactors of their efforts.

Examples of imprint sites are numerous. Civil War battlefields hold the imprint of soldiers; Native American burial and ceremonial grounds ring out with drumming and chanting; and from the Hawaiian temples and volcanoes the goddess Pele takes form. Although the physics at these sites may differ, the common bond among them appears to be intense emotion. A fine example of emotional imprint is found in Chimayo, New Mexico, in a small adobe chapel called the "Lourdes of America." Millions of people come here each year in order to be healed, but it is the faith of the living pilgrims that come to Chimayo that serves as its spirit of place. At Chimayo the imprint of healing and expectation is dynamic due to the faith and expectations of previous generations.

Some sites, such as a shaman cave, can be imprinted by an individual. Over thousands of years tribal shamans may have used a specific cave for vision quests or innerworld journeys. In theory, this would imprint the cave site. The trick was knowing the location of the imprinted cave sites because many were hidden or kept secret—often so foreign imprint would not pollute or attach itself to the spirit of place and so distract from its purity. That's where conscientious teachers came in handy.

In general, there is not any one thing that makes a site sacred. Most often, it is a combination of energies that interact, relate, and compliment each other. The Earth kicks out energies that interact with our brain chemicals, that in turn react in the physical form of mood and activity—in itself also a kind of energy. Each site is unique, just as we are, so there is no given formula as to what will happen at a sacred site, although there are similar flavors of experience. You will probably dream at a dream site. Most folks do. There may also be a common theme to the dreams at some sites. Visitors to Oak Creek Canyon in Arizona often recall dreaming about Native Americans.

Along a similar line of thought, the wellsprings of energies often found on high-elevation mesas do generally give people a charge of energy. In my experience, individuals exposed to these sites experience a kind of turbocharge that is personal and unique. Some people sit quietly and let thoughts and visualisations race through their heads, while others become creative in writing, dancing, painting, or sculpting. There are those who manifest raw intuitive gifts at wellspring sites and use the effect to sharpen their skills. A variety of experiences will emerge from an energy wellspring, but the common bond is an animated rejuvenating charge received by the mind and body.

Answering neatly what makes a site sacred is difficult. The variables are numerous but the bottom line always comes back to faith and physics. Both modern and ancient shamans agree that a sacred site journey is individual, yet guided by spirit of place. To recognize, respect, and utilize the on-site spirit of place takes little effort if one is willing to take the time to observe and study the site before using it for its beneficial properties. Local museums, books, visitor centers, the internet, and tribal public relations offices are wonderful resources to gather information about sites you may be interested in visiting. Remember, knowledge is power. Once you are armed with information, you can take time to view the sacred site with understanding, just as a shaman would. Each site is alive with an imprint and spirit waiting to interact with the human psyche to achieve a higher state of consciousness and grace. And so it is with sacred sites, and has been from the very beginning.

The Sacred Traveler

By Cerridwen Iris Shea

Congratulations! You have the opportunity to take a trip! But what about your spiritual practice? Are you going to take a break? Are you going to promise yourself to maintain your routine, and then feel guilty when you don't? Or are you going to use this as an opportunity to become a sacred traveller and get even more out of your trip? I hope you'll choose the latter.

Planning and Preparation

Whether you're taking a business trip or a pleasure trip, planning is the key to making your travels more spiritual. In general, many

people today can't be bothered to organize their trip. Harried and lacking time, they throw up their hands and say, "Whatever's meant to happen will happen." But, no matter how busy, it is always best to have some control over what's likely to occur during any trip.

To begin, research your destination. What are you interested in doing in this place? Do you need familiar things nearby such as health clubs and fax machines? Or do you want to try something new that you've never tried before? Is a different language spoken? Do you need a passport? Visa? Shots? What are you allowed to bring in?

To find answers beforehand, you should take advantage of a library or travel bookstore in your area to find books, maps, and videos for information. Moreover, you can search tourist boards and chamber of commerce websites. Or try calling a tourist board and asking questions. Read guidebooks, get yourself at least one good map, and don't stop there. Investigate local myths and spiritual practices. Visit relevant forums or chat rooms online. Get a feel for the place from people who live or have traveled there.

Meanwhile, make sure arrangements have been made for care for your pets, plants, and mail back home. As you travel, always keep your keys, money, passport, and tickets in a safe place. Pack carefully, and remember to take an empty bag, or to leave room in your suitcase, for any gifts you pick up on your trip.

THE PORTABLE ALTAR

I have a portable altar that I've put together and use only when I travel. Most of it fits into a large cosmetic bag. Each item is some-

thing I've picked up on previous trips; I make sure it is cleansed and consecrated.

In the portable altar is a purple scarf I use as an altar cloth, a small wooden chalice, two small wooden bowls, a short incense holder, and a round votive candleholder with a scented candle. I also may bring my "travel athame," which is a Celtic scrollwork

letter opener—this travels in my checked luggage only, for the sake of weapons inspections—a few sticks of incense, a deck of tarot cards, and a bottle of rosemary oil. To save room, I try to get some local incense of the region after I arrive, and I fit the bowls and the votive candleholder inside the chalice. The entire package is wrapped in the scarf and put in the cosmetic bag. Sometimes I'll add a few stones and a fetish. As I pack everything, I make sure to bless it all.

On the night before departure, I cast a circle and perform a simple blessing ceremony. I ask that my home and animals be protected during my absence; I ask that I come home safely and that I learn something important on the trip and remain open to any wonders that may come my way. I also give thanks for the opportunity to take the trip, and I bless the vehicle in which I will travel.

DEPARTURE

As I leave my home, I use my key as a blessing tool. As I lock the door, I lock in protection for my home. I envision a glowing blue net of stars that I cast, clockwise around my entire home. The turning of the lock tightens the net, securing the protective energy. My gargoyle sits on the table, facing the doorway, and he is charged with preventing anyone harmful from entering.

I try not to get stressed out about travel delays. If you are delayed, or are too early, don't fret; airports are fascinating places to people-watch and eavesdrop. You can always go into a cafe and have a cup of coffee, or buy a newspaper and read. Leave plenty of time to get to the airport or train station. International flights generally ask you to check in at least two hours prior to flight time, domestic flights one. I always ask my travel agent to give me at least one to two hours between connections.

Once you get on the plane or train or bus, you should take a moment to breathe and bless the trip. Ask your patron deities, or your special travel deities, for protection and blessing on this journey. Then, sit back, relax, and see what new opportunities await you. Remember, getting there is half the fun!

IN YOUR TEMPORARY SPACE

Set up your portable altar on a night table or table in your room. Perform a blessing ceremony as soon as you can, smudging your room, and, preferably the entire place in which you are staying.

Walk around the grounds. Listen to the energies of the residing hearth spirits and the elementals of the land. Find yourself a quiet, sacred space where you can meditate, think, and relate to the energies of the place. Make sure you perform your daily devotionals every morning and every night, even if you are tired. Make an offering to the spirits of the home and the land upon arrival and just before departure. Always leave any place you stay better off than you found it.

Even if you are a solitary, you may want to connect with other like-minded people during your stay somewhere. You may have connected with someone online during your research. Ask this person to meet you for coffee. If they truly are like-minded, suggest a hike or an afternoon's outing, then perhaps trade tarot or other divination readings. Work up to a full ritual.

Other options include getting out the phone book to find pagan supply or book shops. Talk to people there. See what the local energies are like. If you are invited to a ritual with people you recently met, try to find out in advance as much about their practice as possible. If you are going to participate, you need to do so fully, and the only way you can do so is if you feel comfortable with all aspects of their ritual work. They should not feel they must adjust their ritual for you, and you must not feel pushed into something that feels wrong. Open communication from the beginning can save heartache and anger later on. Start by saying politely, "Thank you for inviting me. Do you mind if I ask a few questions?" Then listen to what they say and decide accordingly. This doesn't mean you can't take a risk and try something new, but you should know as much as possible before you start.

One of the most important parts of travel is staying open to new experiences. This does not mean taking unnecessary risks, but it does mean using the power of travel to physicalize your emotional journey. Be sensually aware about new smells, looks, and tastes. Ask questions. Be delighted at unexpected answers.

 Not only will you be better for going someplace new, but any place you touch will be better for having you there.

Returning

When you come home, before you become overwhelmed by picking up the strands of your life, take the time to do a ritual of thanks. Say thanks for your safety, thanks for your new experiences, and thanks that your home was protected. Then, take the time to absorb your journey. Every trip changes you, which means that you, in turn, will change everything around you upon your return. Keep the heightened awareness and openness going for a few days. That is how it is, working with the Goddess. She changes everything She touches, and everything She touches, changes. Touch and be touched. Don't be afraid to change. Merry meet, merry part, and merry meet again!

Some Relevant Travel Deities:

Abeona (Roman)—looks after children as they depart to explore the world

Ariadne (Greek, Celtic)—protection and manifestation

Breasal (Welsh, Cornish)—protects travelers and explorers

Brigid (Celtic)—triple goddess who can help in any endeavor

The Cailleach (Scottish, Irish, Manx)—Samhien, dark moon, weather, storms; not for the faint-hearted

Eulimene (Greek)—provides safe haven for sailors

Euploia (Greek)—brings about a good voyage

Eupompe (Greek)—brings safety to sailors

Fuamnach (Irish)—weather magic

Goll MacMorna (Irish)—will help in dangerous situations

Harimella (Scottish)—protection

Mullo (Breton, European)—protects travellers, especially those who drive for a living

Nehalennia (Breton, Anglo-Celtic)—protects water travellers

Ruadh (Irish)—helps one find own personal adventure

The Wawilak (Australian)—four sisters who wandered the world and created four ceremonies used in initiation rites

THE HANDOFF

BY ELIZABETH BARRETTE

Energy comes in many forms, and most magical practitioners do not work equally well with all of them. Just as no one can cover every world religion, we tend to specialize in practicing styles of magic and spiritualism. Still, diversity does exists, so you may well find yourself someday asking how to accomplish something outside your usual religious or spiritual practice.

These issues crop up often in the Pagan community. Most of us work with others whose skills are totally different from our own—relatives who are Christian, Jewish, or Muslim, coven sisters who request healing energy when we have no experience with healing. At these times, your usual style of practice may not be helpful, and switching wouldn't be much better. We all need ways of bridging the gaps.

My favorite technique for such situations is one I call "the handoff." What you do is pass some energy to someone else for delivery. It works a little bit like an international bank's money-changing service. You want to buy something from a Japanese catalog but the supplier doesn't take American dollars. So you go to the bank and put in dollars, which the bank changes to an equivalent amount of yen. The energy remains the same, but it is now in a suitable form. Many processes in nature operate on this principle; magically, you can accomplish this in a variety of ways.

A good method for handoff within groups is a circle of transmutation. Once you establish a goal, you raise a cone of power and pour energy into it as usual. Individual members need not add a particular kind of energy; they can add whatever they want. A person with strong energy manipulation skills should be in charge of the ritual, so that he or she can change the energy to the proper form before releasing it.

An option for individuals is to engage the services of a messenger. Many deities hold more than one sphere of influence. For example, Brigid's powers include smithcraft, poetry, and healing. She can take the physical labor of hammering and channel it into inspiration. Similarly, a surprising number of powers "hold office" in more than one religion since often a new religion incorporates some or all of the figures from a previous local religion. Thus any such power can translate energy from one tradition to another of their own traditions. Elegba (who appears under various guises in Afro-Caribbean traditions) is associated with the Christian Saints Michael and Peter. Any good guide to deities will include information on spheres of influence. Specialized information often appears in books dedicated to a particular tradition.

When working with the handoff technique, you can draw up pure energy that has no particular signature or style, or you can use your own personal energy or energy that carries its own impressions (like healing energy, or Wiccan energy from an established shrine). Novices find this handy because they can use the energy they are best at raising. However, it helps to use undifferentiated energy if you can, because magic does follow natural laws. Every time you translate energy from one form to another, a little bit gets away from you. Using undifferentiated energy requires only one translation to its final form.

In designing a ritual around the handoff technique, you should consider your own needs as well as those of the recipient. You need to use the accouterments you customarily use for gathering power in your own style, and you also need a symbol of the messenger who will be transmuting and delivering the energy for you. Also choose something to represent the recipient, to make sure the transmuted energy reaches its intended destination.

No special follow-up is required for this technique. As always, you should keep notes regarding what works and doesn't work for you in your magical studies. Remember just how fluid energy really is, and know you can send loving thoughts out into the world where they achieve surprising results.

AVOIDING TOXIC MAGICAL GROUPS

BY ESTELLE DANIELS

Being a good magical practitioner means using consumer skills in evaluating a psychic or magical group before you join it. Most groups are ethical and healthy, but some are not. One has to take constant care to avoid unhealthy situations.

The most important rule to remember when examining a group is use your instincts. Don't argue against your own common sense. If it feels wrong or bad to you, don't let anyone talk you into believing otherwise. If it sounds too good to be true, it probably is. If the claims of the leaders sound overblown or unrealistic, they probably are.

Be willing to investigate and verify claims. If the leader says something like, "I was trained by Merlin Ambrosius who awarded me his special third degree," ask for Merlin's number and follow up. Diplomas can be faked, so a piece of paper is no guarantee. If your request to check up is met with bad feelings, threats, or curses, be wary.

If a person makes mundane claims (for example, "I consult for the local police"), call for confirmation. If the police say, "We have never heard of this person," this can confirm someone is not telling the truth. If the claims are fantastic or unverifiable (like "I was an NSA agent researching psychokinetics"), be wary. There are people who feel compelled to boost their importance. A good teacher or leader is a good teacher or leader, and that's all you should need.

Ask for references. Watch people's reactions. Are they polite, surprised, hostile, or paranoid? The more extreme a reaction is to a benign request, the more it signals warning. If they tell you to take everything on faith, use your instincts. They might try to make you feel bad for doubting or having natural reservations. They might have a million reasons to combat doubts or misgivings. Beware. The more they try to persuade or coerce, the more it could be a scam. Alternatively, the more secretive and enticing it sounds, and the more they appear to resist you, the more barriers you have to hurdle, the more they can be trying to set you up.

How you hook up with a group is also an indicator. Were you referred by a friend, or do you have a contact in the group? This is the best way of assuring the group is okay. However, there are groups that capitalize on this. If an old friend from out of the blue tries to recruit you, be wary. If a friend gets into something, and his or her behavior changes, evaluate whether the change is positive or sinister before you decide to follow.

If you make a contact through the Internet, be extremely cautious. Make sure the first meetings are in a public place of your choice. Bring friends along if you are apprehensive. If it feels wrong, leave and never turn back. Some people count on the anonymity of the Internet to foster their schemes.

Was the contact through a bookstore or coffeehouse? Ask the proprietors about the group or person. If they know nothing, use the same techniques for the Internet. If you answered an ad, be cautious also. If it does turn out to be a scam, inform the paper.

Before you commit, find out what your obligations will be, in time and resources. Find out what you will learn, what the teachers or leaders will do. Get a feel for the group and people. Get a good idea of any financial obligations. If it's a training group, will you be guaranteed a degree? Be honest with yourself. Don't try to make the group something it is not.

Once you are in the group, do not abandon your instincts. Keep perspective. A group that demands all of your time has wrong priorities. Is it you who are choosing to take the time or is the group making demands on you, or both? If it's too much, you may have to drop out. It happens.

Beware of a group that states all books are wrong except theirs. Ask about the rules up front. If the rules are nebulous or changing, watch out. If punishment for breaking the rules seems out of proportion or is threatening, run away. If you are required to undergo some ordeal, make sure you have some idea of what it entails. Psychological and verbal challenges are common, but requirements to imbibe unknown substances or inhale unfamiliar things are not. Tell the group you have allergies and must know always what you are ingesting. If you are made to feel vulnerable in some way (no clothes, in an unfamiliar place), be sure you feel okay about it. If you are isolated for a day or more, be very wary. This can be a possible attempt at psychological reprogramming.

If you are coerced or pressured to have sex with anyone affiliated with the group, run away. There are unethical people everywhere, and sex in exchange for something is a common coercion. Romance does happen, but in the context of a magical or religious group, it should be carefully examined.

Are threats made by group members? This can range from threats of cursing you if you leave, to threats of terrible disasters befalling friends or family from supernatural forces. These are more common in religious-based groups, but magical groups can do this also.

If you leave a group and group members cause problems for you, take action. If a crime is committed, go to the police. If you explain the circumstances, most law enforcement personnel will understand, and since the time of Jim Jones they are more educated about these scams.

Don't beat yourself up if you did make a mistake. Take the experience as a lesson, and make sure you do not repeat it. Learn the warning signs and keep them in your mind.

I hope you will never have a bad group experience, but if you do, use these guidelines. If you keep your eyes open and examine people and claims with a critical eye, you should avoid the worst manipulations.

Runes in Spellwork

By Paul Tuitéan

There is little primary source data on how ancient rune-masters performed magic, divined the future, or cast spells. Still, various authors, using available information and personal inspiration, have written systems of runic divination. They have not, however, been able to do the same with spell-casting, and little information is currently available on how to "send the energies" you call up, or to "cast a spell." This article is an attempt to address this lack.

It is known from old stories such as *Egil's Saga,* and from a portion of the poem *The Hávamál* from the Poetic Edda known as *Odin's Rune Poem* that runemasters of the tenth through twelfth centuries performed "spellcasting," probably using the Younger Futhark rune alphabet. But we do not know in any detail what these runemasters did. From around 1980, the older, and more obscure, Elder Futhark has almost totally supplanted all other runic systems. So the dilemma posed to anyone working magically with runes today is that we are trying to recreate a magical system we don't understand, using a symbolic system we know nearly nothing about.

Still, there are a few facts that allow us to rediscover, or more accurately "reinvent," the magical uses of the runes:

1. Possibly the correct interpretation of stanza 139 of *Odin's Rune Poem,* wherein Odin finds the runes, is that Odin discovered the symbols of the futhark and did not invent them. This gives the runes their own existence—separate from and possibly predating the Norse gods.

2. There is an old saying: "The runes are the runes." This is commonly understood to mean that the meanings of the various characters of the futhark are fixed. Thus we can assume that the true meanings of the runes have not been tamper with

through the centuries. This allows us to rediscover runic meanings and to reinterpret them for modern times.

3. Since the late ninteenth century, many people have tried to discover "the scientific laws of magic," but they have generally failed. By comparing magical systems from around the world, we know there are universal "rules" that the "arts magical" seem to work best with.

Here is a "re-invented" system of runic spellcasting that follows both the rules of magic, and the realities of the runes.

STEP 1: COMPOSE YOUR SPELL

Using any style of runes, first plan out what you are doing. Choose a central phrase or statement around which to build your spell, and translate it into the runic alphabet—for instance, "Praise the Gods." By substituting the runes of the Elder Futhark for our modern English letters we get: ᚲᚱᚨᛁᛊᛖ ᛏᚺᛖ ᚷᛟᛞᛊ. Write your statement or carve it into wood.

STEP 2: PLACE YOURSELF IN SACRED SPACE

Develop a focused state of mind. Gather everything you need for casting. Unplug the phone, put on some relaxing music, light a candle, and recite *The Hávamál* (reproduced at the end of this article) as an invocation. I recite this poem before rune work because it alerts my sub-conscious mind that I am doing something magical.

STEP 3: TRACE OR CUT YOUR RUNES

Now you will either write in paper or recarve in wood each of the runes that you have in your spell. You should concentrate on the meaning of each rune and perform what I call a "heads-up-display" technique. You visualize each rune floating about six inches in front of your forehead. Retrace and concentrate on the rune ᛈ, *perthro* (traditional meaning, birth); then the rune ᚱ, *raido* (riding); ᚨ, *ansuz* (a god); ᛁ, *isa* (ice); ᛋ, *sowulo* (the Sun); ᛗ, *ehwaz* (horse); ↑, *teiwaz* (the god Tyr); ᚻ, *hagalaz* (hail); ᛗ, *ehwaz* again; ✕, *gebo* (gift); ᛟ, *othila* (inherited land); ᛞ, *dagaz* (day); and finally ᛋ, *sowulo* again.

STEP 4: STAIN OR COLOR YOUR RUNES

Retrace the runes of your spell with the color you want them to be. A simplistic color code is: prayers or "priest's runes" are done in white; spells or "warrior's runes" are done in the primary colors—e.g., red, yellow, or blue; and curses or "thrall's runes" are done in black. Concentrate and place each word in your "heads up display."

STEP 5: PROVE OR SACRIFICE
TO YOUR RUNES

Magically charge the spell. Retrace the runes of the spell with a "sacrificial wine." Many Norse practitioners use mead or cider for this. Retrace and put in your "heads-up display" the entire spell, concentrating and visualizing "Praise the Gods," or "ᚲᚱᚨᛁᛋᛗ ↑ᚻᛗ ✕ᛟᛞᛋ."

STEP 6: SEND YOUR SPELL

Finally, revisualize everything. Use a gesture (foot stamping, head nodding) to signal that the "heads-up display" moves away into the distance. Then, to give a chance for the spell to work, forget about what you have just done.

STEP 7: THANK THE POWERS

Put out the candle and thank the gods and the runes.

The Hávamál

Stanza 138. *Wounded I hung on that wind swept tree,*
and there for nine long nights,
pierced by a spear, Odin consecrated to Odin;
I offered myself to myself:
Bound and knotted to that mighty tree,
whose roots men know not.

139. None gave me bread, none gave me drink;
I looked down, I took up runes:
Crying out their names I fell from that great tree.

140. Nine lays of power I learned from the famous Bölthorn,
Bestla's father:
He poured me a drink of precious mead,
drawn from the magic Óthrœrir.

141. Well-being I won and wisdom too,
I grew and joyed in my growth:
From a word to a word, I was led to a word,
from a deed to another deed.

142. Runes you will find, and readable staves,
very strong staves,
very potent staves,
staves that Bolthorn stained:
Made by mighty powers,
graven by the prophetic God.

143. For the Gods by Ódin, for the Elves by Dáin,
by Dvalin, too, for the Dwarves;
by Asvith for the hateful Giants,
and some I carved myself:

144. Know how to cut them, know how to read them,
know how to stain them, know how to prove them,
know how to evoke them, know how to consecrate them,
know how to send them, know how to consume them.

145. Better not to ask, than to over pledge:
As a gift demands a gift,
better not to send, than to slay too many.

—translation by D. Johnson

MAKING A WAND

BY BREID FOXSONG

A wand is a one of the primary Wiccan tools. There are two types of wands, stemming from two different magical traditions. Metal wands, associated with the direction south and element fire, are used in ceremonial magic to control spirits and conduct energy. Wooden wands, associated with the direction east and the element air, are used in natural magic to tune into and utilize the surrounding natural forces. You can also make a wand from bundled herbs or other natural materials.

The creation of a wooden wand is a highly personal task. Your choice of wood is important, as each type of wood has its own properties. Although it is not absolutely necessary that your wand be made from a specific type of wood, as with any other tool, the closer you come to matching the property with the job, the better off you are. Traditionally, most all-purpose wands are made of willow or hazel. You will find a list of woods and their generally accepted properties at the end of this article.

You should try to measure your tools to your body in order personalize the wand. Ideal dimensions for the wand, according to tradition, are a diameter of about the size of your pointer finger and a length equal to the length of your forearm and hand. The length and width can vary according to what you are comfortable with. Remember that you are better off cutting too long rather than too short. You cannot reattach a cut piece. There are commercially made wands available, but making a wand yourself gives you a greater link with your tool. If you cannot cut your own wood, you can buy a dowel at any hardware store.

If you can cut the branch yourself, try to do it on a Wednesday, when the Moon is waxing, at or around midnight, sunrise, midday, or sunset, as these are considered the most magically powerful times. Look for a branch that is straight, with no blemishes. Remember that the bark is probably one-eighth inch thick, so factor that in. You want to be sure that you will not damage the tree when you take the wand, so check that your tools are well sharpened and clean. Take some time to talk to your chosen tree. Explain what you need and why you need it. Listen to the answers you get, sometimes the tree will offer a specific branch, or it may deny your request. You will get more power from freely offered wood than you will by ripping any old branch off a tree.

If you can combine your wand-getting with a needed pruning, all the better. Plan to leave a gift of fertilizer or future care for the tree.

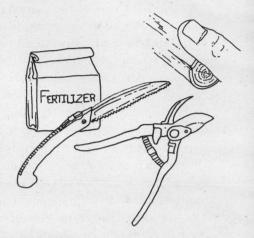

When you have finished talking to the tree, use your athame (or a pair of blessed pruning shears) to sever the branch cleanly. Concentrate on your intentions and your desires as you cut. Be sure to seal the cut in the tree with tar or tree sealant so as not to allow disease to enter into the tree. Thank the tree again and take your new wand home.

Once home, trim the branch of all twigs, branches and bark. Make sure that you gather up all the scrap wood to return to the tree as compost. Cut away any small knots and smooth the wood down with coarse sandpaper. Remember to sand with the grain of the wood, never across it! Progress gradually to finer grades of

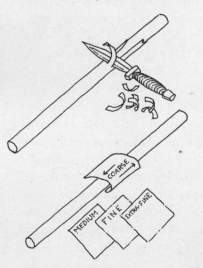

sandpaper until the surface of the wood feels silky smooth. Coat your new wand with beeswax to polish it or oil it with a natural oil such as linseed. This will keep the wood from dying out and cracking.

Some Wiccans like to engrave runes or symbols on their wands. That is a personal choice and depends on your personal teachings and inner feelings. You can paint designs or runes on your wand as well, dedicating it to a specific task or to aid you in your work. Remember that this is a very personal tool, there is no single right way to create it. Use your intuition and imagination so that the wand reflects your magical purposes. It is possible too to make a combination of a wood and metal wand by placing a piece of copper or silver at the tip. Or add a crystal. Be creative!

Although you can make your wand out of almost any wood, be sure to research the wood's affinities so that you know what you are working with. For example, European mountain ash, or rowan, is often associated with magic or enchantment. And in particular, rowan has the specific magical power to break enchantments or to absorb magic. You might want to consider how each wood will affect a circle or a magical working before you choose it for your wand.

SOME PROPERTIES OF WOODS

Birch—New beginnings, feminine power

Rowan (mountain ash)—Magic, protection, absorbing magic

Hawthorn—Protection, wishes, fairies

Oak—Power, male strength, stability

Hazel—Wisdom, divining

Apple—Love, giving

Ivy—Fertility

Fir/pine—Birth/rebirth

Poplar—Success

Yew—Death

A New History
of Witchcraft

By Jenny Gibbons

History changes. Or rather, our knowledge of the past changes. Every few decades, scholars discover new information—such as new carbon-dating data, or a new primary source such as the Dead Sea Scrolls—that revolutionizes our understanding of history.

Witchcraft studies recently went through such a revolution. During the 1970s and 1980s, historians began to study the Witch-trial records. Prior to this time, our knowledge of the persecution of Witches was mainly based on Witch-hunting propaganda: manuals, sermons, and other dogmatic information. Historians have studied a handful of trial records from larger, more infamous cases, but it was not until about twenty years ago that scholars began to compile serious databases of every known Witch trial. Through their efforts, a wealth of new information was found. Today, we can list approximately thirty times as many Witch trials as we could twenty years ago. This new evidence has shown us that almost everything we thought about Witch hunting was wrong. For the first time in history we have a good idea what the average trial and the average Witch looked like.

In the past, people tended to see the burning times as a dualistic fairy tale. There were good guys (Witches, Pagans, wise women), and there were bad guys (the Inquisition, Witch-hunters, male doctors). The bad guys were said to have done awful things to the good guys. The truth actually is a bit more complicated and uncomfortable; that is, every section of society bears some of the blame. No one group committed all the horrors; no one can claim their hands were clean. Not even traditional Witches.

For many of us Witches, that's a hard pill to swallow. But when we turn a blind eye to the truth simply because it's painful, we lose the lessons that history can teach us. And the people who suffered through the burning times deserve better.

Here is a short list exposing some of the formerly unknown truths about what some of the involved groups did and did not do during the burning times.

THE CHRISTIAN CHURCHES

What They Did—The churches laid the groundwork that made the persecution possible. During the Middle Ages, the Catholic Church taught that there was no such thing as neutral magic. All magic was evil, and all of it came from Satan. While there weren't many Witch trials during the Middle Ages, this teaching set the stage for the tragedy to come. Moreover, in the eleventh century the Church suppressed religious diversity by executing "heretics." Their methods—such as burning at the stake—became the traditional method of killing a Witch. When Protestant churches arose during the religious turmoil of the Reformation, they carried on in the Catholic Church's footsteps, prohibiting magic and violently persecuting religious minorities.

What They Didn't Do—During the Middle Ages, when the Church controlled most Witch trials, very few Witches were killed. Witch hunting didn't skyrocket until the Early Modern Period in the sixteenth and seventeenth centuries after the Reformation split "the" Church into warring Protestant and Catholic sects. Even then, church courts killed very few Witches—generally less than one percent of the people they tried. Most Witches were killed by local, nonreligious courts. People were put to death by their own neighbors.

THE INQUISITION

What They Did—The Inquisition encouraged the stereotypes that drove the panics. The earliest Witch-hunting manuals were written by inquisitors.

At the height of the persecution of Witches, most manuals were written by nonreligious authors. However these later writers built from the earlier writings of the Inquisition. In fact, the most influential anti-Witch manual of all times was written by two inquisitors: the *Malleus Maleficarum* of Heinrich Kramer and Jacob Sprenger. Nonreligious courts seized upon this text and followed many of its horrific guidelines. The Inquisition inspired others to commit atrocities, even if their own trials were generally more restrained.

What They Didn't Do—The Inquisition didn't kill many Witches. When it was first created in the early thirteenth century, the Inquisition was not allowed to try Witches as the Church did not consider Witchcraft a heresy. This changed in the early fourteenth century. Yet even then the Inquisition did more talking than killing. Scholars could only find a few hundred Witches who were definitely killed by the Church and Inquisition from 1300–1500. By the time of the main persecution in the mid-sixteenth century, the Inquisition no longer existed in most countries. Odder still, the places where the Inquisition did try Witches (Spain, Italy, and Portugal) had some of the lowest death tolls in Europe. In Spain, the Inquisition actually opposed Witch trials.

Local Authorities

What They Did—It was the local authorities who killed the vast majority of Witches, mostly in community-based courts. Some of these courts were virtual slaughterhouses, killing ninety percent of all accused Witches. Germany offers the most horrific evidence of the dangers of local courts. Most countries had a national court that squelched the excesses of the local courts. But since Germany did not, it killed nearly half of all the Witches who died in these times. Panics were not uncommon in Germany, and all of these panics occurred in local courts.

What They Didn't Do—The local authorities didn't kill millions of people. Historians are confident that somewhere between 40,000 and 60,000 Witches died. This is mainly because, in the past, no one had counted the number of Witch trials in court records. There are millions of trials from this period, and only a small number have anything to do with Witchcraft. Estimates of the numbers of Witches executed were based on wildly varying guesswork. Once historians actually began to count the number of executions, they found that trials were far less common than they thought. To date, fewer than 15,000 definite executions have been found. Compensating for lost records and unrecorded deaths, this suggests that the death toll was nowhere near the millions once suggested.

Of course, the true horror of a Witch trial cannot be found in the cold statistics, but in the sad tales of Witches like Anna Gamperle, tortured to death in front of her husband and sons. That is, each individual unjustified death is a tragedy that we should remember, even if the number of tragedies is not so great as we once thought.

National Governments

What They Did—Contrary to what most people believe, Witch hunting was worst where the Church and State were weakest. Governments generally don't like panics and chaos. The persecution of Witches, then, was worst when and where the authorities couldn't stop it in places along national borders, at times during periods of civil war, and in loose confederacies like Germany and Switzerland. There are some exceptions, such as in Scotland, where King James introduced Witch hunting. But in most areas, a strong government decreased Witch hunting.

What They Didn't Do—The national governments didn't kill many Witches. National courts killed more Witches than Church courts did, but nowhere near as many as the local courts. In many areas, roughly thirty percent of the Witches tried by national courts were killed.

NEIGHBORS AND COMMON FOLK

What They Did—Neighbors and common folk accused the majority of Witches. Most Witches were accused by their neighbors, not by the Church or professional Witch-hunters. Since killing a Witch was believed to be the easiest way of breaking a perceived spell, average people commonly blamed misfortunes on Witchcraft and therefore often welcomed Witch hunting. In fact, when courts would not kill Witches "fast enough" the public frequently took the law into their own hands and lynched suspects.

What They Didn't Do—The common people did not blindly accept the Church's demonology. A close examinations of trial records turned up a surprising fact: many Witches were not convicted of the same crime that they were accused of! Witches were usually accused by their neighbors, then tried by the Church or state. These two groups disagreed over what Witchcraft was. To most people, Witchcraft was harmful magic, and they accused Witches of committing magical crimes—like cursing and killing live-stock. To intellectuals of the Church and state, Witchcraft was heresy, or Satanism. Once they had a Witch in custody, they questioned him or her mercilessly about an allegiance to the Devil. There were often no traces of the Devil in the original charges, but by the end of the trial, the Witch stood convicted of full-blown Satanism.

This difference is important for it shows that people were not accusing Witches because they were forced to. They had their own concerns that were very different from the Church or state's. Also, they remind us that we have to be very careful before we assume that the diabolic aspects of a Witch trial are part of folklore.

TRADITIONAL WITCHES

What They Did—One of the most shocking facts to emerge from the new trial data is that many traditional Witches actively supported the persecution. During these times, most common people divided Witches into "black" and "white" categories (despite that the Church insisted that all Witches were evil). "Black" Witches cursed people. "White" Witches (also called wise women and cunning men) were healers and diviners who specialized in undoing the baneful spells of their "black" sisters. Witches blamed misfortunes on harmful magic, and they helped Witch-hunters discover the identities of "evil" Witches. This did not lead to much persecution during the Middle Ages, but at the height of the Witch scare traditional Witchcraft suddenly became deadly. People looked for remedies against "black" magic beyond simple protective charms. Many people took suspected practitioners of baneful magic to court. Thus, many of the people named were put to death. In France, for instance, twenty-five percent of all Witches put on trial were accused by a wise-woman or cunning man.

What They Didn't Do—They didn't die in great numbers. Contrary to popular opinion, most Witches were not herbal healers or traditional magic-user. Healers and traditional magic-users made up a small percentage of Witches (perhaps around twenty to thirty percent). Most traditional Witches, in fact, lived through the burning times in absolute peace and safety. They were never accused of Witchcraft, simply because, as today, most people were able to distinguish between "good" magic and "bad."

To learn more about the real history of these times, Brian Levack's *The Witch Hunt in Western Europe* and Robin Briggs' *Witches and Neighbors* are excellent summaries of the new evidence collected from trial records.

THE MAGICAL EMERGENCY KIT

By John Michael Greer

O ne important lesson of the Mysteries is that the magical realms have their dangers and pitfalls as well as their blessings. This is a lesson, unfortunately, that too many novice magicians learn the hard way.

As magical practitioners have known since ancient times, the parts of the universe we encounter with the magical senses are every bit as diverse as the parts we encounter with our physical senses. If you visit another city, for example, you may encounter lovers, friends, strangers, muggers, and politicians; if you go hiking in a forest, you may meet mosquitoes and skunks as well as deer and singing birds. In the same way, the universe of magic is inhabited by a vast range of beings and forces. Some of these may be friendly to you; others may be hostile, and still others won't be interested in you at all. In other words, the human voyagers you encounter in your magical journeys will be of many different sorts, and not all of them may be friendly or trustworthy.

Dealing effectively with potential trouble in magic is not necessarily a simple matter. Good intentions will help, but they're not enough by themselves. Accurate information, which can be learned from books, from other magical practitioners, or from your own experience, is a good deal more useful.

Furthermore, there are several items of use in your magical journey. As in any journey, you need a good street map, a few coins for phone calls, and a bottle of pepper spray to help you navigate your way through a modern city; or some insect repellent, rain gear, and good hiking boots in the forest. In the same way, certain pieces of magical equipment will help get you through the rough places in the realms of inner experience.

In fact, it can be useful to assemble these things in a magical emergency kit, which can be packed into a convenient box or shoulder bag, kept in or near the room where you do most of your personal magical work, and carried with you when you attend group workings or festivals. That way, your protective and guiding tools can be used in the event of psychic or magical attack, when a ritual goes awry, or at any other time when magical energies become disrupted or unbalanced.

To some extent, the contents of your magical emergency kit will depend on the tradition of magic you practice, and on the skill and experience you've developed in it. Much will also depend on your own strengths and weaknesses. Still, the following items should probably find a place in your kit.

A steel-bladed athame, ritual dagger, or trident. Most systems of Western magic make use of the subtle-energy effects of iron and steel for protection against hostile or disruptive energies. Whatever specific tool your tradition uses for these purposes, one should be part of your kit. It should be ritually consecrated, and kept wrapped in silk or linen to protect it.

A portable censer, charcoal, waterproof matches, and a folding fan. Incense is one of the more useful tools in any magical emergency. Having these items ready will ensure that you can use incense in any situation. The fan directs the incense smoke where it's needed.

Blessing incense. The actual type will vary somewhat depending on your tradition, but frankincense is nearly always a good bet. Rosemary, sage, and vervain are also common. All incenses should be kept in airtight containers.

Banishing incense. Again, your choices should be guided by the type of magic you practice. Cedarwood, mugwort and myrrh are generally good options.

Red oil. This is an ancient bit of natural magic well worth bringing back into common use. Take a cup or more of St. John's wort flowers, as fresh as possible, and put them in a clear glass jar; pour in olive oil while stirring, until the oil just covers the flowers. Put in a place where the jar will receive direct sunlight for at least a few hours each day, and let stand for 2–4 months. If the flowers are fresh, the oil will turn blood red. Strain, and store the oil in a cool, dark place. A drop of red oil rubbed onto the forehead will banish disruptive energies and help restore peace even in the most trying times.

Salt. Many magical traditions use this to purify and banish. Good-quality kosher salt or sea salt are best.

A small bowl or cup, and a sealed container of incense ash. These, together with salt and clean water, can be used to consecrate holy water for use in blessings and purifications. Pour the water into the cup or bowl, and add a pinch each of salt and ash. Then hold both your hands over the water and speak an appropriate blessing, concentrating on your intention. Holy water can be sprinkled around the edge of a circle to purify it. Any left over at the end of a working should be poured onto the earth.

Protective talismans or amulets. Different schools of magic have different versions of these common tools, ranging from little bags of herbs and graveyard dust to pasteboard disks covered with geometrical diagrams and Hebrew letters. Whatever the details, something of the sort is well worth having in your kit—kept in silk or linen to keep its charge at full intensity.

These objects, plus any other items you may choose to add to the collection, will give you options in most of the difficult situations that come up in magical work. The best kit in the world, though, will be useless if you do not know what to do with it. Take the time to make sure you know how to use every item in your kit. If any of the items are meant to be used in ritual workings, the ritual should be memorized and frequently practiced before you have to rely on it.

WORKING WITH ELEMENTALS: FIRST PRINCIPLES

BY CLARE VAUGHN

To begin at the beginning, I should explain what elementals are. Many legends exist about elementals, their natures, their purpose, and their interactions with humankind. But according to various traditions, these beings belong to the four magical elements of earth, air, fire, and water. Elementals dwell in the elements as humans dwell on Earth; they spring from them as we spring from the chemical elements of Earth. The traditional names given to elementals are salamanders (fire), undines (water), sylphs (air), and gnomes (earth).

Magical traditions teach that elementals are collective beings. They do not have individual souls, and are in the process of acquiring individual personalities. Elementals are not truly capable of independent choice and are guided from the higher consciousness of elemental kings, who are in effect the collective intelligence of their respective peoples. Traditionally, Djinn is named as the king of the salamanders; Paralda, of the sylphs; Nichsa, of the undines; and Ghob, of the gnomes. Above the four elemental kings are the four archangels of the elements: Raphael, of air; Gabriel, of water; Michael, of fire; and Auriel, of earth. Above these is the divine.

Elementals can also receive guidance from human beings who interact with them. According to several sources, they can even acquire individual souls through prolonged work with humans. Collectively, elementals are a younger sibling to the human race. This is partly why we can exercise influence over them and affect their development. This is also why we have a measure of responsibility toward elementals. Any contact made with them must be made with this in mind.

When contacting elementals, recall that their essential natures are bound in their elements, and they should be treated accordingly. The ways in which elementals of different types interact with us and with each other relate directly to their natures. Some accounts take descriptions of elemental natures to extremes, claiming that sylphs and gnomes are incompatible with each other, and likewise salamanders and undines. But this is a limited view. Fire and water, earth and air exist not in enmity but in polarity. The interactions between polarizing pairs are not always harmonious to human perceptions, but they are always balanced. The marriage of fire and water is after all one of the great secrets of alchemy.

Magically, working directly with elementals provides for humans a depth and richness that no other practice can match. The elementals are perfect guides to their realms. Furthermore, elementals generally do benefit by working with human beings in an unforced relationship. Bound servitude is not good for them, any more than it is for us, but in a voluntary partnership elementals thrive. It can speed their collective evolution, and sometimes lead to the development of souls in individual elementals. Over a period of time, elementals may evolve into fully individual ensouled beings.

Humans also benefit by working with elementals. That is, we have much to learn from contact with the elements themselves and from the process of achieving balance that results when we work with all four elements in turn. Many people grow and change positively through their contact with elementals. They may have increased sensory awareness, sharpened perceptions of the natural world, greater understanding of energy patterns and flows, and a wider knowledge of the magical realms. Thus both sides gain when humans and elementals develop a working relationship are on both sides.

A DRUID HEALING SPELL

Used by Druids of the Order of the White Oak, Ord Na Darach Gile

BY ELLEN EVERT HOPMAN

Three are the colors associated with the Celtic goddess Brighid: White for the white cows of Boann, her mother, and for the White Mare of the Otherworld; red and white for the red-eared dogs of the Otherworld; and black, red, and white for the cat, the snake, and the oystercatcher. Black, red and white are the original colors of creation and of the goddess according to tradition.

When healing is needed, three lengths of white, red, and black wool may be passed through the smoke of a sacred fire or dipped in sacred water. Sacred fire is fire that has been kindled using a crystal and the concentrated rays of the sun; fire kindled by friction, by flint and steel, or gathered from a lightning strike. Sacred water is wild water from a stream, from a holy well, from beyond the ninth wave of the ocean, or water exposed to the light of the Full Moon or of the Sun on a holy day.

The lengths of wool are twined together and tied with nine knots. Then may they be tied about a wound or about the neck or a limb of one who needs healing. As the knots are tied in the wool, the following charm, or any healing charm of ancient tradition, may be recited.

> *May you repel every ill, every ill wish, every evil.*
> *As this thread goes round thee may you be well forever.*
> *In the name of Brighid, in the name of the Three, in the name of all the powers together.*
> *Power of air be with you, power of fire, power of storm.*
> *Power of Moon be with you, power of Sun, power of star.*
> *Power of sea be with you, power of Earth, power of stone.*
> *I appeal to Brighid to cast off every harm!*

A Simple Rite to Remind You That You Are a Being of Light

By Janina Renée

Fundamental to many ancient and New Age mystical traditions is the belief that we are essentially spirit beings, and even though we are clothed in flesh, we also have bodies of light. However, due to the limitations of our flesh as well as the pressing demands of daily life, it can be difficult to hold this idea in mind, and to be mindful of our connection with a greater world of spirit. On those occasions when we do feel this connection to spirit, we are inspired and energized, and we experience a revitalized sense of possibility.

Following is a rite to refresh your awareness of the freedom, power, and expansiveness of feeling that you can savor by achieving but a moment of recognition and reconnection with your spirit nature. This is a rite that you might perform when you want to regain your spiritual focus—especially if you feel you need extra energy and are stressed, depressed, and weighed down by matter and by the cares of the world. You may also want to do this as a way of gathering your awareness and starting your day out energized, or as an inspirational meditation when you have a little quiet time.

The basic ingredients for this rite are a candle and a crystal or gemstone. These can be kept on hand specially for this purpose, as you will probably want to perform this rite every so often. A white candle is appropriate because white represents spiritual energy

and light. However, you may use a silver or gold candle if you prefer to work with the qualities of lunar or solar energy that they represent. It is good to anoint your candle with a fragrant oil, such as sandalwood, benzoin, or any other fragrance that suggests spiritual ideals to you. For your gemstone, use a clear, pointed quartz crystal, or any other gemstone that suggests spiritual power to you. (My own preference is a polished piece of rutilated quartz—the fine gold rays within the crystal orb evoke an energetic quality of light for me.) When you feel the need to perform this rite, it is good to create ritual time and space by taking a bath and creating a focus area that is clean and free of distraction. You may further define this space by burning incense and playing music that sets a mood. However, if you are pressed for time, this can also be done as a quickie, using only the candle and the crystal.

When ready, light the candle, then cup the crystal in both hands and recite:

> *I am a spirit of light, with a body of light.*
> *I am of the form and substance of light.*
> *I am a being of energy,*
> *I am a creature of magic.*

Visualize yourself as a spirit of light indeed, your body ethereal and luminescent, with a glow that pulsates and radiates from within you. Now, turn the crystal over in your fingers, and hold it up to the flame, pondering it with a calm mind. Appreciate the beauty of the stone, which is fascinating even for its imperfections. Visualize it pulsating with light and power that vibrates. Hold the stone up in your left hand and say:

Light transforms me.
Light flows through me.

Move the stone to your right hand and say:

Light flows from me, directed
outward,
to give life to my desires.

Now, with both hands, press the stone to your solar plexus area and say:

I am energized and revitalized.
I am one with my own being of light and power.
And I revel in the joy of being,
For I am a free spirit.

Remain in this position for a brief period of time, with your eyes closed, and call back to mind the visualization of yourself as a spirit of light. Hold the visualization in your mind, then reopen your eyes when you feel that you are finished and refreshed. Extinguish the candle, and slip the crystal back into its bag or container, if it has one.

Note: After you have performed this rite a few times, the candle, the crystal, the visualization, and the affirmations become co-identified with ritual intent, and any one of them will serve as a hypnotic key to revive your experience. Thus, if you are at work or elsewhere and cannot light a candle or go through the ritual motions, simply close your eyes and visualize your spirit self, or recite the words in your mind, or carry the crystal in your purse or pocket, fingering it when you get a chance. These actions can refresh you as though you'd performed the entire ritual.

Planets That Go Backward

By Silver RavenWolf

A planet that appears to move backward in the heavens for a period of time is said to be retrograde. I've found retrograde periods uniquely helpful when working magic and considering magical timing.

All the planets in our solar system appear at one time or another to stop—this is called making a "station"—and then move backward. After a time they stop again, or station, and appear to move forward, or turn "direct." Because some planets have faster orbits than others, the time they stop (station), turn retrograde, stop, and turn direct varies from planet to planet.

But in fact, planets never really go backward—it just looks like they do. Retrogrades are all an illusion created by the orbit of our own Earth. Logically speaking, you would think that an illusion wouldn't affect reality. But retrogrades have a profound affect on us. If you think about it another way, there are actually many illusions that affect reality. If we consider the human mind we know that if you "believe" something, then you can create that something in reality. This is what magic is all about.

So what does a retrograde really mean to magical timing? When a planet turns retrograde it is the universe's way of saying, "Hey! Hold up a minute! Time to take a breather. Sit back and just chill!" Of course, we can't stop living just because a planet has decided to surf backward for a while, but in magical timing there are ways to use these retrogrades to our advantage.

To be honest I love to observe how people act during planetary retrogrades. It's sort of fun to sit there, watch everyone run around with eyes twirling in their sockets, while you just relax and smile like a Cheshire cat because you and the universe are sharing an amusing secret, and you were prepared for it.

MAGICAL TIPS FOR RETROGRADES

To take advantage of planetary retrogrades magically, you first need to get yourself a good astrological almanac. In it, you will see symbols for each planet and a little "R_x" symbol indicating the time it turns retrograde and a "D" beside the planet when it turns direct.

Once you've determined the time for each planet's backward passage, the basic key for a retrograde is: "Don't start anything in the subject area that the retrograde planet corresponds to." While you can finish things up, if you start something that pertains to that planet's energy while that planet is furiously backpedaling in the universe, then what you have started will more than likely have to be done all over again when that planet turns direct.

Second tip: The day that a planet stations (stops) before it either goes backward (retrograde) or forward (direct) all heck is going to break loose involving the subjects that the planet corresponds to. Be prepared.

Third tip: The day a planet goes direct your magic in the area of that planet's rule will act like a slingshot. Although Witches and magical people always try to be specific when working magic, be extra careful when a planet turns direct. Check and double-check what it is you truly want to accomplish. The old adage, "Be careful what you wish for," holds a great deal of meaning here.

RETROGRADE PLANETS AND MAGIC

Although all planetary retrogrades have a general meaning, each will be different in some way for every person because of: (1) your personal astrological blueprint—

your natal chart; and (2) what house of life the retrograde planet is currently visiting. These two factors can get fairly complicated, and if you haven't really gotten into astrology the glyphs in your almanac may look like gibberish. Still, you don't need to know everything to practice general magical timing. If you come to like astrology, later on you can study on your own.

Below I have described the general retrograde effects for the three fastest moving planets—Mercury, Venus, and Mars—in relation to magical timing. Although the slower-moving planets can have long-term effects on certain parts of your life, their energies are not as noticeable because of the length of time they take to effect your everyday activities. Mercury, Venus, and Mars retrogrades, however, are quite noticeable in your day-to-day magical activities.

MERCURY

Mercury is the planet of communication, short distance travel, early education, and siblings. Primarily, Mercury is about how we communicate with others; anything communications-oriented is subject to snafus when Mercury stations and turns retrograde. Computers go down, phones don't work, cars poop out, travel plans are canceled, your alarm clock dies at 2:00 A.M.—the list can be endless. A note you sent to a friend is misinterpreted and now she's mad at you. Furthermore, aside from the Moon, Mercury is the fastest planetary body in the heavens. Mercury is named after the Greco-Roman god Mercury—he who is fleet of foot; he moves at a lightning pace, and he flips backward and forward about three times a year so you will often encounter these problems.

In magic, work with Mercury rather than against him. Think before you speak. This is a time to read, study, contemplate, work on projects you started earlier, and tie up loose ends on things already ongoing. This includes magic involving investigative procedures, learning, stopping the flow of gossip, or reorganizing your notes for the big term paper that's due next month. As computer problems often crop up during the Mercury retrograde, this will not be the time to buy new software or try to debug your system. Also, be careful of picking up computer viruses. If something is moving too fast and you want to slow it down, especially in the realm of communications, you can always place the Mercury retrograde symbol (☿℞) on a yellow candle, asking that as the candle burns, the problem slows down until you have time to deal with that situation properly, or until you have the answer you need to proceed in a fair and honorable way.

Magical friends of mine have noticed that brief arguments flare up between themselves and people they love the day before Mercury stations to turn either way. On this day you might choose to sprinkle protection powder around your house, boil a little basil in water on the stove to create sympathy, and avoid altercations with those you care about. Because Mercury is such a fast energy, these fights blow up and blow over quickly, yet the hard feelings may remain until you resolve the problem over the course of the retrograde, or during the following Mercury retrograde. When Mercury's fancy footing does the backward shuffle you are free to think in an imaginative, independent way. Use this energy for vision questing and daily meditations.

VENUS

Venus is the planet of love and relationships, but she also governs fast cash, material items to which you have a psychological attachment, and your short-term savings. When Venus turns retrograde, she basically pouts, is irritable, and downright difficult. Because she affects relationships, her stationing can have the same awkward effect on your relationships as stumbling Mercury. Your mother might not be as easy going as she usually is, your boyfriend may seem to be looking in a different direction, and your boss may have suddenly become an unreasonable soul.

A Venus retrograde happens only every year-and-a-half and lasts about forty days. During this time people are often attracted to the bizarre, unusual, and obscure. If it's weird, a Venus retrograde will expose it, for good or ill. A Venus retrograde is a good time to evaluate yourself and how you react to your parents, spouse, boss, teachers, and friends. If you are trying to find a lost friend or family member, the Venus retrograde is the right time to start looking magically and mundanely. Magic practices for love and relationships should concentrate on yourself—on doing your best to become a better, caring, open-minded person. Other magic during this time can include learning how to save money, how to spend money, and how to decide what you should and should not value in your life. Talking to your guardian angel or totem animal during a Venus retrograde about yourself, your life, and universal love will bring you rewards.

During these forty days, people may be crabby, overly shy, socially inept, or downright rude; yet, Venus is the goddess of creativity and things of beauty. If you don't like what you see in the mirror, then work to change it. If you hate the color of your apartment and had considered repainting it, repaint it now. As you paint, concentrate on feelings of harmony and self-assurance.

If can't seem to hold on to your money, draw the Venus retrograde symbol (♀℞) on a white candle, and place that candle on top of the money you do have. Ask that you learn to slow down on your spending and hold on to your present savings. If you think that a love relationship is moving too fast, draw the Venus retrograde symbol on a blue candle. Place the candle over a picture of yourself. Ask that the relationship slow down until you can think clearly about who you want to associate with and why you are really interested in that person. Ask for clarity of thought. Venus will grant your desire.

MARS

Mars is a particularly feisty fellow. He's the gasoline that fuels all sorts of things, ranging from athletics to war. Another Greco-Roman god, he doesn't take "no" for an answer in the nicest terms, but he is very useful when we need action and lots of it! Mars turns retrograde approximately every two years and two months, so when he suddenly stops short and retreats most humans are left with their mouths hanging open—just as it's a shock when someone puts water in your gas; forget the "vroom," we are now permanently set in putt-putt mode.

While a Mars retrograde doesn't exactly act like other retrogrades (what do you expect, he's the macho guy who likes to do things his way), and while his retrograde period can really confuse matters, in fact this time period can be quite useful, especially if you are a magical person. Since activities slow down, we can learn how to apply our energy in a productive way, rather than wasting it on things that may have no real purpose in our lives. In particular, matters involving karma—every action having a reaction—can be dealt with now.

Because Mars moves more slowly than the other planets we have discussed, he will probably hit only one department in your life in particular, and because Mars deals with challenges and aggression, you may be presented with a bump in life you weren't particularly ready for. Old angers, resentment, and arguments have a tendency to flare up during a Mars retrograde. How you handle that aggression determines whether or not you will grow spiritually and take one step up that ladder of universal love. During a Mars retrograde it is very hard to hold your anger at bay, and after the retrograde you may see things that you missed because you were so busy looking at the problem that you forgot to look beyond for the solution. During a Mars retrograde you can't force people to behave in a specific way—you shouldn't anyway, but it is more pronounced during this time—and issues of right and wrong will seem muddy and mixed up.

Magically, the smartest thing to do during a Mars retrograde is talk to Spirit every day about your mission in life. Mars energy, channeled properly, is not a bad thing. Remember, he's the gas in your cosmic engine. You would think that since Mars retreats and the general pace of life slows down, people would be more complacent. Instead, they seem to go around squealing over the tiniest things. Indeed, this is often the time when we must face our cosmic bullies.

In the end, Mars retrograde energy can be channeled into personal fortitude and actually provide you with the necessary cautionary roadblocks so you can think before you act. During a Mars retrograde, Spirit will show you who your friends are and who doesn't care a wit about you.

Money Growth Box

By Cerridwen Iris Shea

Finally, I found a simple way to get the energies moving toward a more positive financial outlook. It's a baby step to be sure, but the seeds are sown and it looks like there might actually be a harvest this year!

For the first time this year, I experimented with something I call a "money growth box." And I find after all these years it is having a positive effect on my entire life. I am feeling less frantic about finances, and so am better able to improve my overall financial situation.

The box I use is a small wooden one, about four inches in each dimension, that I once received as a birthday gift. I suggest using any box made out of a natural material, such as wood, leather, stone, china, pottery, and the like. I left mine the way it was, but if you wish you can decorate it with money symbols. During a New Moon, cleanse the box and purify it with representatives of the four elements—salt, incense, fire, and water. Say something like, "Money grows from money, and my money grows here, spreading abundance throughout my life."

Add a bit of cat hair in the bottom of the box for luck. Light a few green candles annointed with patchouli oil and some patchouli incense, both of which work well in spells having to do with material goods. Use whichever other correspondences you have found work best for you. On top of the cat hair, put one dollar. Then shut the box and leave it alone.

Each night, for three Moon cycles—New Moon through Full Moon—all the way through to the third Full Moon, put one dollar into the box, saying, "Money grows from money." That's all. Just one simple dollar. If you are so short of cash that you can't spare even one dollar, put in the largest coin you can afford. Don't stop and count the money that's accumulating. Just add the day's dollar on top, speak the affirmation, shut the box and leave it alone.

On the third Full Moon, remove the money from the box and give thanks for it. Put one dollar back in the box. Count the money. Give half of it to the charity of your choice. Spend the other half on yourself. In this, it is very important to spend it on something that makes you feel as though you value yourself—a small gift or token—not on a bill or on something that is a required expense.

For the two weeks of the third waning Moon, leave the box alone. On the fourth New Moon, start the process all over again for another three months.

During this ritual time, I found that I was never short of cash. In fact, it was quite the opposite. Not only did I find myself with extra cash to pay off debts, I found that I had cash to put into my savings account, and also that opportunities to earn additional money came my way. Putting money aside every week for my bills became easier. I became more relaxed about money, more aware and open to new opportunities.

One dollar a day doesn't sound like much, but little bits add up to bigger bits. Money doesn't grow on trees, as they say, but money does grow from money.

PSYCHIC DREAM PILLOWS

BY CARLY WALL

Dreams are our way to tap into our unlimited potentials every night. Each one of us holds great psychic and intuitive powers in our subconscious; if we could only find a way to open the door to unleash that power, we would tap into a great source of magical energy. And in fact, there are many ways to work magically with our dreams.

As our ancestors knew only too well, it is much easier to do this through the dream state. In olden times, many cultures worked with dreams to train their shamans and to survive. If one member of a tribe was a good dreamer, he or she was assured safety from harsh weather conditions, could find new sources of food and water when these became scarce, and could predict when the next attack would come from a neighboring tribe.

Today, we may not have to worry about these particular problems, but we can benefit greatly from dream work. If we work consistently with our dreams, we will soon have psychic experiences. We'll be able to answer any question we have, to dream of our next big job promotion, to see what the future holds, to search out for our true love in our dreams and discover ways bring to them back to us, ask for solutions to problems bothering us, and to get answers to health problems.

I've been working with my dreams for over twenty years. The first thing I learned when I started this practice, was who was meant to be my true love. Just a few weeks afterward, he showed up at my doorstep and now we've been married for more than eighteen years. I've also been shown the path to go in my career; I've been given titles for the books I've written, and I've been shown ways to heal myself and loved ones. It truly is an easy and valuable magical tool.

To begin this practice, the first thing you have to do is create a haven for sleep. Clear away the clutter in the bedroom; take away the television. Clean the room from top to bottom to brush away any negative psychic accumulations. Start yourself off fresh. Next, purchase a dream journal. It can be as simple as a notebook or as complex as a bound blank book. I like to use a daily appointment book that has the dates in it and not too much room to ramble on. And while you are at it, get a special pen to go with the journal. What you will do is record your dreams every morning. Try to get in the habit of jotting down the important details to help you remember your dreams.

Now, as you fall asleep each night, you should make an effort to program your subconscious mind by asking it to solve a problem or show you the way to something. Repeat your request as you fall asleep. You may have to do this for a week before you reach your subconscious mind, but be assured, the answer will come.

Typically, your dream answers will come to you in symbolic form. You must become good at interpreting these symbols for yourself. If something seems unclear, ask the next night for another dream to clarify. As you work more and more with your dreams, the symbols will begin to fall away and your dreams will become crystal clear.

To speed up the process, I use what is called a psychic dream pillow. Regular dream pillows contain herbs which help one to get to sleep. Psychic dream pillows are a little different. These contain certain herbs that have a reputation of freeing up the psychic potential within you.

Traditionally, what you would do to make a psychic dream pillow is sew a square pouch, add the herb and then stitch it closed. To simplify matters, however, at some herb shops you can purchase little pouches used for herbal bath bags. These are the perfect size for your psychic dream pillows, plus they have a drawstring you can pull closed. When the herbs are spent, you can merely toss out the old and add the new. Another simple method is placing a handful of the herb in the middle of a square of cotton material and gathering the ends together and tying it closed. Whatever method you use is fine. You just want to be able to contain the herbs so that they don't get all over your bedding, and yet are still able to impart their magical scents. When you've made your psychic dream pillow, you will place one under your pillow or in your pillowcase, so that as you sleep and toss or turn, you'll release the herbal scents all night long.

Do take care, however, to use these sparingly. It is possible to overdo it with the scents, and so render them powerless on your overloaded senses. You can also become averse to the scent if it is used overwhelmingly. As a general rule, reserve these dream pillows for use during a two to three-night stretch only. Then, place them in a plastic bag for use later. Experiment with different scents and different combinations. Use a few drops of pure and natural essential oil to make the scents stronger. And replace with fresh herbs when you feel the scent is gone after a few months.

Below is a listing of some herbs which may be of most help to you on your dream quest. Try mixing and matching, if you will, to find the best combinations for you:

Bergamot (*Mentha citrata*)—The scent of prosperity and fortune. Use if you want to dream of financial stability, lottery numbers, or a change in careers.

Calendula (*Calendula officinalis*)—This scent helps increase psychic and health awareness. If you want to discover how to heal someone, use this scent.

Cedar (*Cedrus atlantica*)—This scent is one of spirituality. It helps in all religious concerns, and helps one attain a connection to the divine.

Cinnamon (*Cinnamomum zeylanicum*)—A scent which helps increase psychic awareness and prosperity. Use sparingly with other herbs.

Clary Sage (*Salvia sclarea*)—Helps to increase peacefulness and deep dreams.

Eucalyptus (*Eucalyptus globulus*)—A scent for health, purification, and to chase away negative energy.

Frankincense (*Bowellia carterii*)—Has a long history of psychic, magic, and religious use. Helps increase deep breathing. Takes you into other realms of spiritual consciousness.

Hops (*Humulus lupulus*)—Produces deep sleep with dreams emphasizing health concerns.

Juniper (*Juniperus communis*)—An herb of purification and protection. Helpful in spiritual quests.

Lavender (*Lavandula officinalis*)—Calming, helpful in reaching the depths of the subconscious mind. Also good for blending with other scents. Helpful for health and love concerns.

Lilac (*Syringa vulgaris*)—Helps recall past lives.

Marjoram (*Oraganum marjorana*)—The scent of peace and restfulness. It helps reach into the depths to connect with our psychic selves.

Mugwort (*Artemisia vulgaris*)—Good for psychic awareness and astral dreams. Also helps increase visions and prophetic dreams.

Patchouli (*Pogostemon patchouli*)—For sexual energies and prosperity.

Rose (*Rosa centifolia*)—Warm and loving energies. Helpful for enhancing beauty and love relations.

Sweet Woodruff (*Asperula odorata*)—Protects the against nightmares. Enhances a relaxing sleep.

Vervain (*Verbena officinalis*)—Prophetic dreams are enhanced. Chases nightmares.

Theatrical Ritual

By Jami Shoemaker

A friend of mine once asked: "Why is Pagan ritual always so dramatic?" I quipped in response: "Because it's more fun that way." But afterwards, I wondered if the dramatic ritual developed because we believed that the gods would sit up and listen more closely if we made a great show of stomping around the circle and shouting their names. In truth, there is a very good reason why Pagan ritual is often laced with a theatrical quality: ritual and drama are two branches from the same ancient tree that bear the fruit of transformation.

We have all experienced the transforming power of theater. Drama has the ability to create a heightened sense of reality. It acts as a mirror, reflecting back to us our nature as human beings—from ecstatic joy to tender love to the depths of darkness. The origins of Western theater are uncertain, but there are several different theories as to its beginnings. The most popular appears to be the "ritual theory," that proposes theater evolved from religious rituals such as those connected with fertility and the spirits of the seasonal cycle.

Ritual can leave us deeply moved, and it can express all that we have experienced and cannot otherwise put into words. It takes us on a profound journey to places within ourselves, and we return forever changed. There is a fine line between theater and ritual, yet it is important to keep in mind the difference. The distinction lies in the difference between art and life. More practically, we might say that theatre requires an audience. And ritual—since it is not created with an audience in mind—requires participation from everyone.

Theatrical Elements in Ritual

Theater asks that you "suspend disbelief." That is, as an audience member, you agree to forget the fact that you are sitting on a hard folding chair in a small, crowded auditorium so that you can let yourself get caught up in the action. You allow yourself to be carried away by the story, believing that the canvas backdrop actually is a mansion, that the train heard in the distance by the actors is indeed coming nearer, that sorrow truly exists in the heart of the player.

When we engage in ritual, we ask the same—that those who attend play along with us. We ask that they believe an orange crate covered with a scarf is actually an altar of the gods, that the sudden wind in the trees is the voice of the Goddess, and that the words we speak have the power to move mountains. For what is the good of ritual, if not fueled by belief? Through ritual, as through drama, the ordinary becomes sacred; the mundane, divine.

Tools of the Trade

As magical people, we have many tools at our disposal. The most powerful of these are our minds and hearts. If you've ever watched good actors, you will notice that they appear to lose themselves in their roles. They seem to become the characters they are portraying on stage. This is far more than a case of "pretending." This is achieved through a combination of concentration and surrender. Actors concentrate to remain entirely focused on the moment at hand; they also surrender to allow themselves to step into a character's soul.

In ritual, we take on the mantle of priest or priestess, initiate or seeker. We allow a part of ourselves, our spiritual selves, to come forth. And when we approach every action and every word with respect, and allow ourselves to experience sacredness, we become absorbed in the moment. Our personal experience becomes profound, and our reverence is an inspiration to others.

As with actors on stage, our bodies may also serve us well in ritual. Movement is a form of language, and there is much to learn from exploring the many ways you can express yourself through movement. No matter how big your "role" is, try always walking with confidence and being mindful that you are stepping on sacred ground. Magical people understand, too, that the fingers, hands, and arms are extensions of the will. Use them confidently and positively. Gestures not only look good in ritual and bring attention to an action, they move the energy to where you direct it. Experiment with movement. Even a brief introduction to martial arts forms, dance, or movement techniques can go a long way in relaxing the limitations most of us put on our physical expression. Know that being open to the power of gesture and movement will make your body more effective in ritual.

Learn to project your voice. This comes from breathing deeply from your belly and raising your voice when you speak. Projecting not only ensures that everyone can hear you, it actually gives you confidence when speaking. Whether you are calling the gods from the center of the circle or singing a half-remembered chant from the sidelines, don't be afraid to use your voice. Remember, there is great energy in sound, chant, and music, and there is tremendous power in allowing your own voice to be released.

Other tools of ritual are more obvious. The "props" of magic are our athames, chalices, cauldrons, and candles. In ritual, we treat these as the sacred objects they have become. Who, among Witches, has watched the dramatic plunging of the athame into the chalice and not held their breath? These are simply gestures and props, yet together they represent the most sacred act of the gods. Again, it is the mindfulness and reverence with which we use them, which makes the moment meaningful.

Finally, the costumes, makeup, jewelry, and masks we don as ritual garments offer us endless variety. Like the actor, we use these elements to become something more than our ordinary selves. Slipping into a ritual robe prepares you for ceremony; it focuses your attention on the thing you are about to do; it reminds you who you are—a practitioner of magic. Special clothing, masks, or makeup help us to move between the worlds, calm any rambling thoughts, and tap into the spirit of a god or goddess. They also serve as visual "prompts" for others, setting the stage and bringing an aesthetic quality to ritual.

TIPS FOR THE DRAMATICALLY INCLINED

To start, always plan ahead. Take time to put your ritual together, select or write the "script," gather tools, examine a site, and consider any other details. Determine how many people will be participating, how people will interact, the overall desired result, and the experience you want the participants to walk away with. Be organized. Know what you want to accomplish, and convey this to all who are involved. Know where all your tools, props, and costumes are, and have a designated place for everything. Give clear directions. Delegate if you have more than you can handle. At the same time, know that "when the spirit moves" during a ritual, anything can happen. Like a live performance, there is always the chance of something totally unexpected happening. Go with it. This is when some of the most amazing and memorable things can happen.

Rehearse the ritual. Check the timing. Balance spectacle with participation, making sure the ritual actually involves all attendees. Run through the ritual so those who have roles know their functions and have a sense of the continuity of the actions. Do the drummers know their cue? Can the priestess actually walk in that gown you want her to wear?

Consider the setting and the lighting. If the ritual is set outdoors and starts in the evening, will it be dark just at the moment you want everyone to see the most important symbol or gesture? If set indoors, what are your space limitations? If you have neighbors close by, do you have a noise level to consider? In this case, perhaps a silent ritual, rich in visual symbolism would be most effective.

Include some visual appeal. Costumes, makeup, masks, props, and setting can have a tremendous impact on the overall effect of the ritual. "Setting the mood" is essential, and can trigger a more profound ritual experience.

Have verbal appeal. We are moved by beautiful music, by poetry, by words of truth. Eloquence is always welcome in ritual, but be careful not to extend into the obscure. Keep scripted parts of the ritual simple, yet meaningful. Make sure those delivering lines understand what they are saying, and can deliver them with conviction. As an alternative, consider the power of silence. Some of the best rituals I've taken part in were silent. Or make use of random environmental sounds such as the hoot of an owl, or the sudden crackling of a candle flame—they can be more effective than verse.

Draw upon the universal. The most effective ritual—and the greatest of dramas—spring from universal human themes like love, sorrow, joy, and the search for something greater than ourselves. The Pagan pantheons lend us infinite possibilities for storytelling and inspiration.

Always have fun. As serious as we may be about our beliefs, our practices, our rituals of worship, and our faith in the gods, always remember that laughter and enjoyment are essential elements of life, and therefore, essential elements of ritual. There will be mistakes, false starts, and unexpected occurrences. This is what makes a live performance exciting, and it's what makes ritual genuine.

The common elements of ritual and theater allow for a great intermingling of the two. All ritual need not be dramatic. Some of the most amazing rituals I've participated in have been simple, spontaneous workings I've done alone, or shared with one other person. However, most group ritual situations can benefit from the conscious infusion of theatrical elements such as those discussed above. In the end, bringing the tools of theater into the ritual setting can greatly enhance this sacred and transformative art of worship.

THE WHIRLING DERVISHES

BY JIM WEAVER

Accompanied by the ethereal sound of the reed flute, a chorus at one end of the hall begins to chant. Then, following a 700 year-old mystical tradition, men wearing tall felt hats and long flowing white skirts begin a whirling dance around the floor. With their arms extended and their large white skirts floating outward forming brilliant white circles, the trance-like turning, or "sema," mesmerizes the viewer.

The whirling dervishes, as they are known in the West, are part of the great Moslem religious order founded in Konya, Turkey, during the 1200s by the Persian-born poet and mystic, Mevlana Celaleddin Rumi. In the Moslem world they are known as the "Mevlevis," in honor of their founder, Mevlana.

Since ancient times, dance has been used in many religions as a way to give thanks to the gods. To Mevlana, dance was a way for the dervish to be relieved of earthly cares and passions; to be united with the order of the universe.

Every article of ceremonial clothing worn by these dervishes during the dance and each precise dance movement has deep mystical significance.

The tall hats are said to represent tombstones. Tall brimless hats have long been associated with magical orders. It's interesting to note that many dervish sects were interested in the occult and did work magic. The hats may have a deeper meaning than we'll ever know. Before the turning begins, each dervish wears a black robe. The robe represents the grave and earthly attachments. As the robe is removed, it signifies the shedding of earthly ties. The white jacket and long skirt symbolize the future—which is always shrouded in mystery.

As the dervishes begin to turn, they raise their arms. The right palm must face up; the left palm down. It is believed the divine energy enters the right palm and is directed through the body to the left palm, where it enters the earth, similar in the way power is grounded during magical ceremonies.

The circle was a divine shape to Mevlana. Each dancer turns in a circular motion, while his skirt fans out to form yet another circle. It is clear Mevlana must have known about the magical importance of the circle as well as the power of movement. To show their place in the cosmic order, as they spin, the dervishes represent the turning of the planet.

Each December the whirling dervishes still perform in Ronya in memory of Mevlana's death. The ceremony draws many lovers of Mevlana.

Mevlana was born in Persia; however, he settled and taught in the Turkish cultural center of Konya. It is here he is buried in an exquisite green-tiled mausoleum.

Mevlana was not a fanatic. He believed in a faith based on universal love and tolerance; he sought to encompass humankind in this faith. His love lives on in the hearts of those who still perform the sacred dance he created. The love and tolerance that was at the core of his teaching is exemplified here in one of his most famous quotes: "Come," he said. "Come again, whoever you may be, unbeliever or fireworshipper. Come. Come again."

THE SACRED HILL OF TORTUGUERO, COSTA RICA

BY BERNYCE BARLOW

Deep in the jungle, near the northern Caribbean coast, close to the Nicaraguan border, is a Mayan sacred site called Tortuguero. Tortuguero means "place of the turtle" and is an ancient nesting grounds of many species of turtles, including the green and leatherback.

At one time Tortuguero was a busy Mayan temple site used for ceremony and magical rites. Because there are no roads to Tortuguero, it can only be reached by boat access on the many canals that connect with the rivers of Costa Rica. Today, the village of Tortuguero continues to honor the turtle and shares that honor with a handful of tourists who navigate the jungle waterways to the nesting grounds and ruins.

One of the most sacred places at the refuge is an extinct volcano called Tortuguero Hill that can be seen from the sea. Mayan priests built a temple near a cave that is sunk deep into the hill. In the cave is an altar and an image of a sea turtle carved into rock that was placed on the hill altar. Two stone crocodiles were placed on either side of the turtle as guards.

The turtle was a Mayan staple. Shells, claws, leather, meat, and eggs provided the village with daily necessities, much like the buffalo did for native North Americans. The crocodiles in the Mayan calendar represented primordial forces of energy and the possibilities of human emergence from the waters of primitive thought and action. Its ability to protect and guard was secondary to its role as a reflection of human potential emerging from the murky depths of primitive action.

For thousands of years, each July the turtle on the altar would reverse itself ninety degrees and face inland, calling her children home to nest. This was a special time for the village, and many ceremonies celebrated the safe arrival of the sea turtles to Tortuguero. The turtles came by the thousands to lay their eggs at night on the beaches, then return at sunrise to the ocean. When nesting season was over the altar turtle would again reverse herself toward the sea, keeping a safe watch until the time was right to call her daughters inland again.

It is believed that the turtles use the magnetic grid of the Hill to guide them to their nesting place. Strong magnetic energies draw us into ourselves. Many sacred sites display this type of energy. Our ancestors used these magnetic properties to enhance altered states for prayer and ceremony. And so it was and still is with Tortuguero, whose energy and magic was not only called upon by the Mayan priesthood and population but by the turtle daughters of the sea.

Triple Aspect Candle

By Kirin Lee

This is a great ritual candle or an elegant centerpiece for an altar. You may choose the color for a particular season, or use a color suitable for all year. You will need sand (river, beach, sandbox); tapered cups without handles (such as short glasses); a tall thin jar (like an olive jar); paraffin; stearic acid; wire-core wicks; dye of your choice; scented oil of your choice; and wax for a wax bath.

Directions

1. Fill a small laundry tub with sand. Ideally, the sand should be at least ten inches deep. A wooden or cardboard box will work well for this, too. Dampen the sand and firmly pack it. Keep in mind that different types of sand give different looks.

2. Using tapered cups or glasses, press three holes in the sand vertically to form a triangle. The holes should be four to five inches apart.

3. Press the olive jar lengthwise into the sand to connect the holes you made in step 2 like an artery. Your jar will need to be tall enough to reach from hole to hole. A sawed-off piece of broom handle or toilet paper tube may work if you are careful. The connecting "arteries" should not be as deep as the holes.

3. Using your fingers, carefully pack the edges of the connecting sections smooth.

5. Heat the paraffin to 240°F using direct heat. Avoid burning or scorching the paraffin. When the paraffin is ready, add stearic acid. Use two teaspoons for each pound of paraffin. You can save time by using candle-making wax already containing the acid. This can be purchased at craft stores.

6. Add the dye. Wait until you are nearly ready to pour the wax before you add the scent.

7. Slowly pour the wax into the sand mold. By doing it slowly, you will avoid damaging air bubbles.

8. In about thirty to forty minutes, a well will form in each hole section of the mold. Use a pencil or stick to put a hole in each well at the center. Insert a wick in each pencil hole, then refill the wells with hot wax. Make sure the wicks are straight. Short wicks give you a refillable candle. When the inner wells have burned down, you can add small votive candles.

9. When the wax is completely hard, lift the candle out of the sand and brush off any loose sand.

10. Dip your candle in and out of hot, clear wax with a low melting point to give it a glazed look. This wax should not contain stearic acid. Melt this wax in a container deep enough and wide enough to cover your candle. Use low heat to avoid burning or scorching. Wearing rubber gloves to protect you from burns is a good idea. Hold your candle by two of the wicks and dip it several times in the hot wax. Don't leave it in too long or it will melt. Dip the candle in room temperature water right away to add more shine. Let your candle sit a few days before using.

April 1: Trickster's Birthday

By Elizabeth Barrette

Almost every culture includes an "upside down" holiday. Often this comes at a period between the old year and the new, or between the changing of two seasons. It is a time, in general, for releasing tension by making fun of the rules that govern the rest of the year—a trickster's holiday, if you will.

April 1, or "April Fool's Day," once served this purpose, but it has degenerated in recent times to an excuse for idle, and often destructive, pranks. Perhaps it is time to reclaim this holiday for its original role and celebrate the birth, and exploits, of the trickster figure in all guises.

This outrageous archetype of the trickster plays an important part in creating the world and keeping it going. It is trickster's job to make things up, shake things up, and screw things up. In many creation stories, the trickster is the one who gets the ball rolling, often interrupting a gathering of staid deities and adding a note of chaos to their deliberations. The trickster prevents things from stagnating and shows us that it's okay to make mistakes.

Almost all pantheons include some kind of trickster figure, but this whimsical deity can take on any form or name imaginable. In many pantheons the trickster is a skilled shapeshifter. Sometimes he appears as an animal, other times as a human, often strange or deformed in some way. The Norse know him as Loki, the Greeks as Hermes, and Africans as Legba. Native American forms include Raven, Coyote, and Jackrabbit. In China and

Japan we find Inari, the clever fox-spirit. There are representations even in our culture, such as Wile E. Coyote and the Roadrunner of cartoon fame, who between them display nearly all the classic trickster traits.

Depending on the culture of origin, trickster may manifest as male, female, or some odd combination of the two. Many trickster figures are cross-dressers, salacious clowns, or herma-phrodites. They often behave inappropriately—as defined by cultural sex and gender roles. Some even change from one sex to the other. All of this highlights their status of standing outside the norm. Some cultures believe that humans with unusual sexual characteristics are "touched" by trickster energy, making them especially powerful shamans or magicians. In many cultures, sacred clowns are trickster figures bringing divine energy into human form.

Tricksters possess many skills, powers, and attri-butes; however, some traits appear frequently enough to give us a basic archetype. More often than not, a trickster is clever, funny, unkempt, lewd or raunchy, lying, full of himself, greedy, graceless, cheating, and shortsighted. He may be sexually rapacious to a ludicrous degree. Some trickster figures can appear as any age they choose. Trickster may appear beautiful or ugly—or both. Most tricksters like to play pranks, tell jokes, and concoct wild schemes; most work some form of magic. Some tricksters are forever coming up with great ideas that go wrong; others continually wreak havoc inadvertantly, only to find that somehow things turn out right in the end.

This April 1, take some time to invite trickster into your life. Think about old habits or patterns you would like to break— maybe you take yourself too seriously, or maybe you hate your job. Tricksters can shake things loose if you ready for anything; you never know what will happen once you open the gates.

A good way to start is by reading about the trickster in myths, legends, and other stories. Most of these will be funny nonsense stories, but some are more serious. Collections of contemporary cartoons are good too. Try comparing and contrasting stories from different cultures. Retell one of them with a trickster from another land, or make up some trickster tales of your own.

You can also learn about trickster energy by imitating some of trickster's ways. Jot down all the social rules you can think of (shaking hands with your right hand, eating soup with a spoon) and then pick one to give up for a day. Greet every person you meet by telling a funny joke. Wear a silly item of clothing (a helicopter hat or a huge garish tie) or wear clothing that doesn't match. Reverse the meaning of everything you say (for instance, say "Goodbye" when you mean "Hello"). Take up a whimsical hobby such as juggling, mime, or making balloon animals. Paint a clown face on yourself. Embrace absurdity.

This kind of activity can make for a terrific party if you want to get your Pagan friends involved. Invite everyone over for a real whiz-bang Trickster festival. Show comedies and parodies. Serve strange food, like cracker sandwiches with different mystery fillings or Jello molded in exotic shapes. Have everyone make a simple mask with construction paper and string, then swap masks at random intervals. Hold a spoof ritual—you can make up your own or use an old favorite like the "chocolate ritual." Put party bulbs in your lamps, a different color for each room. At the end of the evening, have someone dressed as a stage manager remove the guests one at a time by hooking them with a cane.

There are times in our lives when we all take ourselves too seriously. The trickster and the sacred clowns remind us that life is often crazy, crude, and laughable. This chaotic, whimsical energy helps keep cultures and individuals from ossifying. So when trickster's birthday rolls around, set aside some time to play with change and inanity. The results may amaze you.

Energy Rocks

By Estelle Daniels

Many people use rocks for their energies. It is best to determine for yourself how rocks can work for you.

When teaching students about rocks and their energies, I emphasize that not all rocks work the same for all people. For example, clear quartz crystals are widely recommended as energy batteries, but I don't use them that way. When I want an energy battery I use smoky quartz, topaz, or amber. In general, you have to try your own experiments to see which rocks work for you. The first thing to do is get a field guide to minerals with easy-to-understand explanation of rocks and their properties and color pictures.

Most rock books categorize by color. This is an easy identifier, and there is some validity that each color has certain energy vibrations. However, color is only one of many factors. Not all rocks of one color have the same feel; though malachite, green tourmaline, green jade, and chrysoprase come in very similar shades, their energies and uses are very different.

The next step is to get some rocks and work with them. This can take some time. Start with a few rocks, add to your collection over time, and you will discover new and interesting things. Carry them around in your pocket. Note how you feel, and what energies, images, or uses they seem to bring to mind. Use your field guide and learn about chemical composition, crystal system, hardness, and other properties of each.

One exercise I love is to take a piece of iron pyrite (fool's gold) and a piece of galena. Both use the cubic crystal system, and both are metallic. Pyrite is FeS (iron sulfide) and galena is PbS (lead sulfide). I like to feel how they each run energy in a distinct way despite their similar weight and superficial feel.

Try comparing malachite and azurite. They have very similar chemical compositions and the same crystal system, but their colors are different. Malachite is green and azurite is blue. Their difference is an extra electron in the copper ions. In fact, azurite oxidizes or rusts into malachite, which is why they often occur together. Maybe you don't feel any difference. That's okay—there are no absolute rights or wrongs here. Another source of information is a psychic rock book such as *Cunningham's Encyclopedia of Crystal, Gem, and Metal Magic.*

When I have narrowed my choices somewhat, I try several approaches to study the properties of stones. One is to go into trance while holding the rock and meditate on it, trying to feel its energies. Or I place the stone on an energy point of my body and see how it affects my energy flow. A very safe technique is to place a stone under your pillow and concentrate on the energy of the stone before you go to sleep. It may take a few nights, but you can get good results. Write down your dreams immediately on waking. You can also wear a pendant with the stone and see how life changes over a week; take care not to wear other new jewelry while trying out the new stone.

I have discovered my choice of favorite stone changes over time; new and interesting rocks replace the old ones. Though it is likely my needs and preferences are different than in the past, through time I become better at sensing and using the energies of rocks and can make more subtle and refined distinctions. What I dismissed as a boring mineral a few years ago might suit some more presently pressing need. I find that I end up being drawn to what I need when I need it. As with everything else, too, there are fads and fashions in rocks, and what's abundant and fashionable one year may become scarce. In general, however, I try to avoid fads, often waiting a year or two till prices for new rocks go down considerably.

Let your mineral collection grow while keeping everything safe. A box will serve you well in this, and when you need a rock your box becomes a magical toolbox. You may also end up giving away specimens, especially as healing or protective charms. Having a stash of relatively inexpensive but effective pieces can help those in need.

In the end, you will find you end up favoring some stones and being turned off by others. This is fine, because you are developing your own energy tastes in rocks. That's what this is all about.

Native American Dreamcatchers

By Lynne Sturtevant

In the beginning, Mother Earth was lush and green. The First People understood the language of the animals and the spirits of nature were in harmony. The People and the animals were strong and happy, but time passed and things changed. The human beings could no longer rest. Nightmares descended every night and stole their sleep. The People begged their Clan Mother to make the dreams go away. But the old woman did not tell them the horrible nightmares were haunting her too.

The seasons changed and the human beings grew weaker. The men could not hunt or fish. The women stopped gathering plants, and the corn died on the stalks. During the endless nights, Clan Mother searched her long memory. She had spent her life learning the secrets of plants and the healing stories, but nothing had prepared her for the night terrors. Each morning, she walked in the woods and listened to the breeze, straining to hear the voices of her ancestors or of the Corn Mother. The wind was empty and the spirits were silent.

On the night of the Full Beaver Moon, Spider Woman looked down upon the People and saw their torment. She took pity and visited Clan Mother. "Watch me and do as I do," Spider Woman said. With her strong jaws, she cut a slender branch from a sapling. With her eight legs, she bent it into a hoop. Then she began to spin. Around and around she went filling the hoop with her web. When she reached the center, she left a small hole. Spider Woman scattered berries through her sticky, glistening web. Then she took three soft feathers from her leather pouch and attached them to the bottom of the hoop. She turned to Clan Mother. "This is a magic dreamcatcher. Hang it where the human beings sleep. Dreams will be drawn to the web. The bad dreams will be caught and held fast until first light destroys them."

Clan Mother said, "If the People cannot dream, we will die."

"The dreamcatcher only traps bad dreams. Good dreams emerge through the hole in the center and slide down the feathers into the sleeping human beings."

The dreamcatcher faded away, and Clan Mother knew Spider Woman had come to her in a vision. When the sun colored Father Sky pink, Clan Mother taught the People to make dream-catchers and they have been free of nightmares to this day.

MAKE A DREAMCATCHER

1. Buy or make a hoop. Craft stores sell metal and wooden hoops of various sizes. They are usually displayed with the needlework, macrame, or quilting supplies. If you don't like the hoop's finish, wrap it with suede laces or yarn before you begin tying the web. You can make a hoop from a flexible green stick. Tie the ends of the stick together and let it dry a few days. It will shrink as it dries, therefore you'll need to tighten the knot by holding the ends together before your begin the web.

2. Create the web with embroidery floss, fine yarn, or heavy thread. To determine how much you'll need, measure the circumference of the hoop (the distance around the outside) and multiply by eight. Set aside extra floss to attach decorative items and to hang the finished piece. Tie one end of the floss to the hoop and secure it with a double knot. Then tie half-hitches about an inch apart completely around the hoop (see figure on page 97). Each subsequent row is attached to the web. To begin the second row, tie a half-hitch in the middle of the first loop of the first row. Continue building row upon row working your way to the

center. Leave an opening for the good dreams to pass through and tie off with a double knot. If you want to include beads in the web, thread them onto the floss as you work. The beads will slide unless you tie knots above and below them to hold them in place.

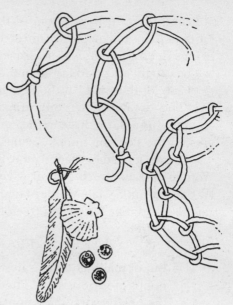

3. Attach decorative items to the hoop with additional floss or glue. Beads, small charms, pieces of suede, and natural items like feathers, pine cones, and acorns work well. Tie a hanger to the top of the dreamcatcher and place it in a window or over your bed. Sweet dreams!

STONE PEOPLE LODGE MAGIC

BY BERNYCE BARLOW

Throughout the ages, body purification baths using hot rocks, water, and steam have been a custom observed by many civilizations. Methods varied as to the kind of structure used as the "sweathouse," but the intent and often the ceremonies that developed around this concept were universally similar. The most obvious reason for sweat baths is to keep the body clean and rid of toxin buildup, but there are magical applications to this type of purification that date back thousands of years.

Within the practice of shamanism there is a concept called "mystical heat." Mystical heat refers to the extreme internal warming of the body and has been recognized as a path to creativity and power by many cultures. It is considered the fire within us, one that sparks and kindles the soul. Indeed, some stories say that the inspiration for creation occurred after a profuse sweating of the creator spirit.

Stone People lodges are an elementary tool in manifesting mystical heat. The monks and nuns of Tibet effect this phenomena through breathing techniques and yoga. Some shamans in India sit very close to large fires. Japanese holy men bury themselves in hot sands; northern Europeans build saunas. No matter the technique used to raise the internal thermometer, the end result is to achieve a state of heightened awareness and spiritual transcendence through intemperate body heat. In this heated state it is believed one has the ability to create more magic, manifest more energy, and disconnect from the physical in order to connect with higher powers. Mystical heat is said to purify the mind, body, and soul, at times through spiritual ecstasy.

Another application of the magical properties found in all Stone People lodges are the rocks, respectfully called Grandfathers. Lava rocks are traditionally used because they are born from the womb of Mother Earth. The cycle of cooled molten lava being refired brings the Grandfathers to life to talk their medicine. When water is poured on the red glowing Grandfathers, they pop and sizzle, filling the lodge with curative sounds, healing energy frequencies, and deep medicinal vibrations that regenerate and purify our bodies and energy fields. Our bodies are made up of whirling protons, atoms, and molecules all bumping into each other with plenty of space among them. Those spaces "in between" can be filled with all kinds of good medicine like sound, music, color, energy, or scent. In a Stone People lodge the "in between" space is filled with all of the above. In return were are healed. Is this not true magic?

One magical aspect of a North American Stone People lodge has to do with the spirit robes and prayer ties that are displayed during ceremony. These robes and prayer ties are a sacred and integral part of a mystic lodge. The prayer ties are small cotton squares approximately two by three inches in size. They are often different colors, representing certain directions or spiritual concepts. Lodge participants place a pinch of tobacco into each square then tie it into a small bundle using cotton thread, sinew, or a thin strip of wet bark from a tree like willow. Each bundle represents a specific prayer, and there can be many bundles on a strand of string. Traditional prayer tie strands vary with the tribal nations. Some strands can carry as many as 700 ties depending on the ceremony. In most cases the ties are burned or set out in nature four days after the lodge ceremony so spirit can do what it will with the prayers. Until then, the ties often hang in the lodge or are placed on the altar directly in front of the lodge. During ceremony, it is taught by some that spirits come and sit in the bundles when invited to do so, becoming active participants in the purification rite. It is also taught that spirits not only reside for awhile in the prayer ties but in the spirit robes hung in the inner lodge.

Spirit robes are strips of colored cotton that are placed in the lodge honoring the spirit life of the four directions, Father Sky, and Mother Earth. Most robes are about a foot long and wide, and hung so spirits may put them on and be welcome in the lodge. The colors do depend on the culture, but the intent is the same. The robes are also burned or set to nature at the same time the prayer ties are.

Aztec sweat huts applied healing magic through steam purification and special combinations of herbal and medicine teas used internally and externally to achieve a specific result. Some teas were made to purify the organs, and others to detoxify muscles or to flush clean the blood. Antifungal and antiseptic washes were also made for external cleansing during a sweat. At times hallucinogenic teas were created to induce a vision or enhance spirit contact. (Author's note: Please do not get inventive about ways to heat up your body. Check with your personal doctor and local shaman before inducing a mystical heat ecstasy state, otherwise you may cook your own goose, if you catch my drift!)

Working with the elements, the Stone People have contributed to the physical, mental, and spiritual well-being of humans. As it was in the beginning, the principles of earth, fire, water and air mingle together within the steamy womb of the sweat lodge.

THE SHIP OF YOUR LIFE: MAGICAL FIGUREHEADS FOR YOUR HOUSE

BY DAVID HARRINGTON

Ancient mariners knew that the sea was a dangerous, unpredictable place. Their vessels were frail, so from early times they bolstered the physical and magical protection of these ships with sacred symbols and animals.

Among the earliest protective images painted on the prows of ships, for instance, were the Eyes of Horus. These eyes looked out for danger, and also made the ship one with the divine energy of Horus. Other Egyptian vessels sometimes were adorned with the high, graceful gooseneck prow, a symbol of the great sun god Ra, "The Great Cackler." Later ships were decorated with images of beautiful women, a remnant of ancient Goddess worship. Ships were all thought to be "female" in nature—nurturing and protecting, yet also capable of fierce attack.

Today, while some of us are fortunate enough to have our own boats, most of us live as "landlubbers"; our homes are our "ships." In many cultures even today homes are often christened, as are ships, with evocative names such as "Windswept," "Heart's Ease," "Willow Cottage," and so on. Houses, like pets, in fact will sometimes tell you their inner names if you take the time to listen. That is, if you live in a house that was built some time ago, it will have acquired its own energy and personality.

"Figureheads" have been incorporated in the homes from many cultures. The gargoyles that protect sacred buildings are a form of figurehead. Old style Chinese roofs are bristling with dozens of small ceramic figures, each from folklore, that protect the inhabitants both by repelling negative energy and by attracting the negativity to themselves rather than to the inhabitants of the house. In Greece, most domestic roofs sport a terracotta image. Sometimes these are just symbolic scrolls, but most of them are stylized images of Aphrodite, with a beautifully modeled head and torso showing her life-giving breasts. Often, the edge of the flat-roofed houses will be lined with *akroterions,* forming a toothlike row warding off all negative outside energy. In Bali, where every child is encouraged to be an artist, the home decorations are immense and creative, usually made of brightly painted carved wood showing the faces of fantastic birds and creatures.

CHOOSING YOUR HOME'S FIGUREHEAD

Figureheads for the home can take many forms. Cast-metal door knockers in the shape of animals are effective talismans, and the metal enables them to hold a charge of magical energy. Mailboxes, which are a portal between the outside world and your inner living space, can be painted or decorated as a protective image. Garden sculptures present a wonderful array of pagan gods and goddesses, Chinese dragons, Germanic gnomes, and Celtic leprechauns—all symbolic of magical power. In the end, choose items you feel comfortable with symbolizing the protection of your home.

Goddess figures and fountains—Any feminine figure can be blessed with divine energy, and all will be protective if you charge them with that intent. In addition to protection, images of Aphrodite, will bring a loving environment or help to maintain one. Chinese Kuan Yin figures confer peace.

God figures and door knockers—Foliate masks, or "Green Men," encourage growth, fertility, and protection. Like gargoyles, these imposing images announce that the area is magically active and ready to protect the inhabitants. Animal images can represent both male and female energies, but some animals are clearly masculine. Stag, wolf, and stallion images can sometimes be found as door knockers, and are just some of the many forms appropriate for magical protection.

If you know you are not going to be in your home for very long, you can dedicate the image itself rather than connecting it energetically to the physical dwelling. In this case, you bless and enchant the image with the idea that it will project protection wherever you are. If you are in a home permanently, you can connect the energy of the image to the existing energies of the house. In this case, the image that you use should probably stay with the house if you ever do leave it. If you expect that it will be unappreciated by the new owners or residents, bury small images somewhere on the property. In this case, the protective figurehead will continue to protect its other half, the physical house itself, even if the occupants are unmagical.

Topiary trees can be used as living totems of magical power. They can be trained or trimmed into many animal forms. Let your imagination run wild. Many hedges and shrubs can be formed into easy, rounded, low-lying animal forms, such as turtles (excellent for house protection as the turtle carries its own house), alligators, and hedgehogs. If you are no artist with the plant shears, don't worry. Even the impression of an animal form will be magically powerful and evocative, even if those who see it aren't quite sure what it's meant to be. In China, confusing evil spirits helps keep them away.

HOME NAMING CEREMONY

For this important ritual, meditate on the idea of your home's name for several days. Walk around your home several times, letting it speak to you. Observe any interesting features. Find out the names of the plants or trees growing nearby, and ask your neighbors if they remember when these things were planted. Think about the microclimate surrounding your area. Listen to the birds, and find out their names.

When you have discovered your home's name, gather your family and friends. Walk around the exterior of the home, softly chanting its new name. Do the same inside, burning a protective, blessing incense such as myrrh as you go from room to room. End the procession by the "hearth"—either a fireplace or kitchen stove—and hang a piece of paper nearby with the name of the home on it. This name can also be later inscribed or painted on a piece of wood and hung outside, nailed to a post, or placed where others can see it. Mark the day of your home naming ceremony on your magical calendar, and each year reenergize and reconfirm the naming.

HOME FIGUREHEAD BLESSING CEREMONY

This ceremony is designed for a home you will plan to live in for a long time. Start by taking the image which you are using to symbolize the protection of your home. If the object is big, such as a statue or fountain, array it and the area around it with flowers, decorative objects, and ritual tools. If you use a particular magical path or faith, feel free to sanctify the space in whatever way you wish. Otherwise, simply take a vessel of water, and add a few leaves, flowers, or twigs from the area around your home to the water. Hold the vessel to your heart and then hold it to the sky, concentrating on your image of the divine. Say these or similar words:

> *I call upon the power of my sacred and eternal home,*
> *the deities of our true spirits*
> *to bless this place on earth, this life's home.*
> *Let the power be placed in this divine image,*
> *(speak of the image itself, for instance "this powerful Wolf,")*
> *Ever vigilant, ever powerful,*
> *potent against any negativity.*
> *protecting all who reside within this home.*

If you have named your dwelling, use the name instead of "this home." Sprinkle the image with the water. Place it where you have decided in your home. Enjoy its magic!

African Ritual Cleaning

By Lilith Dorsey

The coming of spring brings thoughts of regeneration and cleanliness. One of the best things to do during this time is to perform a ritual cleaning. The Orisha, African gods and goddesses of the Yoruba, will not enter a dirty house, so if you are seeking their guidance be sure that your environment is clean at all times. Cleanliness is an important consideration for all altars and shrines in your home.

Traditionally, the cleansing of a home is begun during the waning Moon. This serves to remove negative energy from the premises, and to stop the energies that are hindering your success. A simple way of doing this is with either sea salt for general cleansing and protection or black salt to keep away unwanted visitors. Many African traditions would also include a water blessing in the form of Florida water, angel water, kolonia, or coconut milk. These items should be combined in a large wooden bowl, and then used to bless the home. For added effectiveness a broom of fresh daisies or white carnations can be used to distribute the mixture. Special attention should be given to corners, windows, and doors. This type of cleansing is often repeated after the Moon phase has shifted to waxing with an attraction wash such as High John, Drawing, or Seven African Powers. When cleaning your Orisha shrines be sure to remove the items only one or two at a time, so as not to disturb the

energies there. Any altar cloths should be washed in a ritual bath as well.

In Santeria, ritual cleaning often consists of baths and floor-washes. All herbs used in the religion are classified as either bitter or sweet. Combinations of bitter herbs are used for several nights in a row and then followed by a similar course of sweet herb baths. For more information on these formulas, see Carlos Montenegro's *Magickal Baths of Santería* or Luis Nunez's *Santería: A Practical Guide to Afro-Caribbean Magic*.

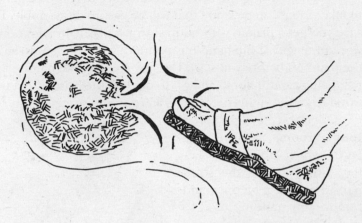

One old African-derived custom uses a coconut for house blessing. First, pick a green coconut that you think resembles your appearance. Rub it with powdered eggshell (cascarilla), and kick it from the farthest corner of the house through all of the rooms, and out the front door. Try not to touch the coconut with your bare hands, and if at all possible kick it into the woods. This should be done after the cleansing described above, or whenever you feel the energy in your house getting a little uneasy. You will be surprised how much better your place feels when you are finished. Whichever method you use, ritual cleansing is a necessary and rewarding process both in the physical and astral realm.

MAKING A BESOM

BY BRIED FOXSONG

All you need to make your own besom is a pair of scissors, some strong cord, colored yarn, a large-eyed mattress needle (about eight to ten inches), a curved carpet needle and, of course, a new broom. Don't use an old broom, you need a new one in order keep any "old dirt" from the circle.

When choosing the broom, remember that you're going to take it apart, so pick one that will be easy to disassemble. Be sure you get a broom with natural straw; plastic bristles don't work in magic. If the handle is painted, you will want to strip the paint off before you start. Use any commercial paint stripper, being careful not to allow it to drip on the bristles. Let the wood dry thoroughly before you start on the straws.

Once you have prepared your broom, remove the cords which hold the straw flat. Check inside the straw part when you get it open and remove any wadding used to shape the broom. Bunch and repack the straw so that your besom will be round and bushy. If the straw on the inner binding is immovable, consider adding your own padding of bundled herbs, a talisman, a protection charm, to round out the besom.

Next, string your mattress needle with a length of strong cord. Pull the straw into a round bundle, and, starting five inches from the neck, push the needle through the straw and out the other side.

Leave a "tail" of about cord about four inches long to tie off when finished. Wrap the cord around several times and then stitch it through the straw again. Pull tight as you go. Whip the cord around the straw and stitch through several times to hold the whipping in place. Tie off the end of the cord to the tail in a tight knot.

Thread your curved needle with colored yarn. You will use this to whip the whipping, sewing around it to fasten it down. Go all the way around the broom, then repeat the other way, making a crisscross pattern. You can thread ribbon or colored yarn through the straw and either tie it off for color contrast, or allow it to trail decoratively. In order for the yarn to stick firmly, use a strong glue. If you want to paint the handle, remember that this is a magical tool and should be dignified. Some paint a rune or charm on the handle; some carve or paint their besom's name in runes or personal symbols. Others decorate it as they would a staff.

Using your Broom

To bless your home—Place your besom on the floor in the middle of your home. Take a small candle, drop some hot wax on the handle and mount the candle on the handle. Then say: "Broom sweep clean. Sweep out evil. Sweep out discord. Sweep out anger. Broom sweep clean. Sweep in joy. Sweep in harmony. Sweep in prosperity."

When the candle burns out, sprinkle a pinch of salt on your doorsills. Sweep the salt into your kitchen and out the back door. If you don't have a back door, sweep the salt up in a dustpan and dispose of it outside.

To guard the house—Place the broom across the door at midnight and say: "Guard well this threshold. Guard well this door. Make sure that my enemies will cross it no more." It will prevent foes from entering.

To guard you during sleep—Also good for astral travel or meditation. Place your besom under your bed or a small besom under your pillow and say: "Besom, guard thine own."

Happy sweeping!

MAGICAL MAINTENANCE

BY CERRIDWEN IRIS SHEA

In most things, we all start out with the best of intentions. We are excited at first; ripe for discovery. We throw ourselves into this new thing wholeheartedly, and we really get going, only to find, after several weeks have passed, that our interest has flagged.

In magical practice, it may be that we haven't done a daily devotional. A layer of dust has gathered on the altar, and we can't recall which crystal goes with what spell. In short, life often gets in the way of our new interests. Between work, lovers, children, and other people, it can be difficult to make time for spiritual things. What to do?

If you accept that your spiritual well-being is important to you—and well it should be—then maintaining your spiritual practice means work. In fact, as far as spiritual things go, there's always more work to be done. Just as you have to maintain the pets, your household, your car, and all manner of things, so you have to maintain your spiritual practice. Your spirituality is just as important as everything else in your life; by maintaining your spirituality, you maintain yourself.

That doesn't mean you can't take "time outs" or that you are a "bad person" if you lapse. Life does get in the way at times, and we all get overwhelmed. But, when something does go wrong, taking a minute to look at your life can be a good and wise thing. If your life seems to be falling apart, chances are good that you have let your spirituality lapse. You may feel that you let your spiritual practice lapse because your life fell apart. Trust me, if you can continue your practice during the tough times, you will be able to get through them a stronger soul.

Instead of berating yourself for slipping up, simply get back on track. Though you may need to work your way back up spiritually, as you would have physically had you stopped going to the gym, all will come in good time.

To start your magical maintenance, you need to give yourself time and space. This can be something as simple as turning your morning shower into a ritual or devotional to greet the day. That is, you may want to light a candle and incense and play music while you shower. If you get ambitious, turn your bathroom into a sanctuary. Read up on water goddesses and decorate the room with appropriate colors, objects, and images. Your morning bath or shower can become a cleansing ceremony that prepares and protects you for the day. Your evening bath or shower can assure a good night's rest.

Meanwhile, the kitchen is your hearth, the center of your home. Let everything you do in the kitchen be sacred. When you stir, stir clockwise, visualizing love and warmth, giving thanks to the Mother for her abundance. Breathe or speak a blessing as you prepare or serve food—even your morning cereal. Hang beautiful and fragrant herbs in the kitchen; cut up an apple, sprinkle with cinnamon, and toss in a pot of water to simmer on the stove and scent the whole room. Use scented floor washes. Vacuum and mop as often as necessary. Turn spring-cleaning and fall-cleaning into full rituals, including everyone in the household. Allow your spirituality to be inclusive instead of exclusive.

In time, you should walk around your home and feel the furniture. Rearrange the rooms until things feel right. If the rooms are used by the entire family, allow everyone to have a say. Change sheets and towels frequently—clean laundry is sacred. Imagine all negative energy draining away in the rinse cycle, and the positive energy of the Sun entering the clothes in the dryer. If you are fortunate enough to have an outside wash line, you can invoke the Sun's energy into the clothes as they dry. Scrub the pet bowls. Clean the cat box. Water the plants. Throw out what's dead, and nurture what is still alive. All of this is an outward expression of your inner journey. Get fresh flowers or seasonal decorations and spread them around the house. Smile at yourself every time you see your reflection in the mirror, especially as you are going out of the door. Take a look at your altar. How does its energy feel? Can you clean the wax drippings off the candleholders and wash the altar cloth? If necessary, you might even remove everything from the altar and sprinkle some anointing oil on the base of the altar. Start again from square one. Put on a fresh cloth. Rearrange what you want on the altar, removing everything but what you need and want in the present time. Reconsecrate everything. Look at the bits and pieces you've removed from the altar. See what needs to be cleaned and put away. See what needs to be returned to the earth. See what needs to be released. Do it.

You may even go so far as to go through your magical drawers or boxes where you keep your magical tools. You may be surprised how much you've accumulated through the years. Take time now to remember when you started out, with all that energy and enthusiasm and even envy for long-time practitioners who had all that cool stuff. Well, guess what—now you're one of them. You've got plenty of cool stuff that you have to take care of.

When in doubt, reconsecrate. If it looks dusty, lonely, and unused, it probably is. Bits of unfinished spells should be released and gotten rid of. Jewelry and statues should be cleaned. Books need to be dusted and rearranged. Take a deep breath and look around. Isn't that better? Now you can actually concentrate when you meditate, when you do your devotionals, and when you thank the deities.

Of course, not everyone lets it slide to that extent. But even in your daily work, there are things that need maintenance. You do want to keep your books, statues, and tools dust-free. Tarot cards should be cleansed after each use and put out under a Full Moon every three to six months to rejuvenate. Cards can be cleansed by passing them through incense, or, if you are somewhere and don't have access, with sacred breath. Same with stones or any other oracle you use.

Any jewelry that you wear constantly should be cleaned with good solid cleaner once a year and then reconsecrated with an oil with a personal scent made specifically for or by you. You should go through all of your boxes and drawers at least once a year to see if anything got shoved aside. Tie up loose ends, figure out if something needs to be reorganized or removed. At times, something will ask to be given away.

Rearrange your altar whenever it feels right. One woman I know rearranges it every morning, as part of her morning devotional. It's a way for her to start each day fresh. Another woman I know rearranges her altar for each sabbat. I don't have a set schedule. I rearrange whenever I feel the need. It's a very individual process.

Treat your magical objects with tenderness and reverence and they will assist in giving you focus, comfort, and forward motion in all aspects of your life. Maintain your magical space and tools lovingly and mindfully, and the rewards will be returned at least threefold.

FLOWER POWER

By Marguerite Elsbeth

Flowers are an integral part of the tapestry of life, woven into the fabric of religion, mythology, and folklore. They have been carved and painted on cave walls since ancient times, and serve mankind as a source of beauty, inspiration, food, medicine, and magic. Each type of flower, in fact, has its own meaning, depending on its essential nature, shape, and color.

FLOWER SYMBOLISM

Flowers in general symbolize new beginnings, beauty, transition, and death. Most flowers have an outer covering of leaflike sepals protecting an inner whorl of brightly colored, scented petals. It is due to their rounded shape that flowers are associated with the center of the universe as well as the soul. Alchemists once called meteors and shooting stars Celestial Flowers, and considered them to be symbolic of the Work of the Sun, or self-transformation.

FLOWER COLORS AND THEIR MEANINGS

An old wive's tale claims that red and white flowers in the same vase are unlucky, while blue and orange flowers may be a calming influence on homes and hospital rooms. Another says that yellow flowers mean love mixed with jealousy, or that you will have more children than you can handle. Color plays a role in determining the significance of a flower. What do flower colors really mean?

Red flowers represent animal life, initiative, energy, and passion. If a flower is orange or yellow, it signifies vitality, ego, will, individuality, purpose, creativity, and friendship. Blue flowers are associated with emotion, nurturance, responsiveness, spirituality, sensitivity, and dreams. Purple or violet flowers indicate prosperity, optimism, generosity, and luck. Pink stands for affection, artistry, beauty, attraction, and peace. White flowers represent purity, well-being, and protection.

FLOWER FOLKLORE

Apple blossoms in April signify a good apple crop; yet if the trees don't bloom until May, the yield will be poor.

African marigolds have a pungent smell and will ward off blackfly and other insects when planted in a garden.

Darling pea and darling lily are said to have the power of binding someone in place for seven years.

Foxglove is known as a fairy plant, and has names such as fairy weed, dead men's bellows, bloody man's fingers, and witch's thimble. The Celts believed that foxgloves in the house were unlucky, and should never be taken aboard a ship. If a foxglove is picked, it will offend fairies who live in the flowers, bringing bad luck or even death to the picker and his or her family.

Honeysuckle brings bad luck in Wales if brought to the home, but foretells a wedding in other parts of Britain.

Lilac is considered unlucky, except when worn around the neck or in the lapel to protect against drunkenness.

Lily is the ultimate fertility symbol. Lilies are also a symbol of death, and at one time were placed on the graves of young innocents.

Primrose is said to bring sickness and sorrow when kept indoors, though its secretions are effective in relieving female hormonal discomfort.

Roses became symbols of love and desire when the love goddess Aphrodite presented a rose to her son Eros. Eros gave a rose to Harpocrates, the god of silence, to induce him not to gossip about his mother's amorous indiscretions, making the rose an emblem of silence and secrecy. The Romans believed that decorating tombs with roses would appease the spirits of the dead.

FLOWER CURES & REMEDIES

Centaury stimulates the appetite, aids digestion, eases heartburn, and relieves gas pains when brewed as a tea from the dried flowering plant.

Chicory owes its magical reputation to the lovely blue of its flower, which may have caused it confused with the Luck-Flower of German folklore. Whoever carried it could make rocks open before him, and so gain entry into the Otherworld.

Cowslip flower tea is a recommended cure for insomnia when taken at bedtime.

Dahlias were used by Aztecs as treatment for epilepsy. Prior to the discovery of insulin, diabetics were given a substance called diabetic sugar made from dahlia tubers.

Daisy has an eye, as their English name—day's eye—suggests, and for this reason the flowers were once used to cure eye trouble. The Assyrians thought that a mixture of daisies and oil would turn gray hair dark again. According to a

116

Celtic legend, children who died at birth scattered daisies on the earth to cheer their parents.

Dandelions were once blown upon in order to tell the time of day. Now we scatter their seeds to make a wish come true. A tea made from dandelion leaves may be used as a tonic to purify the blood. Boiling its roots makes a strong diuretic. The blossoms can be made into wine and the roots can be ground, roasted, and brewed into a coffeelike beverage.

Elderberry is used in the treatment of dropsy. Blossoms mixed with congealed oil make good ointment in burns and scalds. Boil elderberry blossoms together with peppermint leaves to make a soothing tea for common colds and digestive upsets. Elder flower water was once used to clear freckles.

Hawthorn flowers or berries can be prepared as a soothing gargle when infused with hot water.

Nettle juice is an excellent blood purifier, and soft nettle pulp makes an effective poultice for sciatica.

Red poppy has a long reputation as a sedative, although unlike the opium poppy, it contains no narcotics. The blossoms and seeds may be added to cough syrups; the flowers may be used in teas, wine, and ink.

Rose hips may be used for the prevention of scurvy due to their high vitamin C content.

FLOWERY DREAMS

A significant amount of dream flora lore is related to love and marriage. But dreaming of certain flowers may be considered an omen of things to come. Out-of-season flower dreams are thought to bring bad luck, while dreams of blooming flowers bring good luck. Flowers that bring good dream omens include jasmine, lily, laurel, marigold, pear, and thistle. It is thought to be unfortunate to dream of birch, white flowers, cherry, dandelion, plum, and withered roses. Dreams of apricot and apple blossoms may indicate long life, while elder and plum blossoms the possibility of illness. Red roses in full bloom signify love and marriage.

SAY IT WITH FLOWERS

A language using flowers instead of words was formalized in a dictionary written in seventeenth-century France. During the Victorian Era, beautiful and poetic thoughts were shared through coded love letters using this language of flowers. Sometimes entire messages were communicated by bouquet through flower color, positioning, and presentation. For example, a rose bud with leaves and thorns would normally convey, "I fear, but I also hope." Or, if the rose was presented stem first, the meaning would be, "You must neither fear nor hope." Use the list below next time you send or receive a spray of blossoms:

FLOWER	KEYWORD	MEANING
Azalea	Moderation	Slow down! You're moving too fast!
Begonia	Warning	Beware, someone is watching you.
Clover	Promises	I will be true to you.
Daffodil	No	Better to find someone new.
Flax	Thank You	You are very much appreciated.
Fuschia	Caution	Your lover may have another.
Gardenia	Sweetness	You are fresh as the morning dew.
Geranium	Deceit	Do not trust your lover.
Hyacinth	Admiration	You are gifted and beautiful.
Iris	Passion	You inflame my heart and stir my soul.
Jonquil	Desire	Will you be my love?
Lilac	Innocense	There have been others, yet you are my first true love.
Marigold	Jealousy	Time to tame the green-eyed monster.
Narcissus	Selfishness	You think of no one but yourself.
Orchid	Comfort	I give you the Sun, Moon, and stars.
Petunia	Closeness	I can't live without you.
Red Roses	Love	I love you.
Sunflower	Display	You need not show off to impress me.
Tulip	Vow	I will love you forever.
Violet	Purity	You are modest and sweet.

Sacred Disposal

By Diana Olsen

There's always one detail left over after executing the perfect ritual: what to do with the residue—the wax that melted on your altar cloth, the ash left from the incense, the bits of salt either in a bowl or sprinkled at the perimeter of your circle. All of these may remind you of a ritual well done, but they do present a problem, both energetically and physically, when you wish to move on to your next magical act. Few books really say how to dispose of these items beyond a vague suggestion to bury them. Since burial may not always prove Earth-friendly, please consider the following options for disposing of used ritual items.

I have found several convenient methods for sacred disposal. These methods require me to use more than one "sacred vessel" to sort out my disposal needs. A flowerpot sits on my altar, serving as a ritual litter basket. In case of overflow, I keep the empty glass holder for a seven-day candle next to the altar after cleansing it with a salt-water solution.

I sort the physical debris from ritual into three categories: the recyclable, the nonrecyclable, and the biodegradeable. For those interested in conserving matter or cost, most items can be reused. I advocate cleansing and reusing whatever possible as a courtesy to Mother Earth. Some other occultists may argue that this practice leads to frustrating energy buildups, but I have never had a problem in my personal practices. Among conservation methods, you can try melting down wax from old candles and reusing the wax to make new candles or figures. Also, I always save and cleanse my stones unless I am using them for an offering, in which case I always bury them or offer them in a body of running water.

I always take time to sort my ritual debris. I usually place recyclable items, such as certain types of plastic used for wrapping, in the glass candle container. After the jar is full, I sort out the items into pieces to send to the recycling plant and pieces to cleanse and re-use. Fortunately, few of the standard ritual items that I know of are nonrecyclable. Those rare items that are nonrecyclable, usually residue from package wrappings and so on, I place in a box or garbage bag and send with reservations to the landfill. A quick sprinkling of salt water seems to clear any psychic residue I might send along, and I also mutter a prayer that the items reach sunlight so they have a better chance of biodegrading. I think the only item that has ever significantly caused me this problem was the plastic wrap from candles, but with recent changes in recycling technology even those plastics now go to the recycling bin.

Biodegradeable items, as much as possible, go in the flower pot on my altar. I take leftover wax, wet and dry herbs, and even incense dust and put it in the compost heap in the back of the property where I live. This way their remains can break down, and they can reincarnate as new life.

Remaining salt, juice, and wine are tricky as each has a chemical composition that can damage some plants. These byproducts I try to consume myself, or else I offer them at some dirt crossroads.

In the process of determining how to handle my ritual byproducts I've also learned how to manage typical household damage from ritual products. My favorite technique for removing candle wax from clothing, cloth, and carpet is to place a paper towel over the stain and then set an iron on low over the paper towel. After a few moments, the wax melts into the paper towel and is nicely removed from the inappropriate area. Red or white wine stains come out nicely with a mild solution of sea salt, water, and lemon juice. Burns do not come out well, ever.

After an intense ritual, I don't always have the energy to give my altar the immediate cleaning it deserves. In these case, I have learned to apply a "three day rule." I clean my altar within three days of the ritual, giving it a good cleansing with salt water, sage, and sometimes a candle blessing as soon as I've completely wiped off all the dust. There are exceptions to this rule: if the energy from a ritual was particulary intense or volatile, I try to have it cleaned by the next day at the latest. Ideally, after such an intense ritual, cleaning should occur within two hours.

Cleaning up can usually take a small delay, but it is still important magical maintenance, just as crucial as house cleansings. Energy builds in all the magical workings you do. By cleaning out ritual byproducts regularly and promptly, you can better control the type of energy that surrounds you. In extreme cases of neglected "housekeeping," the buildup can lead spells astray and make room for some poltergeist activity. In milder and much more common cases, the energetic "gunk" acts as a demotivator, leading to a feeling of lethargy or disinterest for the more psychically sensitive in a living area. When this occassionally hits me, I've always found a good, old-fashioned house cleansing sets me back in the mood to do my work. By giving my altar a good scrub, I can further motivate myself to return to my magical practices.

Don't limit your cleaning to ritual tools and your altar. I admit that I personally am a lousy housekeeper, but even then, once a month (New Moon is a good time for this) I do my best to clean up flat surfaces, dust a bit, and bring some order to my natural entropic state. Although the process itself can be exhausting, it eventually rewards me with energy and a positive outlook. The physical cleanliness will reflect itself in the astral and make house cleansings and blessings a quicker and more rewarding process as well.

If you need to clean your altar immediately, a simple solution of water and sea salt that has been blessed will work. I've used this solution in plastic spray bottles, sometimes enhanced with essentail oils like cedarwood for purification or sandalwood for psychic energy. If I have a need to perform ritual two days in a row, a quick spritz across the altar prepares the space for me so I can start on my work before giving the space the intensive cleaning and attention it deservies.

For full ritual closure, you might want to offer a prayer to an appropriate underworld, Earth, or reincarnation deity. Here is a simple prayer that you might want to use:

> *Blessed Gaea, all giving Mother*
> *I return these children to you.*
> *Hold them, love them, consume them.*
> *Until again, they are ready for the world.*
> *So mote it be.*

All things, even disposal, should be done with reverence. Humor is appropriate too, but keep in mind that these objects served your higher purpose well and deserve to be honored for that service. All ritual acts are sacred—even the ritual act of disposing.

Lasting Enchantment

By Nuala Drago

From ancient times to modern, every culture has recognized the magic of flowers. Volumes have been written about their lore, romance, and symbolism. They have been assigned planetary correspondences, and meanings have been ascribed to their colors, species, harvesting, and aromas.

There is small wonder in this, for the beauty of flowers has the power to move hearts and communicate emotion without a spoken word. They vibrate with the energy of love. Their beauty and aroma has the ability to alter the atmosphere, uplift spirits, rouse passion, and incite lust.

It is said that the blood of Aphrodite transformed a white rose into red, creating a symbol of passion for all time. Cleopatra was reputed to have once greeted Mark Antony in a room filled knee-deep with rose petals to intensify her sexual attraction. But, there is one flower of which very little is said, and it is the flower than vibrates with more magical energy than any other. That is the flower you receive from one who loves you.

Why then, are these most potent of blooms allowed to wither and die, to be discarded like so much rubbish? Don't let all that beauty and mystical enchantment go to waste. Preserve and use it! Flowers are easy to preserve no matter which method you choose. You can hang them dry, use a microwave, silica gel, or an oven, but the easiest method of all requires no effort whatsoever. When you are given a lovely bouquet of flowers, display them for a few days and then move them to a cool place out of the sunlight. Leave them in the display container and don't drain the water. Place some newspaper or waxed paper underneath to catch dropping foliage, but then simply leave them alone for as long as it takes.

In a couple of weeks, you should have some crisply dried blossoms that are enchanting symbols of your love and affection to another. Powerful tools, these. Get a pair of scissors and start snipping off the flowers, foliage, and greenery that you want to keep, and that looks attractive, making certain that each item you collect is completely dry.

You don't have to do another thing with them, but there really is so much more you can do. If you have seen the movie *Braveheart*, you know that William Wallace won his lady love's heart when he presented her with the dried thistle she had given him when they were children. Imagine, then, pressing a thin satin ribbon and a dried rosebud into the sealing wax of a love note, to be hand-delivered as a simple love charm.

Don't stop there. Why not make a batch of potpourri or sachet? If you don't wish to wait until you have been given enough flowers by your love interest, it wouldn't be cheating to add some flowers of your choice from your own magical flower garden, or add pine cones, wild ferns, herbs such as cinnamon sticks, and even the blossoms of certain weeds. Choose different varieties for their colors, their meanings to you, their foliage, beauty, size, magical assignations—whatever. Combine them in ways that are meaningful to you, or use them in more traditional ways.

You can scent the mixture with your favorite oil if you wish. Be sure to use a fixative such as orris root powder so the fragrance will last. You can display it in a pretty container, or tie or sew the mixture into a handkerchief, piece of lace, or satin. Tie a ribbon around it and hang it in your closet or place it in a drawer. Wear some in a locket as a love charm or fill two puppets with the mixture, one to represent you and another to represent your love. Tie them together with a beautiful ribbon and put them in a secret place.

Other suggestions for your dried flowers include such things as dream pillows, shadowboxes, circlets to wear during your rituals. These last are easily made by gluing your dried flowers and some greenery or moss to any length of satin ribbon. Adorn a hair comb, barrette, or headband. Decorate a picture frame with moss, rosebuds, and baby's breath. Some of the blossoms may be protected with a clear acrylic spray to make them less fragile.

Make floral water to use as a body splash by adding about a quarter cup of unflavored vodka to a pint of distilled water. Add flower petals and buds and a few drops of a specific oil such as rose, orange, or lavender, and keep them tightly bottled to uncover whenever you wish to enjoy their mood-altering fragrance.

Decorate candles to float in your bath water. Decorate food by using fresh, dried, or sugared flowers. However, not all flowers are edible, so consult a good book and stay with the ones you know are safe—such as organic violets, rose petals, and nasturtiums.

Imagine. Fantasize. Mental images are very powerful. Use fresh flowers as well as dried ones. I can't think of a better reason for starting your own magic flower garden. If some flowers are too exotic to grow, and it is unlikely that you will find them fresh or ever receive them as a gift from your love, don't despair. You can still buy their essential oils. Essential oils and dried flowers make wonderful incense.

There is no limit to the seductiveness of flowers if you unlock your creativity and open yourself to their magic. They are magnets for elementals and spirits of nature and will bring beauty, joy, and lasting enchantment into your life if you share their uplifting energy with those you love.

Elemental Etiquette
Or, Put Down That Whip and Chair!

By Clare Vaughn

Magical practitioners have long been stereotyped as lording it over poor hapless spirits by binding them to our wills. But the truth of the matter is that we work with spirits in a variety of ways, and in a majority of cases binding any spirit to one's will is right out of the question.

The stereotype arose chiefly out of the belief, common for centuries in the Christian world, that all nonphysical beings except angels were demonic. Therefore, all spirits supposedly needed to be handled with the harshest possible control measures in order to protect the magician working with them. Magicians who pursued Goetic magic did indeed (and still do) invoke demons, using the magical equivalent of a whip and chair. This approach, however, has very little to recommend it.

Magicians who performed angelic magic took a very different approach—requesting God to send angels to assist them, then requesting the angels to ask lesser spirits to help, and so on down the levels of being. From the viewpoint of magical philosophy, this top-down approach repeats the process of creation and thus works in harmony with the natural flow of divine energies.

Pagans, in working with nature spirits, were more likely to operate on a system of truce and barter, exchanging courtesies and favors while establishing a state of mutual tolerance and cooperation. The details of the system have varied considerably from place to place, but the essentials remain the same. This pattern of behavior establishes a cyclical flow between the parties involved.

So how do you approach elementals if you want to work with them? Magicians and Pagans can learn from each other here. Both the top-down and the cyclical flows have important advantages, and when combined produce a healthy and functional method for working with elementals. The essentials of this method can be summed up in just a few simple rules:

1. Approach elementals in the name of a deity who governs or is related to the element in question. Qabalistic magicians can use the divine names *alhim* (fire), *al* (water), *yhvh* (air), and *adni* (earth). Pagans can select a god or goddess from whichever pantheon they prefer to work with. Greet and part from the elementals with blessings in the chosen name.

2. Treat elementals with courtesy and respect, always. Cooperate with them, and seek their cooperation. If they ask you for help, give it unless it would conflict with your code of ethics. If you want to do a magical working in their territory, discuss it with them. If they object, stop.

3. Do not be afraid to ask questions; however, never demand information or answers from elementals. Likewise, never ignore them. Listen to them, whether you have questioned them or not. You can learn a great deal in this way. In their own realms, elementals have great powers and great wisdom.

The keys, as you can see, are courtesy, respect, and working by way of divine agency. Courtesy and respect should be extended to any being with whom you work. Being rude and ill-behaved in the nonphysical world will get you much the same response it would get here in the physical world.

Working by way of divine energy is partly a protective measure. Not all nonphysical beings are benign, let alone harmless, and approaching by way of divine names and energies is equivalent to having an umbrella on a cloudy day; if you need protection, it is ready at hand. Another reason to approach by way of divine names, however, relates to energy effects. Remember that even a simple greeting given in a divine name invokes the deity whose name is used. The downward flow thus created infuses a fresh current of energy into the cyclical pattern of a mutual relationship. This infusion of energy could be compared to the effect of sun shining on a pond. It is the final component necessary to a vital ecology.

To Know, to Will, to Dare, and to Keep Silent

By Estelle Daniels

The phrase that I have used as the title to this article is borrowed from ceremonial magic and contains the ingredients for a successful spell. But what does it mean exactly?

To know means to have an intellectual and practical knowledge of what you are doing, of the proper spell-work for a particular situation, of the proper methods for handling difficult tasks, of the proper ways to execute your intentions. Most importantly, it means to know what you want to accomplish. The more concise you can make a statement of purpose, the better and more effective your spell will be. To gain world peace is a noble goal, but one which is beyond the scope of most practitioners. To keep drug pushers off my block is a more realistic goal that can be accomplished.

In knowing, avoid "not" or "can't." Rather than having as your magical goal: "To have a workplace that is not abusive and harassing," try instead "To foster a workplace that is healthy, pleasant, and happy." Filter all spells through your younger self before you put it into effect. That way you can focus on the main elements of each spell—the key words and phrases and concepts. Meanwhile, keep books on spells to foster ideas and increase what you know. Seventy-five percent of the work in a spell comes before you start putting up the circle. Researching and assembling the materials take up most of the time. If it's worth doing a spell, it's worth putting in the time to do it right. Good preparation is certainly part of "to know."

To will refers to the magical will. This is the spirit in the self that makes it possible for you to generate enough emotional and psychic energy to accomplish your purpose. You can be very learned and have all the spell work lore in your head and be perfectly practiced, but you have to put your own emotional energy into the thing, or it won't go anywhere. We all know people who have the ideas and talk a blue streak about doing this and that project, but when it comes down to it they have little enthusiasm for actually accomplishing anything. The will is the energy battery you draw from when you raise the power for the spell. If that battery is drained, or never got charged in the first place, the thing won't go. Simple as that.

To dare means to have the gumption to actually get off your couch and do it. You can be learned and burn with intensity, but until and unless you actually go get the stuff, do the research and preparation, and do the spell, nothing will happen. Sounds pretty basic, doesn't it? Well it is, yet this is where many spells die. Talk is cheap. Action and the investment of time and energy are what count with spellwork. Until you act, the spell will be nothing more than a particularly vivid daydream. Yes, thoughts are real and can have an effect on the world, but for an effective spell you have to go through the motions. You can't wait around until you have your own private temple and altar and a perfect relationship with your deities. Make do with what you have; and utilize your absolute intent. Make the best of your time, energy, and resources. Even if you can't afford actual granulated frankincense, charcoal, and a brazier, a stick of frankincense incense will do. If you don't have your own permanent stone altar, a nice altar cloth spread over a any convenient surface will suffice.

To keep silent is the last ingredient and just as important as the other three. You have to be able to understand what you want and what you're doing, have the energy to make it happen, have the gumption to get up and actually do what's necessary, and then, once accomplished, shut up about it. I have seen wonderful spells executed yet never come to fruition because the person couldn't keep quiet.

There are a number of reasons for this. In order for a spell to accomplish its purpose you have to let it go. If you are constantly talking and dwelling on a spell, you are still tied to it and are in effect constantly calling it back. Furthermore, there are people who may not like the idea of your doing a spell, how you did it, what materials you used, what color robes you wore, which books you read, or who your mentor was and where she came from. They may hinder your spell by either consciously or subconsciously trying to stop it. Others may just pray against you or think bad thoughts about you or your spell. Any and all of these can blunt or deflect a spell's energies.

Finally, it's just bad form to talk about specific spells that haven't run their course. You can upset people generally. Many have antiquated notions about spells and what they are meant to do. You can give people an inflated idea of your opinion of yourself and your influence in the world. You never know who will hear about it through the grapevine and how it will be distorted. What is meaningful and important to you may be considered trivial by someone else, or it may just sound that way if you aren't clear and your audience is not paying close enough attention to grasp your intent. In the end, it may not be harmful when you talk about spells you did in the far-off past—particularly if you are teaching or sharing information—but in general a good and wise rule is to keep silent. If you say nothing, you are a hundred percent assured your words will not be misunderstood.

So there it is: a simple maxim that carries a lot of weight and wisdom. Following these four "rules" can do much to increase your magical effectiveness.

Blessed be.

A Spell to Call Your Soul-Self Home to Your Body

By Janina Renée

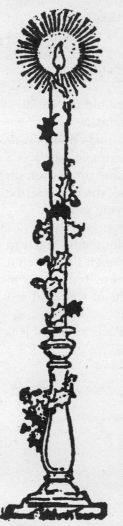

Many cultures recognize a condition called "soul loss," which can occur when traumatic events have fragmented a person's sense of being to the point of depression, fatigue, confusion, and a loss of center. Indeed, treating individuals for soul loss is an important function of shamanic practitioners.

I believe people in our society can suffer from a form of soul loss too, and it doesn't necessarily take a specific event or trauma to precipitate it. The unstable and dehumanizing conditions of many aspects of modern work life causes soul separation by degrees. A lifetime of compromise and hardship can also bring about this extreme state of alienation.

If this theory has resonance for you because you are suffering from such a condition, you should of course be taking whatever steps you can to get into a better environment or line of work, and do whatever else you can to realign your life with the needs of your core self and spirit. However, if you have to bide your time, or if you have recently escaped from a bad situation only to discover that your personal vitality and sense of self haven't yet been restored to you, then the following rite can help.

Gather candles, as many candles as you can get your hands on: old, new, and partially used, of every shape, size, color, and fragrance. In addition to whatever other candles you can find, be sure to include one in "your color"; that is, whichever color you feel best expresses your personal essence. If you are uncertain, or

131

don't have a strong color preference, a list of "astral" colors is appended to this article. Beg candles from friends, explaining your need to them. The act of begging for candles is a Mexican tradition, and adds an important quality to the magic that isn't easily explained. (I believe it has to do with the fact that other people contribute to the construction of one's sense of self, so other people have the power to help repair the self.) Later, you will want to keep some extra candles on hand in case you need to return the favor.

When you have an evening of quiet, assemble the candles, then anoint them with a fragrant oil, such as sandalwood or benzoin, or with any scent that is pleasing to you or suggestive of your personal essence. Then, with an incising instrument such as a small knife or an awl, inscribe your name, many times over, on the surface of each candle. For added panache, you can inscribe your name in runes or any other magical lettering system.

Next, light all the candles except your special essence, or astral, candle, which you will reserve as your focus. You can arrange them in any manner that you wish, though I've found it effective to place one in every corner of the house or dwelling, in keeping with the idea of calling your lost bits of soul and self home from the far corners of the astral world.

Now, set the focal candle in some central place, and light it as you recite the following invocation:

> I call myself back to myself:
> wandering soul, and wandering selves,
> and missing fragments of soul and self.
> I bid you return to me now,
> soul, and self, and spirit,
> unite with me—heart, and mind, and body.
> I call you through corridors of time
> and space and being.
> Fly swiftly home through days and years
> and seasons and cycles past,
> drawn in, gathered in, invited back,
> home to warmth, and home to love,
> and home to light and comfort.
> Rejoin me now, be one with me,
> whole in self and soul and spirit!

So it is, and so shall it be.

Then, allow all of the candles to burn for a time as your resume your normal activities. You can relight the candles every evening and on dark mornings, if convenient, though it isn't necessary to repeat the recitation ceremony unless you want to. You may burn the candles until they are all burnt down, or until you have achieved a reenergizing sense of integration.

Note: Due to space limitations, I don't want to get into a discussion of the differences between the concepts of soul, self, and spirit. In fact, my own definitions are fairly loose, because these aren't tangible objects that we can describe and dissect, nor can we confidently delineate where one begins and the other ends. Therefore, for the purposes of this rite, use your own intuitive sense of what these words mean.

ASTRAL COLORS

The colors that different astrologers attribute to the signs of the zodiac are often described as the "astral colors" of persons born under those signs, and can be used by those persons for all sorts of magical workings. However, if you don't have a strong affinity for the colors ascribed to you, go ahead and use whichever color you think most effective and in harmony with who you are.

Aries—Red, white, yellow

Taurus—Green, brown, pink

Gemini—Yellow, blue, orange

Cancer—White, silver, light blue

Leo—Gold, yellow, red

Virgo—Yellow, green, orange

Libra—Rose, blue, white

Scorpio—Red, black, dark blue

Sagittarius—Purple, indigo, turquoise

Capricorn—Black, brown, dark green

Aquarius—Blue-green, metallic blue, white

Pisces—Foam green, blue-green, salmon pink

A WITCH'S GARDEN

BY ELLEN DUGAN

Picture in your mind for a moment the image of a benevolent Witch who lives in a flower-surrounded cottage. The garden is a place where morning glories and moonflowers tumble over fences. Roses climb over handmade arbors, and magical herbs and flowers thrive in sunny beds. Around back, under old trees the shade gardens offer a quiet spot and relief from the summer heat. Ah… a suburban Pagan myth.

But actually, these images are true. As my aching knees can attest, I am one of those mythical modern Witches. I am a Garden Witch.

Garden Witchcraft is not some new, unheard-of tradition. The lore of herbs and flowers is as ancient as the practice of growing a magical garden. My own garden, however, is in as modern a tract-home neighborhood as you can imagine. Let me assure you, too, that despite all the work, it's very much worth it.

Gardens have always been magical places. You can plant theme gardens for love, prospenty, or protection. Or how about a fairy garden for your children? Magical gardening is a great way to put you in touch with the Earth and her cycles and her seasons. Not to mention it's great exercise, and growing your own veggies and herbs is a great way to save money and eat better.

Here are some Garden Witch suggestions to help you start a magical garden.

To start, try planting coneflowers, brown-eyed susans, yarrow, zinnias and petunias in a sunny spot in your yard. Add monarda, also known as bee balm, and parsley and you'll have a butterfly haven. From the garden you can affect strengthening and love spells, psychic powers, and hex breaking. The parsley adds protection and purification. Monarda adds success and prosperity

For a fragrance garden, plant grandiflora roses or David Austin roses in full sun. Underplant these with lavender, catnip, sage, and allysum. Tall garden phlox would make a good background. This garden's Magical uses include love, protection, purification, beauty, cat magic, wisdom, and protection.

If you have an abundance of shade, no problem. Choose from hostas, white astilbe, ferns, violets, hydrangea, foxglove, lady's mantle, and pastel and white impatiens. Behold, you have assembled the ingredients for a moonlight garden! Magical uses: luck, riches, and health from the ferns; and hex breaking from the hydrangea. Foxglove protects the garden and the home. (Warning! Foxglove is a poisonous plant. I waited until my children were older before I added this plant to my shade gardens.) Violets are sacred to the fairies, and lady's mantle is often used in love spells.

Need more ideas and information? Talk to other gardeners, we like to share. Join a garden club or the Herb Society. Attend free garden seminars. Visit your favorite local nursery and ask questions. Go to the library and see what you can find on plant lore and perennial gardening and read up during the off season.

Now, I want you to go outside and scout out a spot for a small garden for yourself and your family. I bet you could grow tomatoes and herbs in that sunny spot over there in the back yard. Add some organic compost to your soil and get started! I dare you.

The possibilities are truly endless. Go ahead, get your hands in the soil and really ground and center. Lets put the nature back into your Earth religion.

Some suggested titles for magical gardening are: *Cunningham's Encyclopedia of Magical Herbs* by Scott Cunningham, (Llewellyn, 1985), *Garden Spells* by Claire Nahmad (Running Press, 1994), and *Earth Magic* by Claire Nahmad (Destiny Books, 1994).

Garden Mazes

By Cerridwen Iris Shea

There is something fascinating about a labyrinth—its twists and turns and endless possibilities. Whether your eye follows a drawing, or your fingers trace a path in the sand or across a brooch, labyrinths have enraptured humans from Egypt to Greece and from Pompeii to Great Britain. When you put the labyrinth into the three-dimensional context of a garden maze, you take it one step further, adding a tangibly physical experience to the emotional one.

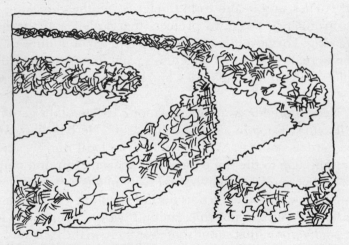

Most people are familiar with the classical, or Cretan labyrinth, known from the legend of the Minotaur. Created from a center cross with four dots, it contains seven rings of paths within eight concentric rings of barriers. It is easy to draw and easy to walk. The design has been carved on stone, chalked on doorways to keep out evil spirits, and incorporated into church design.

There are several theories as to the origin of turf mazes, none of which can be definitely proven. One school of thought suggests that they were cut out by clerics for penitents to roam; another suggests that children carved them into the ground in order to show off their ability to puzzle their peers. Yet a third suggests that people danced through these turf mazes on holidays, possibly serving as the origin of the spiral dance often performed in modern-day Craft ceremonies. In Wales, the creation of new turf mazes ceased when village dancing was banned; several places in the region revived this creation in the 1970's. Shakespeare refers to turf mazes in *A Midsummer Night's Dream* and *The Tempest*—in Elizabethan times, they were used as party games and for romantic assignations. Whether used as a tool to represent death and rebirth, or used as a means of fun, labyrinths make the inner journey a physical journey, and therein lies much of both its appeal and its fascination.

The maze at Hampton Court in England, ostensibly built in 1690, is probably one of the most well-known and popular of these mazes in the world. It was originally planted of hornbeam, but is now primarily yew. A maze at Bicton Park in Devon, meanwhile, is made of upright wooden logs and resembles a large footprint. Six bridges are incorporated into the large maze at Longleat House in Wiltshire.

Whatever the overall shape of the maze when gazed at from above, the two basic internal patterns are unicursal and multicursal. Unicursal means there is only one path, walked once in each direction, to the center and back out. Decision-making and getting lost are not concerns. Multicursal is the type used to make puzzle mazes; it has several twists, turns, and dead ends. If you make a wrong turn, you must retrace your steps and try to figure out the correct path. Getting to the center and getting back out means finding a whole new path. The multicursal design became popular in the seventeenth century, and may have come to England from Holland.

One of the most unusual garden mazes is in Glendurgan Garden in Cornwall, England. Planted in 1833 by Alfred Fox, it rests on a gently sloping hillside. Its shape is slightly oval, and it is created out of waist-high laurel. I visited this maze in the fall of 1999 during a rainy day. Still, the entire garden is one of the most beautifully spiritual places I have ever encountered. Each growing, living plant is given love and care and responds by showering love and care onto the garden's visitors. To walk down the path and see the maze appear before you is a breathtaking sight. To actually enter the maze and get a chance to walk it is uplifting.

The Glendurgan maze's multicursal design means there are plenty of places to take a wrong turn. However, since it is only waist-high, if you choose, you can look ahead and try to figure out the correct way. There is also a very kind garden worker sitting on a bench beside the maze to call out encouragement in case you get hopelessly lost.

Wandering through a maze in the daytime, looking at the raindrops glistening on the deep green leaves, breathing in the scent of so many different flowers, plants, and shrubs, can lift all tensions. At Glendurgan, I felt peaceful and serene. It was okay to make a wrong turn; there was no rush. When I reached the center, I sat in the small thatched gazebo and gazed out over both the maze and the garden. I was filled with wonder at the beauty that surrounded me.

There are so many wonderful paths to explore in labyrinths around the world. Each holds unique gifts for a visitor. In the end, the exploration and the experience of a labyrinth is what brings to mind the joy of the journey.

BABYLONIAN DREAMS AND OMENS

BY KENNETH JOHNSON

Long before Greece and Rome, there was Babylon. The kingdoms of the Tigris and Euphrates were contemporary with ancient Egypt, and they played a vital role in shaping Western civilization. For instance, among other things, the Babylonians invented the art of writing. Not only were the Babylonians important in establishing our civilization, they were also at the forefront of the Western esoteric tradition.

Babylonians were great believers in dreams and omens. They watched the earth and the heavens for signs, and their restless curiosity about the night sky gave birth to the art of astrology. The Babylonians recorded their esoteric knowledge in cuneiform writing on tablets of clay. Today, thousands of these tablets remain, describing every aspect of human existence. Among these are many that deal with the predictive qualities of dream visions derived from the natural world. For instance, in Babylonian tradition various animal dreams meant various things:

If you dream of eating a wild bull, you will have a long life.
If you dream of eating a monkey, you will have success in your undertakings.

While these are a bit dated for our modern experience, other Babylonian omens make more practical sense to us for their observation of natural phenomena. Consider this agricultural omen:

If a north wind blows until the time of new Moon, the harvest will be good.

More interesting, from a psychological and magical point of view, is the idea of reversal. In Babylonian dream theory, seemingly positive events may signify negative circumstances, while apparently negative events often mean that something positive will occur. Here are a few more examples:

If you dream of growing wings and flying away, it signifies a radical change in circumstances.

If you are rich, you will become poor; if you are poor, you will become rich.

If you dream that the whole town falls down around you, and that no one hears you shout, you will have good fortune.

This "reality reversal" may sound strange to us, but it has a sound basis in the world of ideas. The Babylonians, much like our own society, were obsessed with social rules and certain taboos. Perhaps all human beings have felt this way—closed in by rules and regulations and countless social rituals. We often admire people who rebel against the order of things, while we do not have the courage to mount our own such rebellion. In dreams, on the other hand, no one can punish you. If you break free and do the unexpected, no one knows. All of this can be expressed very simply in a phrase from yet another of the Babylonian dream books:

If you dream of breaking rules and laws, great success will follow.

Lest we believe that our ancestors more fatalistic than we, it should be noted that the Babylonians believed one could offset the evils of dreams through a few simple rituals. For example, upon arising in the morning after an unfavorable dream, one may pour a libation of vinegar on the floor and say, "Let the wind carry away the evil promised by that dream." Or simpler still, if you dream of something inauspicious, you can prevent it from happening in your life by saying, even before you get out of bed: "By the Sun and the Moon, that dream was a good one!"

Nut

BY DETRACI REGULA

N ut wraps around the world like a speckled snake, consuming the Sun and Moon as though there were big apples. She is the true Starry Mother, the one who brought forth another bright mother, the Egyptian goddess Isis. Yet we rarely hear about her, and priestesses of Nut, while not unknown, are rare.

Along with her mythological daughters Isis and Nephthys, Nut forms a triad. The two sides of the imposing pylon gates of the heavens were sometimes called "Isis" and "Nephthys," and Nut was said to be the space between—the opening that led into the sanctified space. Nut's association with the beyond, with outer space, is natural. She is not only the stars we see in the night sky, but she is the infinite blackness beyond the stars. She is the explanation that science can not give regarding the darkness of the night sky. That is, given the countless stars, the night should be filled with a dim gray light, yet the darkness of the night is undeniable.

Does Nut give her name to the night she rules? It's tempting to think so, especially in French, where the word for night is "nuit," a version of Nut's name which is also used by Thelemic practitioners. Mythologically said to be the daughter of Shu, the presiding divinity of air, and Tefnut, the sometimes-lion-headed goddess associated with moisture, Nut emanates a primal creative essence that takes precedence over her assigned genealogy. Represented as a sky cow, whose dark back is spangled with white patches, she is a nurturer of life herself.

Her beloved is Geb, the Earth god. Nut and Geb wrap around each other so closely that there is no room on the surface of the earth for humankind, until these two are finally rent apart by Ra so that humankind can survive. Still, there is some falseness to this legend—for the sky still embraces the earth wherever it can touch it directly. We breathe sky every day.

Pregnant by Geb, yet denied by Ra to have her children on any day of the year, Nut is desperate. Finally Tahuti, Lord of Wisdom, embarks on a gambling game with Khonsu, the god of the Moon. The stakes: enough of Khonsu's moonlight to create five new days in the year. Tahuti, with his wisdom of psychology and his ability to calculate mathematical odds, is the easy winner. He presents to Nut the gift of the five days "between the years," not of them. And she prepares to give birth.

But things would still not be easy. One of her offspring, Set, violently leaps from her side, making himself the first born. Her other four children follow: Osiris, Horus, Isis, and Nephthys. One of the five, Horus, is said to actually be the offspring of Isis and Osiris, loving one another while still within her womb.

Yet Nut is so ancient, even the gods and goddesses have difficulty reaching her directly. During the drawn-out battle between Set and Horus, the gods appeal to Nut in desperation, sending her a letter asking her opinion. As the mother of all those involved in the dispute, her viewpoint was thought to be fair. She replies back, also by letter, that Horus is clearly the heir to the throne. After soliciting her opinion, her words are then ignored by the council of gods, dominated by Ra, who is to decide the matter.

Behind the loving hand of Isis on the shoulders of her children is Nut herself, guiding even Isis with a loving touch. No crone is she, as her voluptuous images on the inner lid of sarcophagi attest, but a definite grande dame, a great enchantress, a sacred goddess whose womb has given to us another great goddess in the endless cycle of birth and rebirth.

How to Make a Ritual Robe

By Maria Kay Simms

You can make an great-look-ing ritual robe, even if you're new to sewing. The instructions in this article, plus a little patience and persistence, will result in an easy-to-make, ele-gantly flowing robe to wear when doing your magical work.

Of course, if you've never even repaired a split seam, you might do well to have a more experienced friend show you how to get started with needle and thread, or better yet, a sewing machine. I've watched men who were sure they'd be all thumbs put together robes in which they looked elegant, and they felt a real pride of accomplishment in the bargain.

A sewing circle can be mutu-ally encouraging and fun. My Circle of the Cosmic Muse has scheduled several sewing days in which an extra sewing machine or two was brought in, and we all spent the day helping each other cut, sew, hem, and trim new robes. Especially for pinning a hem straight, it helps to work with a friend.

To Start

The first thing you need to do is look for fabric that is 60 inches wide. With cloth of this length, you will not have to set in sleeves, and you will save a lot of time and effort. Finding 60-inch fabric is not difficult, nor does it have to be expensive. Go to a fabric store and ask the sales person to point out which fabrics are that width.

At this size you'll often find cotton knits—the type of fabric that T-shirts or sweatshirts are made of. This fabric has the advan-tages of being very comfortable to wear, inexpensive, easy to wash, and relatively wrinkle-free. Cotton sheeting will also come in 60-inch width, and is inexpensive, though more prone to wrinkling. Purists insist on natural materials, but frankly, I'd rather have cotton mixed with a synthetic fabric for a "wash and wear" feel. You can also find the width in lightweight desert cloth and some of the luxurious and silky dress materials, but these are more expensive. Also in the more expensive line, but very comfortable and luxurious looking, are brushed, suedelike materials. All of the fabrics I've mentioned come in many colors.

At the fabric store, pull enough of the fabric off the roll so you can see how much it will take to go from your neck to the floor. You need double that amount, plus an extra third of a yard for hem and facings. If you want to add a hood to your robe, get an extra full yard. Ask the salesperson if you need help to the right measure. Be sure to get a roll of thread to match your fabric.

The figure above shows a finished robe that has no cut sleeves, but instead uses the full width of the fabric. This is a more flowing look, usually preferred by women (but also some men). Some of you may prefer having sleeves, such as the variation on the previous page. The illustrations at the bottom of this page show how optional hoods are attached to the robes.

At the store, you'll also find a variety of

trims to use around the neckline or sleeve edges of your robe, or for a tie around the waist. If this is your first robe, it may be easier to make the robe first, and then measure where you want the trim so you'll know how much you need.

STEP BY STEP INSTRUCTIONS

Once you have your cloth, fold the material in half lengthwise, so that it is slightly longer than you are from neck to floor (about 2 inches longer is enough), with the fold at the shoulders. Now fold it in half across the width. The fold is now a line that would go down the center of your body. Cut a small curve across the folded corners, as shown.

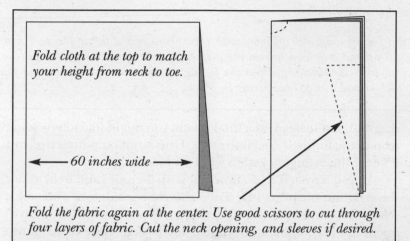

Fold cloth at the top to match your height from neck to toe.

← 60 inches wide →

Fold the fabric again at the center. Use good scissors to cut through four layers of fabric. Cut the neck opening, and sleeves if desired.

Next, unfold the material, put your head through the hole and see if you like the "neckline." If it's not big enough, fold it up again and cut out a little more—being very cautious. You can always cut the hole bigger, but if it gets too big it is more difficult to fix. Once you have the neckline a size that pleases you, you need only to finish it as illustrated in the diagram at the top of the next page. A note, however: If you want a hood on the robe, it must be added before the neckline is finished. For an illustration of this, check the diagrams on page 148. You could fold under the raw edge of the neckline twice and sew it, but it will be neater if you make a facing, following the instructions that caption the

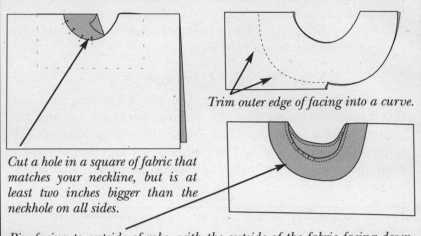

Trim outer edge of facing into a curve.

Cut a hole in a square of fabric that matches your neckline, but is at least two inches bigger than the neckhole on all sides.

Pin facing to outside of robe, with the outside of the fabric facing down. Stitch about a half-inch from the neck edge, and trim the edge one-quarter inch from the stitching. Press the facing to the inside of the robe and top stitch or add trim to hold facing in place.

diagram. But instead, as a final touch, you might like to sew some trim to the finished neckline edge. Trim is not only attractive, but it keeps the facing tucked in where it belongs.

All you have left to do now is sew up the sides and hem as per the diagram on page 147. Turn the robe inside out and sew a seam on each side as shown, leaving adequate space for "sleeve" openings. I recommend trimming the bottom edge corners into a curve, and having a side slit to the knee, so the sides won't drag on the floor. For the same reason, it's best to hem the robe a half-inch from the floor. If possible, have a friend pin the hem straight for you. If not, you'll have to guess, look in the mirror, and then adjust as necessary. A wide hem should be hand sewn; a narrower one will look fine with neat machine stitching. You may not need to hem the sleeve opening if you used the entire width of the fabric, because the fabric edge will mostly likely have a sufficiently finished look.

With all steps, always err on the side of cutting too big, and not too far in on the sides. You can always sew the garment smaller, but if you cut too deeply under the arms, it can be a real challenge trying to fix it.

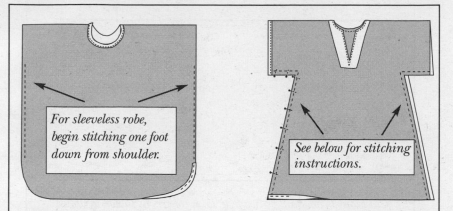

For sleeveless robe, begin stitching one foot down from shoulder.

See below for stitching instructions.

Stitch under the arms and down the sides as shown by the dotted lines—of course stitching with the robe inside-out. It is easier to stitch if you pin first, as shown on the left side of the sleeved robe. Note that the sleeveless robe is cut with curves at the bottom and not stitched all the way down, thus forming a slit on each side. This is to avoid having the robe drag on the floor when your arms are down. When you've finished the sides, press the seams, turn the robe rightside-out, and try it on. Mark the hem at the length you desire and pin. Take off, turn inside-out, and press the hem up along the pin lines. Try it on once again and adjust if necessary. Then stitch the hem to the inside of the robe. You may need to hem the sleeve edges, though the fabric edge may be adequate in the sleeveless robe.

The last diagram on page 148 shows how to add a hood. Cut and stitch as shown. Hem the straight edge and gather the curved edge. A double line of loose machine stitching is recommended for the gathering, so if you accidentally break one line, you'll still be able to continue. Pin the gathered edge into the unfinished neckline of the robe as shown, then when you add the facing, the raw edge of the hood will be hidden inside between facing and robe. You should carefully trim the extra fabric from the seam, being careful not to cut through your stitching, or the seam will be too bulky. Again, adding a row of trim or braid neatly holds everything in place. If you don't trim, you might want to do a neat line of top stitching through all layers.

There are lots of variations for trimming and decorating this very easy basic robe. You could tie-dye a solid fabric, or add occult symbols with fabric paint. I drew zodiacal symbols along the hem of one of my robes, and painted stylized ocean waves on another.

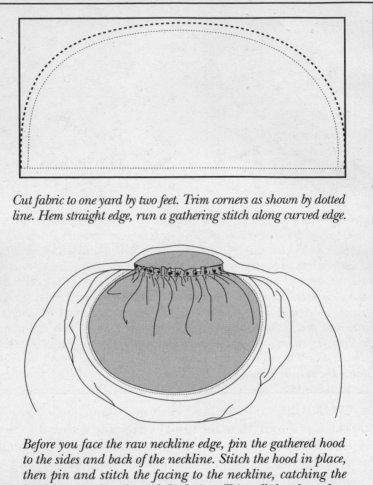

Cut fabric to one yard by two feet. Trim corners as shown by dotted line. Hem straight edge, run a gathering stitch along curved edge.

Before you face the raw neckline edge, pin the gathered hood to the sides and back of the neckline. Stitch the hood in place, then pin and stitch the facing to the neckline, catching the hood between the robe and the facing. Trim all the edges, then press the facing to the inside of the robe. Bind the edges with a decorative binding as describe in the diagram on page 146.

On yet another robe, I laid out, pinned and then hand stitched a braid in the shape of a circled pentagram on each sleeve and used the same braid to trim the sleeve, neckline and hood edges.

Let your creativity flow. Check *The Witch's Circle* for more ideas and instructions for other robe variations. Make a different robe for each season. Most of all, have fun!

Almanac Section

Calendar

Time Changes

Full Moons

Sabbats

Lunar Phases

Moon Signs

World Holidays

Color of the Day

Incense of the Day

ALMANAC LISTINGS

In these listings you will find the date, day, lunar phase, Moon sign, color and incense for the day, and festivals from around the world.

THE DATE

The date is used in numerological calculations that govern magical rites.

THE DAY

Each day is ruled by a planet that possesses specific magical influences:

MONDAY (MOON): Peace, sleep, healing, compassion, friends, psychic awareness, purification, and fertility.

TUESDAY (MARS): Passion, sex, courage, aggression, and protection.

WEDNESDAY (MERCURY): The conscious mind, study, travel, divination, and wisdom.

THURSDAY (JUPITER): Expansion, money, prosperity, and generosity.

FRIDAY (VENUS): Love, friendship, reconciliation, and beauty.

SATURDAY (SATURN): Longevity, exorcism, endings, homes, and houses.

SUNDAY (SUN): Healing, spirituality, success, strength, and protection.

THE LUNAR PHASE

The lunar phase is important in determining the best times for magic.

THE WAXING MOON (from the New Moon to the Full) is the ideal time for magic to draw things toward you.

THE FULL MOON is the time of greatest power.

THE WANING MOON (from the Full Moon to the New) is a time for study, meditation, and little magical work (except magic designed to banish harmful energies).

THE MOON'S SIGN

The Moon continuously "moves" through the zodiac, from Aries to Pisces. Each sign possesses its own significance:

ARIES: Good for starting things, but lacks staying power. Things occur rapidly, but quickly pass. People tend to be argumentatitve and assertive.

TAURUS: Things begun now last the longest, tend to increase in value, and become hard to alter. Brings out appreciation for beauty and sensory experience.

GEMINI: Things begun now are easily changed by outside influence. Time for shortcuts, communication, games, and fun.

CANCER: Stimulates emotional rapport between people. Pinpoints need, supports growth and nurturance. Tends to domestic concerns.

LEO: Draws emphasis to the self, to central ideas or institutions, away from connections with others and emotional needs. People tend to be melodramatic.

VIRGO: Favors accomplishment of details and commands from higher up. Focuses on health, hygiene, and daily schedules.

LIBRA: Favors cooperation, social activities, beautification of surroundings, balance, and partnership.

SCORPIO: Increases awareness of psychic power. Precipitates psychic crises and ends connections thoroughly. People tend to brood and become secretive.

SAGITTARIUS: Encourages flights of imagination and confidence. This is an adventurous, philosophical, and athletic Moon sign. Favors expansion and growth.

CAPRICORN: Develops strong structure. Focus on traditions, responsibilities, and obligations. A good time to set boundaries and rules.

AQUARIUS: Rebellious energy. Time to break habits and make abrupt change. Personal freedom and individuality is the focus.

PISCES: The focus is on dreaming, nostalgia, intuition, and psychic impressions. A good time for spiritual or philanthropic activities.

COLOR AND INCENSE

The color and incense for the day are based on information from *Personal Alchemy* by Amber Wolfe, and relate to the planet that rules each day. This information can be taken into consideration along with other factors when planning works of magic or when blending magic into mundane life. Please note that the incense selections are not hard and fast. If you can not find or do not like the incense listed for the day, choose a similar scent that appeals to you.

FESTIVALS AND HOLIDAYS

Festivals are listed throughout the year. The exact dates of many of these ancient festivals are difficult to determine; prevailing data has been used.

TIME CHANGES

The times and dates of all astrological phenomena in this almanac are based on **Eastern Standard Time (EST)**. They have NOT been adjusted for Daylight

Saving Time. If you live outside of EST, you will need to make the following changes:

PACIFIC STANDARD TIME: subtract three hours.

MOUNTAIN STANDARD TIME: subtract two hours.

CENTRAL STANDARD TIME: subtract one hour.

ALASKA/HAWAII: subtract five hours.

DAYLIGHT SAVING TIME: add an hour. Daylight saving time runs from April 1 to October 28, 2001.

2001 SABBATS AND FULL MOONS

January 9	Full Moon 3:24 PM
February 2	Imbolc
February 8	Full Moon 2:12 AM
March 9	Full Moon 12:23 PM
March 20	Ostara (Spring Equinox)
April 7	Full Moon 10:22 PM
May 1	Beltane
May 7	Full Moon 8:53 AM
June 5	Full Moon 8:39 PM
June 21	Litha (Summer Solstice)
July 5	Full Moon 10:04 AM
August 1	Lammas
August 4	Full Moon 12:56 AM
September 2	Full Moon 4:43 PM
September 22	Mabon (Fall Equinox)
October 2	Full Moon 8:49 AM
October 31	Samhain
November 1	Full Moon 12:41 AM
November 30	Full Moon 3:49 PM
December 21	Yule (Winter Solstice)
December 30	Full Moon 5:40 AM

CAPRICORN ♑

1 MONDAY
New Year's Day • Kwanzaa ends
Waxing Moon
Moon Phase: First Quarter
Color: Lavender

Moon Sign: Pisces
Moon enters Aries 5:14 pm
Incense: Daffodil

2 TUESDAY
Good Luck Day (Macedonian)
Waxing Moon
Moon Phase: Second Quarter 5:31 pm
Color: Red

Moon Sign: Aries
Incense: Cinnamon

3 WEDNESDAY
St. Genevieve's Day
Waxing Moon
Moon Phase: Second Quarter
Color: Yellow

Moon Sign: Aries
Incense: Cedar

4 THURSDAY
Frost Fairs on the Thames
Waxing Moon
Moon Phase: Second Quarter
Color: Violet

Moon Sign: Aries
Moon enters Taurus 1:57 am
Incense: Orchid

5 FRIDAY
Epiphany Eve
Waxing Moon
Moon Phase: Second Quarter
Color: Pink

Moon Sign: Taurus
Incense: Nutmeg

6 SATURDAY
Epiphany
Waxing Moon
Moon Phase: Second Quarter
Color: Indigo

Moon Sign: Taurus
Moon enters Gemini 6:44 am
Incense: Juniper

7 SUNDAY
Carnival
Waxing Moon
Moon Phase: Second Quarter
Color: Orange

Moon Sign: Gemini
Incense: Ginger

8 MONDAY
Full Moon Day (Burmese)   Moon Sign: Gemini
Waxing Moon   Moon enters Cancer 8:09 am
Moon Phase: Second Quarter   Incense: Myrrh
Color: Brown

TUESDAY
Lunar Eclipse   Moon Sign: Cancer
Waxing Moon   Incense: Coriander
Moon Phase: Full Moon 3:24 pm
Color: Orange

10 WEDNESDAY
Business God's Day   Moon Sign: Cancer
Waning Moon   Moon enters Leo 7:44 am
Moon Phase: Third Quarter   Incense: Vanilla
Color: White

11 THURSDAY
Unification Day (Nepalese)   Moon Sign: Leo
Waning Moon   Incense: Ylang ylang
Moon Phase: Third Quarter
Color: Violet

12 FRIDAY
Revolution Day (Tanzanian)   Moon Sign: Leo
Waning Moon   Moon enters Virgo 7:26 am
Moon Phase: Third Quarter   Incense: Clove
Color: Peach

13 SATURDAY
Twentieth Day (Norwegian)   Moon Sign: Virgo
Waning Moon   Incense: Carnation
Moon Phase: Third Quarter
Color: Blue

14 SUNDAY
Feast of the Ass (French)   Moon Sign: Virgo
Waning Moon   Moon enters Libra 9:05 am
Moon Phase: Third Quarter   Incense: Peony
Color: White

CAPRICORN

♑

15 MONDAY
Martin Luther King, Jr.'s Birthday (observed)   Moon Sign: Libra
Waning Moon   Incense: Musk
Moon Phase: Third Quarter
Color: Gray

◖ TUESDAY
Apprentices' Day   Moon Sign: Libra
Waning Moon   Moon enters Scorpio 2:02 pm
Moon Phase: Fourth Quarter 7:35 am   Incense: Frankincense
Color: Black

17 WEDNESDAY
St. Anthony's Day (Mexican)   Moon Sign: Scorpio
Waning Moon   Incense: Sage
Moon Phase: Fourth Quarter
Color: Peach

18 THURSDAY
Assumption Day   Moon Sign: Scorpio
Waning Moon   Moon enters Sagittarius 10:35 pm
Moon Phase: Fourth Quarter   Incense: Basil
Color: Green

19 FRIDAY
Robert E. Lee's Birthday   Moon Sign: Sagittarius
Waning Moon   Sun enters Aquarius 7:16 pm
Moon Phase: Fourth Quarter   Incense: Rosemary
Color: Rose

20 SATURDAY
Inauguration Day   Moon Sign: Sagittarius
Waning Moon   Incense: Maple
Moon Phase: Fourth Quarter
Color: Indigo

21 SUNDAY
St. Agnes' Day (English)   Moon Sign: Sagittarius
Waning Moon   Moon enters Capricorn 9:57 am
Moon Phase: Fourth Quarter   Incense: Dill
Color: Orange

22 MONDAY
St. Vincent's Day   Moon Sign: Capricorn
Waning Moon   Incense: Clove
Moon Phase: Fourth Quarter
Color: Silver

23 TUESDAY
St. Ildefonso's Day   Moon Sign: Capricorn
Waning Moon   Moon enters Aquarius 10:43 pm
Moon Phase: Fourth Quarter   Incense: Coriander
Color: Red

WEDNESDAY
Chinese New Year (snake)   Moon Sign: Aquarius
Waning Moon   Incense: Poplar
Moon Phase: New Moon 8:07 am
Color: Brown

25 THURSDAY
Burns' Night (Scottish)   Moon Sign: Aquarius
Waxing Moon   Incense: Evergreen
Moon Phase: First Quarter
Color: Turquoise

26 FRIDAY
Republic Day (Indian)   Moon Sign: Aquarius
Waxing Moon   Moon enters Pisces 11:39 am
Moon Phase: First Quarter   Incense: Sandalwood
Color: Peach

27 SATURDAY
St. Devota's Day (Monaco)   Moon Sign: Pisces
Waxing Moon   Incense: Chrysanthemum
Moon Phase: First Quarter
Color: Blue

28 SUNDAY
St. Charlemagne's Day   Moon Sign: Pisces
Waxing Moon   Moon enters Aries 11:35 pm
Moon Phase: First Quarter   Incense: Thyme
Color: Yellow

AQUARIUS

≈≈≈

29 MONDAY
Australia Day
Waxing Moon
Moon Phase: First Quarter
Color: Lavender

Moon Sign: Aries
Incense: Gardenia

30 TUESDAY
Three Hierarchs Day (Eastern Orthodox)
Waxing Moon
Moon Phase: First Quarter
Color: Gray

Moon Sign: Aries
Incense: Myrrh

31 WEDNESDAY
Independence Day (Nauru)
Waxing Moon
Moon Phase: First Quarter
Color: Yellow

Moon Sign: Aries
Moon enters Taurus 9:21 am
Incense: Patchouli

"WITCHE LIGHT"

During times of need, give yourself, your family, and your pets a daily protection by visualizing a light blue pentagram in the center of your (or their) forehead. This may be visually renewed as often as needed. It's also a good idea to place these pentagrams at the four corners of your dwelling.

Blue light like this is sometimes referred to as "Witche Light." It is said to be psychic in nature, and to carry much power.

THURSDAY
St. Bridget's Day (Irish)   Moon Sign: Taurus
Waxing Moon   Incense: Rose
Moon Phase: Second Quarter 9:02 am
Color: Violet

2 FRIDAY
Imbolc • Groundhog Day   Moon Sign: Taurus
Waxing Moon   Moon enters Gemini 3:56 pm
Moon Phase: Second Quarter   Incense: Ginger
Color: Pink

3 SATURDAY
St. Blaise's Day   Moon Sign: Gemini
Waxing Moon   Incense: Maple
Moon Phase: Second Quarter
Color: Brown

4 SUNDAY
Independence Day (Sri Lankan)   Moon Sign: Gemini
Waxing Moon   Moon enters Cancer 7:00 pm
Moon Phase: Second Quarter   Incense: Nutmeg
Color: Gold

5 MONDAY
Lincoln's Birthday (observed)   Moon Sign: Cancer
Waxing Moon   Incense: Neroli
Moon Phase: Second Quarter
Color: White

6 TUESDAY
Bob Marley's Birthday   Moon Sign: Cancer
Waxing Moon   Moon enters Leo 7:21 pm
Moon Phase: Second Quarter   Incense: Lilac
Color: White

7 WEDNESDAY
Full Moon Poya (Sri Lankan)   Moon Sign: Leo
Waxing Moon   Incense: Basil
Moon Phase: Second Quarter
Color: Peach

AQUARIUS ♒

THURSDAY
Mass for Broken Needles (Japanese)
Waxing Moon
Moon Phase: Full Moon 2:12 am
Color: White

Moon Sign: Leo
Moon enters Virgo 6:35 pm
Incense: Neroli

---

9 FRIDAY
St. Marion's Day (Lebanese)
Waning Moon
Moon Phase: Third Quarter
Color: White

Moon Sign: Virgo
Incense: Vanilla

---

10 SATURDAY
Gasparilla Day
Waning Moon
Moon Phase: Third Quarter
Color: Gray

Moon Sign: Virgo
Moon enters Libra 6:46 pm
Incense: Pine

---

11 SUNDAY
Foundation Day (Japanese)
Waning Moon
Moon Phase: Third Quarter
Color: Peach

Moon Sign: Libra
Incense: Cinnamon

---

12 MONDAY
Abraham Lincoln's Birthday
Waning Moon
Moon Phase: Third Quarter
Color: Lavender

Moon Sign: Libra
Moon enters Scorpio 9:51 pm
Incense: Geranium

---

13 TUESDAY
Parentalia (Roman)
Waning Moon
Moon Phase: Third Quarter
Color: Red

Moon Sign: Scorpio
Incense: Thyme

WEDNESDAY
Valentine's Day
Waning Moon
Moon Phase: Fourth Quarter 10:23 pm
Color: White

Moon Sign: Scorpio
Incense: Daffodil

FEBRUARY

15 THURSDAY
Lupercalia (Roman)
Waning Moon
Moon Phase: Fourth Quarter
Color: Violet

Moon Sign: Scorpio
Moon enters Sagittarius 5:02 am
Incense: Honeysuckle

16 FRIDAY
Mayo Indian Lent (Mexican)
Waning Moon
Moon Phase: Fourth Quarter
Color: Rose

Moon Sign: Sagittarius
Incense: Coriander

17 SATURDAY
Quirinalia (Roman)
Waning Moon
Moon Phase: Fourth Quarter
Color: Indigo

Moon Sign: Sagittarius
Moon enters Capricorn 3:59 pm
Incense: Evergreen

18 SUNDAY
Parentalia (Roman)
Waning Moon
Moon Phase: Fourth Quarter
Color: Yellow

Moon Sign: Capricorn
Sun enters Pisces 9:27 am
Incense: Patchouli

19 MONDAY
Presidents' Day (observed)
Waning Moon
Moon Phase: Fourth Quarter
Color: Silver

Moon Sign: Capricorn
Incense: Sage

20 TUESDAY
Installation of the New Lama (Tibetan)
Waning Moon
Moon Phase: Fourth Quarter
Color: Black

Moon Sign: Capricorn
Moon enters Aquarius 4:53 am
Incense: Juniper

21 WEDNESDAY
Feast of Lanterns (Chinese)
Waning Moon
Moon Phase: Fourth Quarter
Color: Peach

Moon Sign: Aquarius
Incense: Ginger

♓

22 THURSDAY
Independenc Day (Saint Lucia)
Waning Moon
Moon Phase: Fourth Quarter
Color: Green

Moon Sign: Aquarius
Moon enters Pisces 5:45 pm
Incense: Parsley

☽ FRIDAY
Terminalia (Roman)
Waning Moon
Moon Phase: New Moon 3:21 am
Color: Peach

Moon Sign: Pisces
Incense: Nutmeg

24 SATURDAY
The Flight of Kings (Roman)
Waxing Moon
Moon Phase: First Quarter
Color: Brown

Moon Sign: Pisces
Incense: Musk

25 SUNDAY
National Day (Kuwaiti)
Waxing Moon
Moon Phase: First Quarter
Color: Orange

Moon Sign: Pisces
Moon enters Aries 5:20 am
Incense: Rosemary

26 MONDAY
Shrove Monday (Greek)
Waxing Moon
Moon Phase: First Quarter
Color: Gray

Moon Sign: Aries
Incense: Cedar

27 TUESDAY
Threepenny Day (English)
Waxing Moon
Moon Phase: First Quarter
Color: Gray

Moon Sign: Aries
Moon enters Taurus 3:06 pm
Incense: Eucalyptus

28 WEDNESDAY
Ash Wednesday
Waxing Moon
Moon Phase: First Quarter
Color: Brown

Moon Sign: Taurus
Incense: Frankincense

♓

MARCH

1 THURSDAY
St. David's Day (Welsh)   Moon Sign: Taurus
Waxing Moon   Moon enters Gemini 10:36 pm
Moon Phase: First Quarter   Incense: Evergreen
Color: Turquoise

◗ **FRIDAY**
St. Chad's Day (English)   Moon Sign: Gemini
Waxing Moon   Incense: Dill
Moon Phase: Second Quarter 9:03 pm
Color: Pink

3 SATURDAY
Doll Festival (Japanese)   Moon Sign: Gemini
Waxing Moon   Incense: Myrrh
Moon Phase: Second Quarter
Color: Gray

4 SUNDAY
St. Casimir's Day (Polish)   Moon Sign: Gemini
Waxing Moon   Moon enters Cancer 3:24 am
Moon Phase: Second Quarter   Incense: Sage
Color: Peach

5 MONDAY
Isis Festival (Roman)   Moon Sign: Cancer
Waxing Moon   Incense: Orchid
Moon Phase: Second Quarter
Color: Lavender

6 TUESDAY
Alamo Day   Moon Sign: Cancer
Waxing Moon   Moon enters Leo 5:30 am
Moon Phase: Second Quarter   Incense: Sandalwood
Color: Black

7 WEDNESDAY
Festival of Rama (Hindu)   Moon Sign: Leo
Waxing Moon   Incense: Clove
Moon Phase: Second Quarter
Color: Yellow

PISCES ♓

8 THURSDAY
International Women's Day
Waxing Moon
Moon Phase: Second Quarter
Color: White

Moon Sign: Leo
Moon enters Virgo 5:44 am
Incense: Rose

FRIDAY
Purim
Waxing Moon
Moon Phase: Full Moon 12:23 pm
Color: White

Moon Sign: Virgo
Incense: Jasmine

10 SATURDAY
Tibet Day
Waning Moon
Moon Phase: Third Quarter
Color: Blue

Moon Sign: Virgo
Moon enters Libra 5:47 am
Incense: Almond

11 SUNDAY
Feast of Gauri (Hindu)
Waning Moon
Moon Phase: Third Quarter
Color: Gold

Moon Sign: Libra
Incense: Parsley

12 MONDAY
St. Gregory's Day
Waning Moon
Moon Phase: Third Quarter
Color: Gray

Moon Sign: Libra
Moon enters Scorpio 7:43 am
Incense: Juniper

13 TUESDAY
Purification Feast (Balinese)
Waning Moon
Moon Phase: Third Quarter
Color: Red

Moon Sign: Scorpio
Incense: Basil

14 WEDNESDAY
Mamuralia (Roman)
Waning Moon
Moon Phase: Third Quarter
Color: White

Moon Sign: Scorpio
Moon enters Sagittarius 1:17 pm
Incense: Carnation

164

15 THURSDAY
Phallus Festival (Shinto)   Moon Sign: Sagittarius
Waning Moon   Incense: Myrrh
Moon Phase: Third Quarter
Color: Turquoise

○ FRIDAY
St. Urho's Day (Finnish)   Moon Sign: Sagittarius
Waning Moon   Moon enters Capricorn 11:02 pm
Moon Phase: Fourth Quarter 3:45 pm   Incense: Ginger
Color: Rose

17 SATURDAY
St. Patrick's Day   Moon Sign: Capricorn
Waning Moon   Incense: Poplar
Moon Phase: Fourth Quarter
Color: Brown

18 SUNDAY
Sheelah's Day (Irish)   Moon Sign: Capricorn
Waning Moon   Incense: Clove
Moon Phase: Fourth Quarter
Color: Orange

19 MONDAY
St. Joseph's Day (Sicilian)   Moon Sign: Capricorn
Waning Moon   Moon enters Aquarius 11:36 am
Moon Phase: Fourth Quarter   Incense: Honeysuckle
Color: White

20 TUESDAY
Ostara • Spring Equinox   Moon Sign: Aquarius
Waning Moon   Sun enters Aries 8:31 am
Moon Phase: Fourth Quarter   Incense: Neroli
Color: White

21 WEDNESDAY
Juarez Day (Mexican)   Moon Sign: Aquarius
Waning Moon   Incense: Dill
Moon Phase: Fourth Quarter
Color: Peach

ARIES

♈

22 THURSDAY
Hilaria (Roman)
Waning Moon
Moon Phase: Fourth Quarter
Color: Green

Moon Sign: Aquarius
Moon enters Pisces 12:28 am
Incense: Sage

23 FRIDAY
Pakistan Day
Waning Moon
Moon Phase: Fourth Quarter
Color: Pink

Moon Sign: Pisces
Incense: Basil

☽ SATURDAY
Day of Blood (Roman)
Waning Moon
Moon Phase: New Moon 8:21 pm
Color: Blue

Moon Sign: Pisces
Moon enters Aries 11:43 am
Incense: Chrysanthemum

25 SUNDAY
Hegira (Islamic)
Waxing Moon
Moon Phase: First Quarter
Color: Yellow

Moon Sign: Aries
Incense: Nutmeg

26 MONDAY
Prince Kuhio Day (Hawaiian)
Waxing Moon
Moon Phase: First Quarter
Color: Lavender

Moon Sign: Aries
Moon enters Taurus 8:50 pm
Incense: Lilac

27 TUESDAY
Smell the Breezes Day (Egyptian)
Waxing Moon
Moon Phase: First Quarter
Color: Black

Moon Sign: Taurus
Incense: Pine

28 WEDNESDAY
Wapynshaws of Scotland
Waxing Moon
Moon Phase: First Quarter
Color: Brown

Moon Sign: Taurus
Incense: Patchouli

29 THURSDAY

Youth Day (Taiwanese) Moon Sign: Taurus
Waxing Moon Moon enters Gemini 4:01 am
Moon Phase: First Quarter Incense: Cedar
Color: Turquoise

30 FRIDAY

Seward's Day (Alaskan) Moon Sign: Gemini
Waxing Moon Incense: Sage
Moon Phase: First Quarter
Color: Rose

31 SATURDAY

The Borrowed Days Moon Sign: Gemini
Waxing Moon Moon enters Cancer 9:23 am
Moon Phase: First Quarter Incense: Musk
Color: Brown

PROTECTIVE MAGICS

Though we live in a highly civilized society, there are times when it is wise to guard ourselves, such as when hearing a sound in the house at night or when walking a lonely stretch of road. At such moments, simple, quick protective rites can put our minds at ease and strengthen our psychic armor:

- IN BED:

  When lying in bed at night, visualize yourself completely encased in a glowing purple suit of power through which no energy can pass.

- OUTSIDE AT NIGHT:

  Straighten your back. Breathe slowly. Visualize yourself as a lion stalking the jungle, searching for prey. Transmit the unmistakable image that you're not to be bothered by anyone.

♈

🌑 **SUNDAY**
April Fools' Day • Daylight Saving Time begins at 2:00 am
Waxing Moon   Moon Sign: Cancer
Moon Phase: Second Quarter 5:49 am   Incense: Cinnamon
Color: Peach

2 MONDAY
The Battle of Flowers (French)   Moon Sign: Cancer
Waxing Moon   Moon enters Leo 12:54 pm
Moon Phase: Second Quarter   Incense: Basil
Color: Silver

3 TUESDAY
Ashura (Islamic)   Moon Sign: Leo
Waxing Moon   Incense: Gardenia
Moon Phase: Second Quarter
Color: White

4 WEDNESDAY
National Day (Senegalese)   Moon Sign: Leo
Waxing Moon   Moon enters Virgo 2:46 pm
Moon Phase: Second Quarter   Incense: Eucalyptus
Color: Yellow

5 THURSDAY
Tomb-Sweeping Day (Chinese)   Moon Sign: Virgo
Waxing Moon   Incense: Orchid
Moon Phase: Second Quarter
Color: Violet

6 FRIDAY
Chakri Day (Thai)   Moon Sign: Virgo
Waxing Moon   Moon enters Libra 3:57 pm
Moon Phase: Second Quarter   Incense: Vanilla
Color: White

🌝 **SATURDAY**
Festival of Pure Brightness (Chinese) Moon Sign: Libra
Waxing Moon   Incense: Evergreen
Moon Phase: Full Moon 10:22 pm
Color: Gray

8 SUNDAY
Palm Sunday • Passover begins
Waning Moon
Moon Phase: Third Quarter
Color: Orange

Moon Sign: Libra
Moon enters Scorpio 6:01 pm
Incense: Myrrh

9 MONDAY
Valour Day (Filipino)
Waning Moon
Moon Phase: Third Quarter
Color: Gray

Moon Sign: Scorpio
Incense: Poplar

10 TUESDAY
"The Tenth of April" (British)
Waning Moon
Moon Phase: Third Quarter
Color: Gray

Moon Sign: Scorpio
Moon enters Sagittarius 10:47 pm
Incense: Maple

11 WEDNESDAY
Heroes' Day (Costa Rican)
Waning Moon
Moon Phase: Third Quarter
Color: Brown

Moon Sign: Sagittarius
Incense: Sandalwood

12 THURSDAY
Cerealia (Roman)
Waning Moon
Moon Phase: Third Quarter
Color: Green

Moon Sign: Sagittarius
Incense: Ginger

13 FRIDAY
Good Friday • Orthodox Good Friday
Waning Moon
Moon Phase: Third Quarter
Color: Pink

Moon Sign: Sagittarius
Moon enters Capricorn 7:21 am
Incense: Coriander

14 SATURDAY
Passover ends
Waning Moon
Moon Phase: Third Quarter
Color: Indigo

Moon Sign: Capricorn
Incense: Patchouli

♈

○ **SUNDAY**
Easter • Orthodox Easter   Moon Sign: Capricorn
Waning Moon   Moon enters Aquarius 7:11 pm
Moon Phase: Fourth Quarter 10:31 am   Incense: Thyme
Color: Peach

---

16 MONDAY
Zurich Spring Festival   Moon Sign: Aquarius
Waning Moon   Incense: Rosemary
Moon Phase: Fourth Quarter
Color: Silver

---

17 TUESDAY
Maple Syrup Festival (American)   Moon Sign: Aquarius
Waning Moon   Incense: Dill
Moon Phase: Fourth Quarter
Color: Red

---

18 WEDNESDAY
Flower Festival (Japanese)   Moon Sign: Aquarius
Waning Moon   Moon enters Pisces 8:00 am
Moon Phase: Fourth Quarter   Incense: Daffodil
Color: White

---

19 THURSDAY
Women's Celebration (Balinese)   Moon Sign: Pisces
Waning Moon   Sun enters Taurus 7:36 pm
Moon Phase: Fourth Quarter   Incense: Geranium
Color: Violet

---

20 FRIDAY
Drum Festival (Japanese)   Moon Sign: Pisces
Waning Moon   Moon enters Aries 7:18 pm
Moon Phase: Fourth Quarter   Incense: Ginger
Color: Rose

---

21 SATURDAY
Tiradentes Day (Brazilian)   Moon Sign: Aries
Waning Moon   Incense: Almond
Moon Phase: Fourth Quarter
Color: Blue

22 SUNDAY
Earth Day   Moon Sign: Aries
Waning Moon   Incense: Cedar
Moon Phase: Fourth Quarter
Color: Yellow

23 MONDAY
Children's Day (Turkish)   Moon Sign: Aries
Waning Moon   Moon enters Taurus 3:46 am
Moon Phase: New Moon 10:26 am   Incense: Jasmine
Color: Lavender

24 TUESDAY
St. Mark's Eve   Moon Sign: Taurus
Waxing Moon   Incense: Maple
Moon Phase: First Quarter
Color: Gray

25 WEDNESDAY
St. Mark's Day   Moon Sign: Taurus
Waxing Moon   Moon enters Gemini 10:11 am
Moon Phase: First Quarter   Incense: Rosemary
Color: Peach

26 THURSDAY
Confederate Memorial Day   Moon Sign: Gemini
Waxing Moon   Incense: Orchid
Moon Phase: First Quarter
Color: White

27 FRIDAY
Humabon's Conversion   Moon Sign: Gemini
Waxing Moon   Moon enters Cancer 2:49 pm
Moon Phase: First Quarter   Incense: Coriander
Color: Peach

28 SATURDAY
Floralia (Roman)   Moon Sign: Cancer
Waxing Moon   Incense: Musk
Moon Phase: First Quarter
Color: Indigo

29 SUNDAY
Green Day (Japanese)   Moon Sign: Cancer
Waxing Moon   Moon enters Leo 6:25 pm
Moon Phase: First Quarter   Incense: Basil
Color: Gold

MONDAY
Walpurgis Night   Moon Sign: Leo
Waxing Moon   Incense: Lavender
Moon Phase: Second Quarter 12:08 pm
Color: White

SCOTT CUNNINGHAM'S MAGICAL PRINCIPLES

- Magic is natural.
- Harm none, not even yourself, through its use.
- Magic requires effort. You will receive what you put into it.
- Magic is not usually instantaneous. Spells require time to be effective.
- Magic should not be performed for pay.
- Magic should not be used in jest or to inflate your ego.
- Magic can be worked for your own gain, but only if it harms none.
- Magic is a divine act.
- Magic can be used for defense but should never be used for attack.
- Magic is knowledge of its way and laws and also of its effectiveness. Know that magic works!
- Magic is love. All magic should be performed out of love. The moment anger or hatred tinges your magic you have crossed the border into a dangerous world, one that will ultimately consume you.

1   **TUESDAY**
Beltane • May Day
Waxing Moon
Moon Phase: Second Quarter
Color: Black

Moon Sign: Leo
Moon enters Virgo 9:16 pm
Incense: Pine

2   **WEDNESDAY**
Feast of St. Domenico (Roman)
Waxing Moon
Moon Phase: Second Quarter
Color: Peach

Moon Sign: Virgo
Incense: Clove

3   **THURSDAY**
Holy Cross Day (Mexican)
Waxing Moon
Moon Phase: Second Quarter
Color: Violet

Moon Sign: Virgo
Moon enters Libra 11:50 pm
Incense: Neroli

4   **FRIDAY**
People's Day (Japanese)
Waxing Moon
Moon Phase: Second Quarter
Color: Rose

Moon Sign: Libra
Incense: Nutmeg

5   **SATURDAY**
Cinco de Mayo (Mexican)
Waxing Moon
Moon Phase: Second Quarter
Color: Blue

Moon Sign: Libra
Incense: Lilac

6   **SUNDAY**
Martyrs' Day (Lebanese)
Waxing Moon
Moon Phase: Second Quarter
Color: Yellow

Moon Sign: Libra
Moon enters Scorpio 3:00 am
Incense: Patchouli

MONDAY
Pilgrimage of St. Nicholas (Italian)
Waxing Moon
Moon Phase: Full Moon 8:53 am
Color: Lavender

Moon Sign: Scorpio
Incense: Peony

8 TUESDAY
Liberation Day (French)
Waning Moon
Moon Phase: Third Quarter
Color: Red

Moon Sign: Scorpio
Moon enters Sagittarius 8:05 am
Incense: Parsley

9 WEDNESDAY
Lemuria (Roman)
Waning Moon
Moon Phase: Third Quarter
Color: Yellow

Moon Sign: Sagittarius
Incense: Evergreen

10 THURSDAY
First Day of Bird Week (Japanese)
Waning Moon
Moon Phase: Third Quarter
Color: Green

Moon Sign: Sagittarius
Moon enters Capricorn 4:10 pm
Incense: Thyme

11 FRIDAY
Ceremony for Rain (Guatemalan)
Waning Moon
Moon Phase: Third Quarter
Color: Rose

Moon Sign: Capricorn
Incense: Ginger

12 SATURDAY
Florence Nightingale's Birthday
Waning Moon
Moon Phase: Third Quarter
Color: Indigo

Moon Sign: Capricorn
Incense: Evergreen

13 SUNDAY
Mother's Day
Waning Moon
Moon Phase: Third Quarter
Color: Gold

Moon Sign: Capricorn
Moon enters Aquarius 3:20 am
Incense: Sandalwood

14 MONDAY
Whitmonday (English)
Waning Moon
Moon Phase: Third Quarter
Color: Silver

Moon Sign: Aquarius
Incense: Sage

○ **TUESDAY**
Festival of St. Dympna (Belgian)   Moon Sign: Aquarius
Waning Moon   Moon enters Pisces 4:01 pm
Moon Phase: Fourth Quarter 5:11 am   Incense: Eucalyptus
Color: Black

---

16 **WEDNESDAY**
St. Honoratus' Day   Moon Sign: Pisces
Waning Moon   Incense: Rosemary
Moon Phase: Fourth Quarter
Color: Peach

---

17 **THURSDAY**
Norwegian Independence Day   Moon Sign: Pisces
Waning Moon   Incense: Maple
Moon Phase: Fourth Quarter
Color: Turquoise

---

18 **FRIDAY**
Las Piedras Day (Uruguayan)   Moon Sign: Pisces
Waning Moon   Moon enters Aries 3:41 am
Moon Phase: Fourth Quarter   Incense: Sage
Color: Pink

---

19 **SATURDAY**
Pardon of the Poor (French)   Moon Sign: Aries
Waning Moon   Incense: Poplar
Moon Phase: Fourth Quarter
Color: Brown

---

20 **SUNDAY**
Mecklenburg Independence Day   Moon Sign: Aries
Waning Moon   Sun enters Gemini 6:44 pm
Moon Phase: Fourth Quarter   Moon enters Taurus 12:29 pm
Color: Yellow   Incense: Ginger

---

21 **MONDAY**
Victoria Day (Canadian)   Moon Sign: Taurus
Waning Moon   Incense: Violet
Moon Phase: Fourth Quarter
Color: White

♊

☽ TUESDAY
Heroes' Day (Sri Lankan)   Moon Sign: Taurus
Waning Moon   Moon enters Gemini 6:12 pm
Moon Phase: New Moon 9:46 pm   Incense: Ylang ylang
Color: White

23 WEDNESDAY
Labour Day (Jamaican)   Moon Sign: Gemini
Waxing Moon   Incense: Cedar
Moon Phase: First Quarter
Color: Brown

24 THURSDAY
Culture Day (Bulgarian)   Moon Sign: Gemini
Waxing Moon   Moon enters Cancer 9:42 pm
Moon Phase: First Quarter   Incense: Rose
Color: White

25 FRIDAY
Lady Godiva's Day   Moon Sign: Cancer
Waxing Moon   Incense: Dill
Moon Phase: First Quarter
Color: Peach

26 SATURDAY
The Three Maries (French)   Moon Sign: Cancer
Waxing Moon   Incense: Myrrh
Moon Phase: First Quarter
Color: Gray

27 SUNDAY
Benediction Day (Swiss)   Moon Sign: Cancer
Waxing Moon   Moon enters Leo 12:12 am
Moon Phase: First Quarter   Incense: Coriander
Color: Orange

28 MONDAY
Memorial Day (observed) • *Shavuot*   Moon Sign: Leo
Waxing Moon   Incense: Orchid
Moon Phase: First Quarter
Color: Lavender

♊

MAY

◐ **TUESDAY**
Royal Oak Day (British)　　　　　Moon Sign: Leo
Waxing Moon　　　　　Moon enters Virgo 2:38 am
Moon Phase: Second Quarter 5:09 pm　　Incense: Musk
Color: Gray

30　WEDNESDAY
Waxing Moon　　　　　　　　Moon Sign: Virgo
Moon Phase: Second Quarter　　　　Incense: Jasmine
Color: White

31　THURSDAY
Republic Day (South African)　　　Moon Sign: Virgo
Waxing Moon　　　　　Moon enters Libra 5:41 am
Moon Phase: Second Quarter　　　Incense: Almond
Color: Violet

❧

MORE PROTECTIVE MAGICS

- WHEN SOMEONE TRIES TO READ YOUR THOUGHTS:

  If you believe that someone is trying to read your thoughts or otherwise intrude into your head, visualize it as being stuffed with thick mashed potatoes that make such penetration impossible.

- FOR MANY CIRCUMSTANCES:

  Taste salt, or throw it around you in a circle. (Carrying a small packet of salt from a restaurant facilitates this.)

  Cross your fingers. (This calls upon the force of the Sun.)

  Tighten your muscles and relax them while visualizing protection. (This sends out protective power.)

  Stand. (You're more in control when standing than when sitting or reclining.)

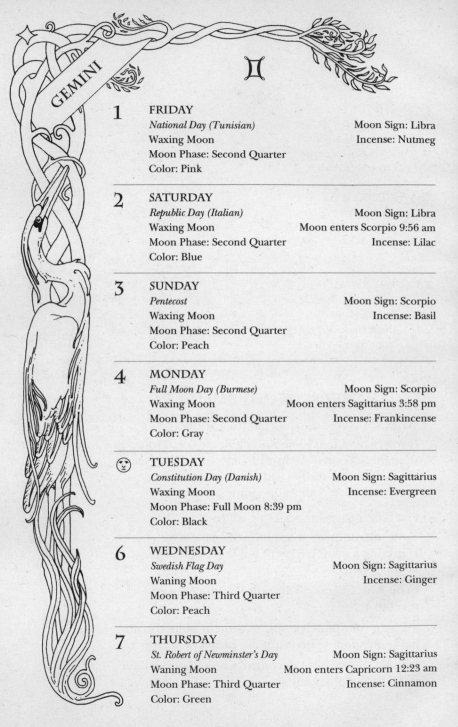

♊

1 FRIDAY
National Day (Tunisian)   Moon Sign: Libra
Waxing Moon   Incense: Nutmeg
Moon Phase: Second Quarter
Color: Pink

2 SATURDAY
Republic Day (Italian)   Moon Sign: Libra
Waxing Moon   Moon enters Scorpio 9:56 am
Moon Phase: Second Quarter   Incense: Lilac
Color: Blue

3 SUNDAY
Pentecost   Moon Sign: Scorpio
Waxing Moon   Incense: Basil
Moon Phase: Second Quarter
Color: Peach

4 MONDAY
Full Moon Day (Burmese)   Moon Sign: Scorpio
Waxing Moon   Moon enters Sagittarius 3:58 pm
Moon Phase: Second Quarter   Incense: Frankincense
Color: Gray

☺ **TUESDAY**
Constitution Day (Danish)   Moon Sign: Sagittarius
Waxing Moon   Incense: Evergreen
Moon Phase: Full Moon 8:39 pm
Color: Black

6 WEDNESDAY
Swedish Flag Day   Moon Sign: Sagittarius
Waning Moon   Incense: Ginger
Moon Phase: Third Quarter
Color: Peach

7 THURSDAY
St. Robert of Newminster's Day   Moon Sign: Sagittarius
Waning Moon   Moon enters Capricorn 12:23 am
Moon Phase: Third Quarter   Incense: Cinnamon
Color: Green

8   FRIDAY
Dragon Boat Festival (Chinese)   Moon Sign: Capricorn
Waning Moon   Incense: Lavender
Moon Phase: Third Quarter
Color: White

9   SATURDAY
Vestalia (Roman)   Moon Sign: Capricorn
Waning Moon   Moon enters Aquarius 11:20 am
Moon Phase: Third Quarter   Incense: Poplar
Color: Brown

10   SUNDAY
Portugal Day   Moon Sign: Aquarius
Waning Moon   Incense: Pine
Moon Phase: Third Quarter
Color: Yellow

11   MONDAY
Queen's Birthday (British)   Moon Sign: Aquarius
Waning Moon   Moon enters Pisces 11:53 pm
Moon Phase: Third Quarter   Incense: Honeysuckle
Color: Lavender

12   TUESDAY
Independence Day (Filipino)   Moon Sign: Pisces
Waning Moon   Incense: Basil
Moon Phase: Third Quarter
Color: Red

☽   WEDNESDAY
St. Anthony of Padua's Day   Moon Sign: Pisces
Waning Moon   Incense: Nutmeg
Moon Phase: Fourth Quarter 10:28 pm
Color: Yellow

14   THURSDAY
Flag Day   Moon Sign: Pisces
Waning Moon   Moon enters Aries 12:03 pm
Moon Phase: Fourth Quarter   Incense: Vanilla
Color: Violet

Ⅱ

15 FRIDAY
Lantern Festival (Japanese)
Waning Moon
Moon Phase: Fourth Quarter
Color: Peach

Moon Sign: Aries
Incense: Ginger

16 SATURDAY
Bloomsday (Irish)
Waning Moon
Moon Phase: Fourth Quarter
Color: Indigo

Moon Sign: Aries
Moon enters Taurus 9:39 pm
Incense: Evergreen

17 SUNDAY
Father's Day
Waning Moon
Moon Phase: Fourth Quarter
Color: Peach

Moon Sign: Taurus
Incense: Clove

18 MONDAY
Independence Day (Egyptian)
Waning Moon
Moon Phase: Fourth Quarter
Color: Silver

Moon Sign: Taurus
Incense: Sandalwood

19 TUESDAY
Juneteenth
Waning Moon
Moon Phase: Fourth Quarter
Color: White

Moon Sign: Taurus
Moon enters Gemini 3:42 am
Incense: Orchid

20 WEDNESDAY
Flag Day (Argentinian)
Waning Moon
Moon Phase: Fourth Quarter
Color: Brown

Moon Sign: Gemini
Incense: Juniper

THURSDAY
Litha • Summer Solstice • Solar Eclipse
Waning Moon
Moon Phase: New Moon 6:58 am
Color: Violet

Moon Sign: Gemini
Sun enters Cancer 2:38 am
Moon enters Cancer 6:40 am
Incense: Daffodil

♋ JUNE

22 FRIDAY
Rose Festival (British)   Moon Sign: Cancer
Waxing Moon   Incense: Rosemary
Moon Phase: First Quarter
Color: Rose

23 SATURDAY
St. John's Eve   Moon Sign: Cancer
Waxing Moon   Moon enters Leo 7:55 am
Moon Phase: First Quarter   Incense: Pine
Color: Brown

24 SUNDAY
Carabobo Day (Venezuelan)   Moon Sign: Leo
Waxing Moon   Incense: Thyme
Moon Phase: First Quarter
Color: Gold

25 MONDAY
Fiesta of Santa Orosia (Spanish)   Moon Sign: Leo
Waxing Moon   Moon enters Virgo 8:57 am
Moon Phase: First Quarter   Incense: Violet
Color: Lavender

26 TUESDAY
Pied Piper Day (German)   Moon Sign: Virgo
Waxing Moon   Incense: Maple
Moon Phase: First Quarter
Color: Black

◐ WEDNESDAY
Day of the Seven Sleepers (Islamic)   Moon Sign: Virgo
Waxing Moon   Moon enters Libra 11:11 am
Moon Phase: Second Quarter 10:19 pm   Incense: Lilac
Color: White

28 THURSDAY
Paul Bunyan Day   Moon Sign: Libra
Waxing Moon   Incense: Geranium
Moon Phase: Second Quarter
Color: White

29 FRIDAY

Saints Peter's and Paul's Day   Moon Sign: Libra
Waxing Moon   Moon enters Scorpio 3:28 pm
Moon Phase: Second Quarter   Incense: Coriander
Color: Peach

30 SATURDAY

The Burning of the Three Firs (French)
Waxing Moon   Moon Sign: Scorpio
Moon Phase: Second Quarter   Incense: Carnation
Color: Blue

~❦~

MAGIC BOOKS

Family spells that had been proven effective over many centuries were often written in small, leather-bound books and guarded from the eyes of strangers. If you're not fortunate enough to have access to such a magic book, you have the opportunity to create one for your own family. Begin this magical operation on the night of the Full Moon.

Choose a small, unlined, bound book. Light a white candle. By its flame, draw a pentagram on the first page. On this page, beneath the pentagram, add the date of the book's creation, your mundane or magical name, and the Moon's phase. Hold it up before the candle and say these or similar words:

> *O stars, O sun,*
> *O moon so bright,*
> *Bless now this book*
> *I've made tonight.*

Raise the book to the north, east, south, and west. Copy at least one successful spell into the book on the night upon which you create it. Such a magic book can become a treasured heirloom, for it reveals the magical and spiritual nature of those who have created it.

♋ JULY

1 SUNDAY

Passion Play at Oberammergau   Moon Sign: Scorpio
Waxing Moon   Moon enters Sagittarius 10:13 pm
Moon Phase: Second Quarter   Incense: Basil
Color: Peach

2 MONDAY

Heroes' Day (Zambian)   Moon Sign: Sagittarius
Waxing Moon   Incense: Peony
Moon Phase: Second Quarter
Color: White

3 TUESDAY

Indian Sun Dance (Amer. Indian)   Moon Sign: Sagittarius
Waxing Moon   Incense: Poplar
Moon Phase: Second Quarter
Color: Gray

4 WEDNESDAY

Independence Day   Moon Sign: Sagittarius
Waxing Moon   Moon enters Capricorn 7:21 am
Moon Phase: Second Quarter   Incense: Parsley
Color: Peach

☺ THURSDAY

Lunar Eclipse   Moon Sign: Capricorn
Waxing Moon   Incense: Thyme
Moon Phase: Full Moon 10:04 am
Color: Green

6 FRIDAY

Khao Phansa Day (Thai)   Moon Sign: Capricorn
Waning Moon   Moon enters Aquarius 6:33 pm
Moon Phase: Third Quarter   Incense: Clove
Color: Pink

7 SATURDAY

Weaver's Festival (Japanese)   Moon Sign: Aquarius
Waning Moon   Incense: Eucalyptus
Moon Phase: Third Quarter
Color: Indigo

183

8 SUNDAY
St. Elizabeth's Day (Portuguese)
Waning Moon
Moon Phase: Third Quarter
Color: Orange

Moon Sign: Aquarius
Incense: Rosemary

9 MONDAY
Battle of Sempach Day
Waning Moon
Moon Phase: Third Quarter
Color: Silver

Moon Sign: Aquarius
Moon enters Pisces 7:05 am
Incense: Basil

10 TUESDAY
Lady Godiva Day (English)
Waning Moon
Moon Phase: Third Quarter
Color: Red

Moon Sign: Pisces
Incense: Ginger

11 WEDNESDAY
Revolution Day (Mongolian)
Waning Moon
Moon Phase: Third Quarter
Color: Brown

Moon Sign: Pisces
Moon enters Aries 7:36 pm
Incense: Musk

12 THURSDAY
Lobster Carnival (Nova Scotian)
Waning Moon
Moon Phase: Third Quarter
Color: Turquoise

Moon Sign: Aries
Incense: Patchouli

◖ FRIDAY
Festival of the Three Cows
Waning Moon
Moon Phase: Fourth Quarter 1:45 pm
Color: Rose

Moon Sign: Aries
Incense: Dill

14 SATURDAY
Bastille Day (French)
Waning Moon
Moon Phase: Fourth Quarter
Color: Blue

Moon Sign: Aries
Moon enters Taurus 6:13 am
Incense: Jasmine

69   JULY

15 SUNDAY
St. Swithin's Day
Waning Moon
Moon Phase: Fourth Quarter
Color: Yellow

Moon Sign: Taurus
Incense: Cedar

16 MONDAY
Our Lady of Carmel Day
Waning Moon
Moon Phase: Fourth Quarter
Color: Gray

Moon Sign: Taurus
Moon enters Gemini 1:26 pm
Incense: Myrrh

17 TUESDAY
Rivera Day (Puerto Rican)
Waning Moon
Moon Phase: Fourth Quarter
Color: White

Moon Sign: Gemini
Incense: Geranium

18 WEDNESDAY
Gion Matsuri Festival (Japanese)
Waning Moon
Moon Phase: Fourth Quarter
Color: Yellow

Moon Sign: Gemini
Moon enters Cancer 4:56 pm
Incense: Juniper

19 THURSDAY
Flitch Day (English)
Waning Moon
Moon Phase: Fourth Quarter
Color: Violet

Moon Sign: Cancer
Incense: Daffodil

FRIDAY
Binding of Wreaths (Lithuanian)
Waning Moon
Moon Phase: New Moon 2:44 pm
Color: Peach

Moon Sign: Cancer
Moon enters Leo 5:43 pm
Incense: Basil

21 SATURDAY
National Day (Belgian)
Waxing Moon
Moon Phase: First Quarter
Color: Brown

Moon Sign: Leo
Incense: Evergreen

185

LEO ♌

22 SUNDAY
St. Mary Magdalene's Day
Waxing Moon
Moon Phase: First Quarter
Color: Peach

Moon Sign: Leo
Sun enters Leo 1:26 pm
Moon enters Virgo 5:29 pm
Incense: Cinnamon

23 MONDAY
Mysteries of Santa Cristina (Italian)
Waxing Moon
Moon Phase: First Quarter
Color: Lavender

Moon Sign: Virgo
Incense: Carnation

24 TUESDAY
Pioneer Day (Mormon)
Waxing Moon
Moon Phase: First Quarter
Color: Red

Moon Sign: Virgo
Moon enters Libra 6:08 pm
Incense: Ginger

25 WEDNESDAY
St. James' Day
Waxing Moon
Moon Phase: First Quarter
Color: Peach

Moon Sign: Libra
Incense: Coriander

26 THURSDAY
St. Anne's Day
Waxing Moon
Moon Phase: First Quarter
Color: Turquoise

Moon Sign: Libra
Moon enters Scorpio 9:17 pm
Incense: Maple

☽ FRIDAY
Sleepyhead Day (Finnish)
Waxing Moon
Moon Phase: Second Quarter 5:08 am
Color: Rose

Moon Sign: Scorpio
Incense: Thyme

28 SATURDAY
Independence Day (Peruvian)
Waxing Moon
Moon Phase: Second Quarter
Color: Gray

Moon Sign: Scorpio
Incense: Frankincense

29 SUNDAY
Pardon of the Birds (French)   Moon Sign: Scorpio
Waxing Moon   Moon enters Sagittarius 3:44 am
Moon Phase: Second Quarter   Incense: Dill
Color: Yellow

30 MONDAY
Micmac Festival of St. Ann   Moon Sign: Sagittarius
Waxing Moon   Incense: Sandalwood
Moon Phase: Second Quarter
Color: Silver

31 TUESDAY
Weighing of the Aga Khan   Moon Sign: Sagittarius
Waxing Moon   Moon enters Capricorn 1:16 pm
Moon Phase: Second Quarter   Incense: Poplar
Color: Black

LOVE SPELL

To discover who your lover will be, go out and look upon the Moon when it is waxing and in its first quarter. Say:

Mother Moon let me see
The person who will love with me

You must do this for seven nights in a row. On the seventh night you should dream of your future lover.

LEO ♌

1 WEDNESDAY
Lammas
Waxing Moon
Moon Phase: Second Quarter
Color: Peach

Moon Sign: Capricorn
Incense: Sage

---

2 THURSDAY
Porcingula (Native American)
Waxing Moon
Moon Phase: Second Quarter
Color: Violet

Moon Sign: Capricorn
Incense: Lavender

---

3 FRIDAY
Drimes (Greek)
Waxing Moon
Moon Phase: Second Quarter
Color: Rose

Moon Sign: Capricorn
Moon enters Aquarius 12:53 am
Incense: Basil

SATURDAY
Cook Islands Constitution Celebrations
Waxing Moon
Moon Phase: Full Moon 12:56 am
Color: Blue

Moon Sign: Aquarius
Incense: Ylang ylang

---

5 SUNDAY
Benediction of the Sea (French)
Waning Moon
Moon Phase: Third Quarter
Color: Gold

Moon Sign: Aquarius
Moon enters Pisces 1:30 pm
Incense: Thyme

---

6 MONDAY
Hiroshima Peace Ceremony
Waning Moon
Moon Phase: Third Quarter
Color: White

Moon Sign: Pisces
Incense: Vanilla

---

7 TUESDAY
Republic Day (Ivory Coast)
Waning Moon
Moon Phase: Third Quarter
Color: Black

Moon Sign: Pisces
Incense: Musk

8 WEDNESDAY
Dog Days (Japanese)   Moon Sign: Pisces
Waning Moon   Moon enters Aries 2:05 am
Moon Phase: Third Quarter   Incense: Sage
Color: Yellow

9 THURSDAY
Nagasaki Peace Ceremony   Moon Sign: Aries
Waning Moon   Incense: Chrysanthemum
Moon Phase: Third Quarter
Color: White

10 FRIDAY
St. Lawrence's Day   Moon Sign: Aries
Waning Moon   Moon enters Taurus 1:23 pm
Moon Phase: Third Quarter   Incense: Ginger
Color: Pink

11 SATURDAY
Puck Fair (Irish)   Moon Sign: Taurus
Waning Moon   Incense: Patchouli
Moon Phase: Third Quarter
Color: Gray

☾ SUNDAY
Fiesta of Santa Clara   Moon Sign: Taurus
Waning Moon   Moon enters Gemini 9:59 pm
Moon Phase: Fourth Quarter 2:53 am   Incense: Cinnamon
Color: Orange

13 MONDAY
Women's Day (Tunisian)   Moon Sign: Gemini
Waning Moon   Incense: Maple
Moon Phase: Fourth Quarter
Color: Gray

14 TUESDAY
Festival at Sassari   Moon Sign: Gemini
Waning Moon   Incense: Poplar
Moon Phase: Fourth Quarter
Color: Gray

15 WEDNESDAY
Assumption Day
Waning Moon
Moon Phase: Fourth Quarter
Color: White

Moon Sign: Gemini
Moon enters Cancer 2:55 am
Incense: Geranium

16 THURSDAY
Festival of Minstrels (European)
Waning Moon
Moon Phase: Fourth Quarter
Color: Green

Moon Sign: Cancer
Incense: Thyme

17 FRIDAY
Feast of the Hungry Ghosts (Chinese)
Waning Moon
Moon Phase: Fourth Quarter
Color: Peach

Moon Sign: Cancer
Moon enters Leo 4:25 am
Incense: Clove

☽ SATURDAY
St. Helen's Day
Waning Moon
Moon Phase: New Moon 9:55 pm
Color: Brown

Moon Sign: Leo
Incense: Cedar

19 SUNDAY
Rustic Vinalia (Roman)
Waxing Moon
Moon Phase: First Quarter
Color: Gold

Moon Sign: Leo
Moon enters Virgo 3:53 am
Incense: Nutmeg

20 MONDAY
Constitution Day (Hungarian)
Waxing Moon
Moon Phase: First Quarter
Color: Gray

Moon Sign: Virgo
Incense: Maple

21 TUESDAY
Consualia (Roman)
Waxing Moon
Moon Phase: First Quarter
Color: Red

Moon Sign: Virgo
Moon enters Libra 3:19 am
Incense: Basil

♍

22 WEDNESDAY
Feast of the Queenship of Mary (British)   Moon Sign: Libra
Waxing Moon   Sun enters Virgo 8:27 pm
Moon Phase: First Quarter   Incense: Ginger
Color: Peach

23 THURSDAY
National Day (Romanian)   Moon Sign: Libra
Waxing Moon   Moon enters Scorpio 4:50 am
Moon Phase: First Quarter   Incense: Jasmine
Color: Violet

24 FRIDAY
St. Bartholomew's Day   Moon Sign: Scorpio
Waxing Moon   Incense: Honeysuckle
Moon Phase: First Quarter
Color: White

◐ SATURDAY
Feast of the Green Corn (American Indian)   Moon Sign: Scorpio
Waxing Moon   Moon enters Sagittarius 9:59 am
Moon Phase: Second Quarter 2:55 pm   Incense: Myrrh
Color: Indigo

26 SUNDAY
Pardon of the Sea (French)   Moon Sign: Sagittarius
Waxing Moon   Incense: Coriander
Moon Phase: Second Quarter
Color: Peach

27 MONDAY
Summer Break (British)   Moon Sign: Sagittarius
Waxing Moon   Moon enters Capricorn 7:02 pm
Moon Phase: Second Quarter   Incense: Rosemary
Color: Silver

28 TUESDAY
St. Augustine's Day   Moon Sign: Capricorn
Waxing Moon   Incense: Evergreen
Moon Phase: Second Quarter
Color: Black

VIRGO ♍

29 WEDNESDAY
St. John's Beheading
Waxing Moon
Moon Phase: Second Quarter
Color: Brown

Moon Sign: Capricorn
Incense: Cinnamon

30 THURSDAY
St. Rose of Lima Day (Peruvian)
Waxing Moon
Moon Phase: Second Quarter
Color: Green

Moon Sign: Capricorn
Moon enters Aquarius 6:47 am
Incense: Basil

31 FRIDAY
Unto These Hills Pageant (Cherokee)
Waxing Moon
Moon Phase: Second Quarter
Color: Pink

Moon Sign: Aquarius
Incense: Parsley

❧·❦·❧

ANCIENT HERBAL SPELLS

• Place thorny rose branches on the front doorstep to keep evil far from your abode.

• Consuming a bit of wild thyme before retiring will grant the diner a sleep free from nightmares.

• Keep money with cedar chips in a small box to attract yet more money.

• To discover the future, take two acorns. Name one "yes," the other "no." Place them in a basin of water and ask your question. The acorn that floats toward you indicates the answer.

• Gather the first anemone flower to bloom in spring and carry with you as a charm against sickness.

• To keep evil spirits from the house, hang dried seaweed in the kitchen.

♍ SEPTEMBER

1 SATURDAY
New Year's Day (Greek)
Waxing Moon
Moon Phase: Second Quarter
Color: Blue

Moon Sign: Aquarius
Moon enters Pisces 7:32 pm
Incense: Daffodil

☺ SUNDAY
Wilhelm Tell Festival (Swiss-American)
Waxing Moon
Moon Phase: Full Moon 4:43 pm
Color: Gold

Moon Sign: Pisces
Incense: Ginger

3 MONDAY
Labor Day
Waning Moon
Moon Phase: Third Quarter
Color: Lavender

Moon Sign: Pisces
Incense: Vanilla

4 TUESDAY
Los Angeles' Birthday
Waning Moon
Moon Phase: Third Quarter
Color: Red

Moon Sign: Pisces
Moon enters Aries 7:58 am
Incense: Sage

5 WEDNESDAY
Roman Circus
Waning Moon
Moon Phase: Third Quarter
Color: Yellow

Moon Sign: Aries
Incense: Dill

6 THURSDAY
Virgin of the Remedies (Mexican)
Waning Moon
Moon Phase: Third Quarter
Color: Turquoise

Moon Sign: Aries
Moon enters Taurus 7:18 pm
Incense: Juniper

7 FRIDAY
Festival of Durga (Bengalese)
Waning Moon
Moon Phase: Third Quarter
Color: Rose

Moon Sign: Taurus
Incense: Nutmeg

8   **SATURDAY**
Birthday of the Virgin Mary   Moon Sign: Taurus
Waning Moon   Incense: Geranium
Moon Phase: Third Quarter
Color: Blue

9   **SUNDAY**
Chrysanthemum Festival (Japanese)   Moon Sign: Taurus
Waning Moon   Moon enters Gemini 4:41 am
Moon Phase: Third Quarter   Incense: Clove
Color: Gold

◯   **MONDAY**
Festival of the Poets (Japanese)   Moon Sign: Gemini
Waning Moon   Incense: Dill
Moon Phase: Fourth Quarter 1:59 pm
Color: Silver

11   **TUESDAY**
Coptic New Year   Moon Sign: Gemini
Waning Moon   Moon enters Cancer 11:09 am
Moon Phase: Fourth Quarter   Incense: Rosemary
Color: Red

12   **WEDNESDAY**
National Day (Ethiopian)   Moon Sign: Cancer
Waning Moon   Incense: Cinnamon
Moon Phase: Fourth Quarter
Color: Peach

13   **THURSDAY**
The God's Banquet (Roman)   Moon Sign: Cancer
Waning Moon   Moon enters Leo 2:16 pm
Moon Phase: Fourth Quarter   Incense: Nutmeg
Color: Green

14   **FRIDAY**
Holy Cross Day   Moon Sign: Leo
Waning Moon   Incense: Coriander
Moon Phase: Fourth Quarter
Color: Peach

15 SATURDAY
Birthday of the Moon (Chinese)   Moon Sign: Leo
Waning Moon   Moon enters Virgo 2:39 pm
Moon Phase: Fourth Quarter   Incense: Pine
Color: Indigo

16 SUNDAY
Independence Day (Mexican)   Moon Sign: Virgo
Waning Moon   Incense: Eucalyptus
Moon Phase: Fourth Quarter
Color: Yellow

☽ MONDAY
Von Steuben's Day   Moon Sign: Virgo
Waning Moon   Moon enters Libra 2:00 pm
Moon Phase: New Moon 5:27 am   Incense: Peony
Color: Lavendar

18 TUESDAY
Rosh Hashanah   Moon Sign: Libra
Waxing Moon   Incense: Lilac
Moon Phase: First Quarter
Color: White

19 WEDNESDAY
"The Scouring of the White Horse" (British)   Moon Sign: Libra
Waxing Moon   Moon enters Scorpio 2:27 pm
Moon Phase: First Quarter   Incense: Poplar
Color: Yellow

20 THURSDAY
St. Eustace's Day   Moon Sign: Scorpio
Waxing Moon   Incense: Patchouli
Moon Phase: First Quarter
Color: Turquoise

21 FRIDAY
Independence Day (Maltan)   Moon Sign: Scorpio
Waxing Moon   Moon enters Sagittarius 6:02 pm
Moon Phase: First Quarter   Incense: Sage
Color: Pink

LIBRA

♎

22 SATURDAY
Mabon • Fall Equinox   Moon Sign: Sagittarius
Waxing Moon   Sun enters Libra 6:04 pm
Moon Phase: First Quarter   Incense: Pine
Color: Gray

23 SUNDAY
Carrot and Cracknut Sunday (British)   Moon Sign: Sagittarius
Waxing Moon   Incense: Thyme
Moon Phase: First Quarter
Color: Orange

☽ MONDAY
Schwenkfelder Thanksgiving (German-Amer.) Moon Sign: Sagittarius
Waxing Moon   Moon enters Capricorn 1:48 am
Moon Phase: Second Quarter 4:31 am   Incense: Honeysuckle
Color: White

25 TUESDAY
Salute to the Sun (Chinese)   Moon Sign: Capricorn
Waxing Moon   Incense: Cedar
Moon Phase: Second Quarter
Color: Gray

26 WEDNESDAY
Feast of Santa Justina (Mexican)   Moon Sign: Capricorn
Waxing Moon   Moon enters Aquarius 1:05 pm
Moon Phase: Second Quarter   Incense: Musk
Color: Brown

27 THURSDAY
Yom Kippur   Moon Sign: Aquarius
Waxing Moon   Incense: Rose
Moon Phase: Second Quarter
Color: Violet

28 FRIDAY
Confucius' Birthday   Moon Sign: Aquarius
Waxing Moon   Incense: Basil
Moon Phase: Second Quarter
Color: Rose

♎

29 SATURDAY
Michaelmas   Moon Sign: Aquarius
Waxing Moon   Moon enters Pisces 1:50 am
Moon Phase: Second Quarter   Incense: Juniper
Color: Brown

30 SUNDAY
St. Jerome's Day   Moon Sign: Pisces
Waxing Moon   Incense: Ginger
Moon Phase: Second Quarter
Color: Peach

◦∾❈∾◦

HECATE

Hecate is perhaps the most famous of the Greek
deities associated with magic. According to tradition,
she was the daughter of Zeus and Demeter, or Perses
and Asteria, or Zeus and Hera.

From the earliest times she ruled the Moon, the
earth, and the sea. Among her blessings were wealth,
victory, wisdom, successful sailing, and hunting, but
she withheld these from those mortals who didn't
deserve them. She retained such powers under the
iron rule of Zeus, and she was honored by all the
immortal deities.

Hecate is best remembered today as a dark goddess who at night sent out demons and phantoms, who
taught magic and sorcery to brave mortals, and who
wandered with the souls of the dead after dark. Her
approach was always heralded by the cries and howls
of dogs. Despite this, she was also invoked for protection and was greatly loved.

Hecate is a complex goddess: giver of wealth and
fortune, and mistress of sorcery. She is still worshiped
today by those unafraid of her awesome powers.

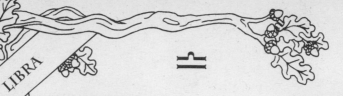

LIBRA

1 MONDAY
Armed Forces Day (South Korean)
Waxing Moon
Moon Phase: Second Quarter
Color: Gray

Moon Sign: Pisces
Moon enters Aries 2:08 pm
Incense: Pine

2 TUESDAY
Sukkot begins
Waxing Moon
Moon Phase: Full Moon 8:49 am
Color: Black

Moon Sign: Aries
Incense: Evergreen

3 WEDNESDAY
Moroccan New Year's Day
Waning Moon
Moon Phase: Third Quarter
Color: Peach

Moon Sign: Aries
Incense: Sage

4 THURSDAY
St. Francis' Day
Waning Moon
Moon Phase: Third Quarter
Color: White

Moon Sign: Aries
Moon enters Taurus 1:01 am
Incense: Gardenia

5 FRIDAY
Republic Day (Portuguese)
Waning Moon
Moon Phase: Third Quarter
Color: Pink

Moon Sign: Taurus
Incense: Sandalwood

6 SATURDAY
St. Faith's Day
Waning Moon
Moon Phase: Third Quarter
Color: Indigo

Moon Sign: Taurus
Moon enters Gemini 10:12 am
Incense: Musk

7 SUNDAY
Kermesse (German)
Waning Moon
Moon Phase: Third Quarter
Color: Gold

Moon Sign: Gemini
Incense: Parsley

198

8 MONDAY
Sukkot ends • Columbus Day (observed)   Moon Sign: Gemini
Waning Moon   Moon enters Cancer 5:19 pm
Moon Phase: Third Quarter   Incense: Sage
Color: Silver

◑ TUESDAY
Alphabet Day (South Korean)   Moon Sign: Cancer
Waning Moon   Incense: Maple
Moon Phase: Fourth Quarter 11:20 pm
Color: Gray

10 WEDNESDAY
Health Day (Japanese)   Moon Sign: Cancer
Waning Moon   Moon enters Leo 9:54 pm
Moon Phase: Fourth Quarter   Incense: Myrrh
Color: Yellow

11 THURSDAY
Medetrinalia (Roman)   Moon Sign: Leo
Waning Moon   Incense: Ylang ylang
Moon Phase: Fourth Quarter
Color: Violet

12 FRIDAY
National Day (Spanish)   Moon Sign: Leo
Waning Moon   Moon enters Virgo 11:58 pm
Moon Phase: Fourth Quarter   Incense: Clove
Color: Peach

13 SATURDAY
Floating of the Lamps (Siamese)   Moon Sign: Virgo
Waning Moon   Incense: Eucalyptus
Moon Phase: Fourth Quarter
Color: Brown

14 SUNDAY
Battle Festival (Japanese)   Moon Sign: Virgo
Waning Moon   Incense: Coriander
Moon Phase: Fourth Quarter
Color: Peach

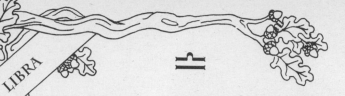

15 MONDAY
Deepavali (Hindu)
Waning Moon
Moon Phase: Fourth Quarter
Color: Lavender

Moon Sign: Virgo
Moon enters Libra 12:26 am
Incense: Chrysanthemum

☽ TUESDAY
The Lion Sermon (British)
Waning Moon
Moon Phase: New Moon 2:23 pm
Color: Red

Moon Sign: Libra
Incense: Thyme

17 WEDNESDAY
St. Audrey's Fair
Waxing Moon
Moon Phase: First Quarter
Color: White

Moon Sign: Libra
Moon enters Scorpio 1:03 am
Incense: Vanilla

18 THURSDAY
Brooklyn Barbecue
Waxing Moon
Moon Phase: First Quarter
Color: Green

Moon Sign: Scorpio
Incense: Sage

19 FRIDAY
Our Lord of Miracles Procession (Peruvian)
Waxing Moon
Moon Phase: First Quarter
Color: White

Moon Sign: Scorpio
Moon enters Sagittarius 3:47 am
Incense: Neroli

20 SATURDAY
Colchester Oyster Feast
Waxing Moon
Moon Phase: First Quarter
Color: Gray

Moon Sign: Sagittarius
Incense: Sandalwood

21 SUNDAY
Feast of the Black Christ
Waxing Moon
Moon Phase: First Quarter
Color: Yellow

Moon Sign: Sagittarius
Moon enters Capricorn 10:11 am
Incense: Cedar

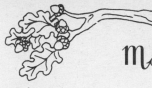

22 MONDAY
Goddess of Mercy Day (Chinese)   Moon Sign: Capricorn
Waxing Moon   Incense: Pine
Moon Phase: First Quarter
Color: Silver

◐ TUESDAY
Revolution Day (Hungarian)   Moon Sign: Capricorn
Waxing Moon   Sun enters Scorpio 3:26 am
Moon Phase: Second Quarter 9:58 pm   Incense: Ginger
Color: Gray   Moon enters Aquarius 8:26 pm

24 WEDNESDAY
United Nations Day   Moon Sign: Aquarius
Waxing Moon   Incense: Eucalyptus
Moon Phase: Second Quarter
Color: Brown

25 THURSDAY
St. Crispin's Day   Moon Sign: Aquarius
Waxing Moon   Incense: Almond
Moon Phase: Second Quarter
Color: Violet

26 FRIDAY
National Day (Austrian)   Moon Sign: Aquarius
Waxing Moon   Moon enters Pisces 8:56 am
Moon Phase: Second Quarter   Incense: Sage
Color: Peach

27 SATURDAY
Allan Day (Welsh)   Moon Sign: Pisces
Waxing Moon   Incense: Violet
Moon Phase: Second Quarter
Color: Blue

28 SUNDAY
Daylight Saving Time ends at 2:00 am   Moon Sign: Pisces
Waxing Moon   Moon enters Aries 9:15 pm
Moon Phase: Second Quarter   Incense: Rosemary
Color: Gold

♏

29 MONDAY
Iroquois Feast of the Dead　　　　　Moon Sign: Aries
Waxing Moon　　　　　　　　　　Incense: Carnation
Moon Phase: Second Quarter
Color: White

30 TUESDAY
Full Moon Day (Burmese)　　　　　Moon Sign: Aries
Waxing Moon　　　　　　　　　　Incense: Pine
Moon Phase: Second Quarter
Color: Black

31 WEDNESDAY
Halloween • Samhain　　　　　　Moon Sign: Aries
Waxing Moon　　　　Moon enters Taurus 7:48 am
Moon Phase: Second Quarter　　　Incense: Evergreen
Color: Yellow

MOON SPELL

Upon seeing the Full Moon, form a circle with the thumb and first finger of your talented hand. Hold it up until the Moon rests within this ring, and say these words in a hushed voice:

Good Moon, round Moon,
Full Moon near:
Let the future
Now appear.

Gaze at the Moon and ask a question; it shall be answered.

THURSDAY
All Saints' Day
Waxing Moon
Moon Phase: Full Moon 12:41 am
Color: Violet

Moon Sign: Taurus
Incense: Peony

---

2 FRIDAY
All Souls' Day
Waning Moon
Moon Phase: Third Quarter
Color: Pink

Moon Sign: Taurus
Moon enters Gemini 4:12 pm
Incense: Thyme

---

3 SATURDAY
St. Hubert's Day
Waning Moon
Moon Phase: Third Quarter
Color: Blue

Moon Sign: Gemini
Incense: Jasmine

---

4 SUNDAY
Mischief Night (British)
Waning Moon
Moon Phase: Third Quarter
Color: Orange

Moon Sign: Gemini
Moon enters Cancer 10:44 pm
Incense: Ginger

---

5 MONDAY
Guy Fawkes' Day
Waning Moon
Moon Phase: Third Quarter
Color: Gray

Moon Sign: Cancer
Incense: Juniper

---

6 TUESDAY
Election Day
Waning Moon
Moon Phase: Third Quarter
Color: Silver

Moon Sign: Cancer
Incense: Basil

---

7 WEDNESDAY
Mayan Day of the Dead
Waning Moon
Moon Phase: Third Quarter
Color: Peach

Moon Sign: Cancer
Moon enters Leo 3:34 am
Incense: Cinnamon

THURSDAY
Queen's Birthday (Nepalese)
Waning Moon
Moon Phase: Fourth Quarter 7:21 am
Color: Violet

Moon Sign: Leo
Incense: Geranium

---

9 FRIDAY
Lord Mayor's Day (English)
Waning Moon
Moon Phase: Fourth Quarter
Color: Rose

Moon Sign: Leo
Moon enters Virgo 6:49 am
Incense: Sage

---

10 SATURDAY
Martin Luther's Birthday
Waning Moon
Moon Phase: Fourth Quarter
Color: Indigo

Moon Sign: Virgo
Incense: Cedar

---

11 SUNDAY
Veterans Day
Waning Moon
Moon Phase: Fourth Quarter
Color: Yellow

Moon Sign: Virgo
Moon enters Libra 8:53 am
Incense: Coriander

---

12 MONDAY
Tesuque Feast Day
Waning Moon
Moon Phase: Fourth Quarter
Color: Silver

Moon Sign: Libra
Incense: Dill

---

13 TUESDAY
Festival of Jupiter (Roman)
Waning Moon
Moon Phase: Fourth Quarter
Color: Black

Moon Sign: Libra
Moon enters Scorpio 10:44 am
Incense: Evergreen

---

14 WEDNESDAY
The Little Carnival (Greek)
Waning Moon
Moon Phase: Fourth Quarter
Color: Peach

Moon Sign: Scorpio
Incense: Parsley

☽ **THURSDAY**
St. Leopold's Day   Moon Sign: Scorpio
Waning Moon   Moon enters Sagittarius 1:51 pm
Moon Phase: New Moon 1:40 am   Incense: Gardenia
Color: White

16 **FRIDAY**
Ramadan begins   Moon Sign: Sagittarius
Waxing Moon   Incense: Nutmeg
Moon Phase: First Quarter
Color: Peach

17 **SATURDAY**
Queen Elizabeth's Day   Moon Sign: Sagittarius
Waxing Moon   Moon enters Capricorn 7:40 pm
Moon Phase: First Quarter   Incense: Ylang ylang
Color: Blue

18 **SUNDAY**
St. Plato's Day   Moon Sign: Capricorn
Waxing Moon   Incense: Clove
Moon Phase: First Quarter
Color: Gold

19 **MONDAY**
Garifuna Day (Belize)   Moon Sign: Capricorn
Waxing Moon   Incense: Vanilla
Moon Phase: First Quarter
Color: White

20 **TUESDAY**
Revolution Day (Mexican)   Moon Sign: Capricorn
Waxing Moon   Moon enters Aquarius 4:55 am
Moon Phase: First Quarter   Incense: Eucalyptus
Color: Gray

21 **WEDNESDAY**
Repentance Day (German)   Moon Sign: Aquarius
Waxing Moon   Incense: Sandalwood
Moon Phase: First Quarter
Color: Yellow

THURSDAY
Thanksgiving Day
Waxing Moon
Moon Phase: Second Quarter 6:21 pm
Color: Turquoise

Moon Sign: Aquarius
Sun enters Sagittarius 1:00 am
Incense: Musk
Moon enters Pisces 4:52 pm

23 FRIDAY
St. Clement's Day
Waxing Moon
Moon Phase: Second Quarter
Color: Rose

Moon Sign: Pisces
Incense: Rosemary

24 SATURDAY
Feast of the Burning Lamps (Egyptian)
Waxing Moon
Moon Phase: Second Quarter
Color: Brown

Moon Sign: Pisces
Incense: Juniper

25 SUNDAY
St. Catherine's Day (French)
Waxing Moon
Moon Phase: Second Quarter
Color: Orange

Moon Sign: Pisces
Moon enters Aries 5:21 am
Incense: Parsley

26 MONDAY
Festival of Lights (Tibetan)
Waxing Moon
Moon Phase: Second Quarter
Color: Lavender

Moon Sign: Aries
Incense: Almond

27 TUESDAY
St. Maximus' Day
Waxing Moon
Moon Phase: Second Quarter
Color: Black

Moon Sign: Aries
Moon enters Taurus 4:06 pm
Incense: Patchouli

28 WEDNESDAY
Ascension of Abdul-Baha (Baha'i)
Waxing Moon
Moon Phase: Second Quarter
Color: Brown

Moon Sign: Taurus
Incense: Poplar

29 **THURSDAY**
Tubman's Birthday (Liberian)   Moon Sign: Taurus
Waxing Moon   Incense: Basil
Moon Phase: Second Quarter
Color: Green

FRIDAY
St. Andrew's Day   Moon Sign: Taurus
Waxing Moon   Moon enters Gemini 12:04 am
Moon Phase: Full Moon 3:49 pm   Incense: Ginger
Color: Pink

THE LORE OF MONEY

*Here are some delightful "old wisdoms," lore,
and spells concerning cash:*

- Always keep a few coins in your home when leaving for a journey. To do otherwise bodes ill.

- If you drop any money in the home, say: "Money on the floor, money at the door." Step on the money and pick it up; more will come to you.

- Finding money is fortunate, but to keep such money invites misfortune. Spend it as quickly as possible, and tell no one of its origin.

- Never leave the house without at least one coin in your pocket or handbag. The best charm of all is a bent coin or a coin pierced with a hole. These coins are both "lucky" and protective.

- If you fold your bills, fold them toward you to indicate that money will come to you. Folding money away from you will result in its absence.

- To ensure that you will always have money and friends, tie a string into a circle and keep it in your pocket, wallet, or purse.

207

1 **SATURDAY**
Big Tea Party (Japanese)   Moon Sign: Gemini
Waning Moon   Incense: Myrrh
Moon Phase: Third Quarter
Color: Gray

2 **SUNDAY**
Republic Day (Laotian)   Moon Sign: Gemini
Waning Moon   Moon enters Cancer 5:30 am
Moon Phase: Third Quarter   Incense: Cinnamon
Color: Gold

3 **MONDAY**
St. Francis Xavier's Day   Moon Sign: Cancer
Waning Moon   Incense: Violet
Moon Phase: Third Quarter
Color: Lavender

4 **TUESDAY**
St. Barbara's Day   Moon Sign: Cancer
Waning Moon   Moon enters Leo 9:15 am
Moon Phase: Third Quarter   Incense: Daffodil
Color: White

5 **WEDNESDAY**
Eve of St. Nicholas' Day   Moon Sign: Leo
Waning Moon   Incense: Pine
Moon Phase: Third Quarter
Color: Brown

6 **THURSDAY**
St. Nicholas' Day   Moon Sign: Leo
Waning Moon   Moon enters Virgo 12:11 pm
Moon Phase: Third Quarter   Incense: Orchid
Color: White

☾ **FRIDAY**
Burning the Devil (Guatemalan)   Moon Sign: Virgo
Waning Moon   Incense: Clove
Moon Phase: Fourth Quarter 2:52 pm
Color: Rose

8 SATURDAY
Feast of the Immaculate Conception   Moon Sign: Virgo
Waning Moon   Moon enters Libra 2:57 pm
Moon Phase: Fourth Quarter   Incense: Musk
Color: Brown

9 SUNDAY
St. Leocadia's Day   Moon Sign: Libra
Waning Moon   Incense: Nutmeg
Moon Phase: Fourth Quarter
Color: Orange

10 MONDAY
Hanukkah begins   Moon Sign: Libra
Waning Moon   Moon enters Scorpio 6:09 pm
Moon Phase: Fourth Quarter   Incense: Ginger
Color: Silver

11 TUESDAY
Pilgrimage at Tortugas   Moon Sign: Scorpio
Waning Moon   Incense: Maple
Moon Phase: Fourth Quarter
Color: Black

12 WEDNESDAY
Fiesta of Our Lady of Guadalupe   Moon Sign: Scorpio
Waning Moon   Moon enters Sagittarius 10:30 pm
Moon Phase: Fourth Quarter   Incense: Sandalwood
Color: Peach

13 THURSDAY
St. Lucy's Day (Swedish)   Moon Sign: Sagittarius
Waning Moon   Incense: Peony
Moon Phase: Fourth Quarter
Color: Violet

 FRIDAY
Solar Eclipse   Moon Sign: Sagittarius
Waning Moon   Incense: Coriander
Moon Phase: New Moon 3:47 pm
Color: Peach

SAGITTARIUS

15 SATURDAY
Ramadan ends
Waxing Moon
Moon Phase: First Quarter
Color: Indigo

Moon Sign: Sagittarius
Moon enters Capricorn 4:48 am
Incense: Frankincense

16 SUNDAY
Posadas (Mexican)
Waxing Moon
Moon Phase: First Quarter
Color: Yellow

Moon Sign: Capricorn
Incense: Patchouli

17 MONDAY
Hannukah ends
Waxing Moon
Moon Phase: First Quarter
Color: Gray

Moon Sign: Capricorn
Moon enters Aquarius 1:43 pm
Incense: Evergreen

18 TUESDAY
Feast of the Virgin of Solitude
Waxing Moon
Moon Phase: First Quarter
Color: Red

Moon Sign: Aquarius
Incense: Parsley

19 WEDNESDAY
Opalia (Roman)
Waxing Moon
Moon Phase: First Quarter
Color: Yellow

Moon Sign: Aquarius
Incense: Poplar

20 THURSDAY
Commerce-God Festival (Japanese)
Waxing Moon
Moon Phase: First Quarter
Color: Turquoise

Moon Sign: Aquarius
Moon enters Pisces 1:09 am
Incense: Maple

21 FRIDAY
Yule • Winter Solstice
Waxing Moon
Moon Phase: First Quarter
Color: White

Moon Sign: Pisces
Sun enters Capricorn 2:21 pm
Incense: Chrysanthemum

☽ **SATURDAY**
Fiesta of Santo Tomas (Guatemalan)   Moon Sign: Pisces
Waxing Moon   Moon enters Aries 1:45 pm
Moon Phase: Second Quarter 3:56 pm   Incense: Lavender
Color: Blue

23 SUNDAY
Larentalia (Roman)   Moon Sign: Aries
Waxing Moon   Incense: Basil
Moon Phase: Second Quarter
Color: Gold

24 MONDAY
Christmas Eve   Moon Sign: Aries
Waxing Moon   Incense: Dill
Moon Phase: Second Quarter
Color: Silver

25 TUESDAY
Christmas Day   Moon Sign: Aries
Waxing Moon   Moon enters Taurus 1:12 am
Moon Phase: Second Quarter   Incense: Eucalyptus
Color: Gray

26 WEDNESDAY
Kwanzaa begins   Moon Sign: Taurus
Waxing Moon   Incense: Sage
Moon Phase: Second Quarter
Color: Peach

27 THURSDAY
Feast of St. John the Evangelist   Moon Sign: Taurus
Waxing Moon   Moon enters Gemini 9:39 am
Moon Phase: Second Quarter   Incense: Honeysuckle
Color: Violet

28 FRIDAY
Holy Innocents' Day   Moon Sign: Gemini
Waxing Moon   Incense: Ginger
Moon Phase: Second Quarter
Color: Rose

CAPRICORN

♑

29 SATURDAY
St. Thomas à Becket
Waxing Moon
Moon Phase: Second Quarter
Color: Brown

Moon Sign: Gemini
Moon enters Cancer 2:40 pm
Incense: Sandalwood

SUNDAY
Lunar Eclipse
Waxing Moon
Moon Phase: Full Moon 5:40 am
Color: Peach

Moon Sign: Cancer
Incense: Thyme

31 MONDAY
New Year's Eve
Waning Moon
Moon Phase: Third Quarter
Color: Lavender

Moon Sign: Cancer
Moon enters Leo 5:09 pm
Incense: Neroli

PROPHETIC DREAM SPELL

To create prophetic dreams, walk outside with a fresh white rose. Hold it up to the Moon between both hands so that the blossom is flooded with moonlight. Say:

Awaken my second sight

Press the white rose against your forehead, saying:

By the power of this rite

Place the flower under your pillow before sleep and remember your dreams.

A BLESSING FOR COMEDIES

BY ELIZABETH BARRETTE

Maui of the Thousand Tricks,
Hero of the First Days,
May you fight always on our side!

When trouble turns in our direction,
May you throw a banana peel in its path;
When you see the other gods
Measuring the days of our lives,
May it please you to fudge the numbers in our favor.

When you hear them plotting to squash us all,
May you tell them bad jokes
Until they die laughing
And leave us alone.

Maui, you hung the sky and snared the sun.
We can never return the favor,
But we hope you like this poetic farce.
Please try not to wreck it before we're through.

MOONLIGHT, WITCHCRAFT, AND MOTHER GOOSE

BY LYNNE STURTEVANT

Mother Goose rhymes are a jumble of riddle, poetry, folklore, political satire, moral lessons, and old drinking songs. Most of these nursery rhymes originated in the fifteenth and sixteenth centuries, but some hint at much older sources. Counting-out chants, such as "eena, meena, mina, mo," may be derived from Druid rituals, and other rhymes contain magical incantations, ancient folk beliefs, and fragments of forgotten tales.

AN UNBROKEN CHAIN

In traditional societies, myths, legends, and lore are preserved and transmitted by storytellers. Although the written word began to replace the oral tradition in Europe centuries ago, rural people continued to tell the tales handed down by their ancestors. Unfortunately, folklorists did not start documenting the old beliefs until the nineteenth century, and many of the stories had already been lost.

In their stampede to interview elderly farm people, scholars ignored another group with a rich and unbroken oral tradition. The members of this group could neither read nor write and they had been reciting the same poems, songs, and chants for hundreds of years, word for word, often without understanding their meanings. The members of this group were children.

As anyone who has cared for a child knows, nursery rhymes must be repeated without variation. If you change or miss a single word, you'll be interrupted by an irritated four-year-old who will insist that you "Start over and do it right!" This behavior pattern is not new, and the demand for endless, exact repetition explains how the rhymes passed unchanged from generation to generation.

MOON RHYMES

Some of the oldest known nursery rhymes are about the Moon. Many are exactly what they appear to be—pleasant jingles, weather wisdom, and practical gardening lore.

> *Girls and boys come out to play,*
> *The Moon doth shine as bright as day.*

> *Pale Moon doth rain,*
> *Red Moon doth blow,*
> *White Moon doth neither rain nor snow.*

> *Sow peas and beans in the wane of the Moon;*
> *Who soweth them sooner, he soweth too soon.*

Not all Moon rhymes are simple and straightforward. Several contain mysterious references that only make sense in the context of old folk beliefs and practices.

THE SINISTER MOON

For thousands of years, people believed that lunacy and countless other maladies were caused by moonlight. Children were so vulnerable they could be harmed without even coming into direct contact with Moon beams. In order to keep their children safe, new mothers never hung wet baby clothes or diapers to dry in the moonlight, and they taught their children to bow or curtsey to the New Moon as an extra precaution. Children were also sternly warned never to point at the Moon regardless of its phase.

When moonlight entered their bedrooms and touched their faces, children recited the following poem.

I see the Moon and the moon sees me.
God bless the Moon and God bless me.

Although the rhyme sounds like an innocent nursery prayer, it is a corruption of an ancient spell to ward off Moon-induced madness. Other versions of the last line are "God bless the priest that christened me," "God bless the sailors on the sea," and "The Moon sees something I want to see."

Adults were not immune to the Moon's evil influence, and a Full Moon on Friday was the most dangerous of all.

Friday's Moon,
Come when it will,
It comes too soon.

In small, controlled doses, moonlight could be beneficial. For example, the Moon could cure warts. People rubbed the afflicted areas of their bodies while staring at the New Moon and repeated the following rhyme three times.

What I see is growing.
What I rub is going.

Other rhymes are actually incantations that were part of romantic divination rituals performed on the night of the New Moon. Before going to bed, young women placed a door key, a prayer book, and the playing cards the ten of clubs, the nine of hearts, the ace of spades, and the ace of diamonds under their pillows. They then repeated one of the following prayers.

Luna, every woman's friend,
To me thy goodness condescend,
Let me this night in visions see
Emblems of my destiny.

All hail to the Moon! All hail to thee!
I pray, good Moon, declare to me
This night who my future husband must be.

Some New Moon rites involved collecting plants. Women placed freshly picked yarrow flowers under their pillows and chanted:

> Good night, fair yarrow.
> Thrice good night to thee;
> I hope before tomorrow's dawn
> My true love I shall see.

THE CRYPTIC MOON

Many rhymes that began as political satire found their way into nursery story books. The meanings of several are well-known. "Georgie Porgie" is about the lecherous King George I. "Mary, Mary Quite Contrary" is Mary, Queen of Scots. "Little Boy Blue" is Cardinal Wolsey, and "Lucy Locket" is one of Charles II's many mistresses.

Not all political rhymes are obvious. At times in the past, composing political satire was a treasonable offense, punishable by death. Authors portrayed powerful people as animals or other nonhuman characters, including the Moon. In addition, veiled satirical rhymes often include strange settings and contradictory or puzzling statements.

The man in the Moon in the following rhyme is probably Charles Stuart, who later became King Charles II. He was the target of numerous unflattering poems and songs. The rhyme describes his dithering and strategic blunders during the English Civil War.

> The man in the Moon
> Came down too soon,
> And asked the way to Norwich.
> He went by the south,
> And burned his mouth,
> While eating cold plum porridge.

When the political rhymes were written, their meanings were clear to everyone. However, some historical characters were so well disguised that their true identities are a mystery to us today. These rhymes have become the subject of intense study and outlandish speculation. "Hey, diddle, diddle" has generated several bizarre theories to decipher its meaning.

Hey diddle, diddle,
The cat and the fiddle,
The cow jumped over the Moon.
The little dog laughed
To see such a sight
And the dish ran away with the spoon.

Although the explanation isn't as popular as it used to be, some historians think the cat and the cow were nicknames for Queen Elizabeth I and the little dog. The Moon, the dish, and the spoon were members of her court.

Most of the analysis has focused on the line "The cow jumped over the moon." The following three theories link the phrase to ancient Egyptian mythology. Each is notoriously far-fetched. According to the first theory, the cow represents the goddess Hathor, who was usually portrayed as having a cow's head. According to the second, the cow is a bull. Its horns and the crescent Moon symbolize the goddess Isis. According to the third, the cat is Egypt, the fiddle is a scarab beetle, the cow is the constellation Taurus, the little dog is the North Star, and the dish and the spoon are the ancient Egyptians fleeing the rising waters of the Nile.

Most scholars reject both the Elizabethan and the Egyptian interpretations and maintain that the rhyme is nothing more than a nonsense poem based on the words to a popular sixteenth-century drinking song.

WITCHES, FAIRIES, AND THE OLD RELIGION

On first reading, the following rhyme sounds like it might be political satire.

The man in the Moon was caught in a trap
For stealing the thorns from another man's gap.
If he had gone by, and let the thorns lie,
He wouldn't be man in the moon so high.

The rhyme actually describes the conflict between early Christians and Pagan adherents of the Old Religion. It is based on the story of a man caught stealing thorn branches and piling them in front of a church to keep people from entering. Thorns are associated with fairies in Celtic lore and they reinforce the man's identity as a Pagan. He was punished for his transgression by being banished to the Moon. It is his image people saw on clear nights, a warning to others reluctant to adopt the new belief system.

Mother Goose rhymes also include charms for protection. Although the following two rhymes specifically mention Witches, they describe traditional Celtic techniques for avoiding trouble with the fairies.

> Rowan tree and red thread
> Hold the Witches all in dread.

Aside from protection charms, references to Witchcraft in Mother Goose are rare, and when they do appear, they are subtle. Even though the word "Witch" isn't used in the following rhymes, both incorporate familiar symbols.

> There was an old woman tossed up in a basket
> Nineteen times as high as the Moon.
> Where she was going I couldn't but ask it,
> For in her hand she carried a broom.

> There was an old woman who rode on a broom,
> With a high gee ho, gee humble;
> And she took her old cat behind for a groom,
> With a bimble, bamble, bumble.

The rhythm of "high gee ho, gee humble" and "bimble, bamble, bumble" hint that the phrases may be spell fragments.

Folklorists have suggested the following rhyme is not about a real person, but rather about an inanimate object. Even if true, the image of ducking, a test used to determine the guilt or innocence of people accused of Witchcraft, is central here. The alleged Witch was bound and thrown into deep water. Those who floated were found guilty and sentenced to death. Those who sank were found innocent.

> *There was an old woman, her name it was Peg;*
> *Her head was of wood, and she wore a cork leg.*
> *The neighbors all pitched her into the water;*
> *Her leg was drowned first, and her head followed after.*

AN OLD WOMAN AND HER BIRD

Who is Mother Goose? Was she a real person or does she represent something else?

> *Old Mother Goose*
> *When she wanted to wander,*
> *Would fly through the air*
> *On a very fine gander.*

Like the words of the rhymes, her portrayal in nursery books has remained remarkably consistent through the years. She is always an old woman. She wears a tall, pointed hat and flies through the air, symbols as familiar as the broom and the cat mentioned earlier. Her character may be based on a village elder, healer, wise woman, or storyteller. Then again, Mother Goose may be much, much older.

Her companion and namesake is a bird, a well-documented symbol of the ancient Mother Goddess. The bird mother of the nursery rhyme may be a dim reflection of the oldest mother of all. Even though she has traveled from a time so remote it is all but unimaginable, as long as little children remember her and repeat the rhymes, the grand old lady will continue to soar.

> *And Old Mother Goose*
> *Her bird saddled up soon,*
> *She mounted his back,*
> *And flew up to the Moon.*

SACRED ARCHEOLOGY

BY CHAS S. CLIFTON

Many people know that Stonehenge and other European megalithic monuments appear to have served as astronomical and ritual calculators. But controversy still surrounds the suggestion that a series of archeological sites in the American West may represent an attempt to create similar ritual calendars.

The sites of the Ogham corridor—the nickname of a swath of land reaching from the Oklahoma panhandle into southeastern Colorado—do not involve huge standing stones. But a group of researchers thinks they have a Pagan European origin, an idea that violates conventional American history and enrages many archeologists.

And in a time when Celtic art, music, and spirituality are all enjoying renewals, perhaps it is only these sites' remoteness that has protected them from being overrun by seekers of ancient wisdom. Certainly they pose an intriguing question: did pre-Columbian explorers enter mid-North America as much as two thousand years ago? And did they stay long enough to make astronomical observations connected to their religious practices? The answers to such questions are, at best, merely conjectural.

The Ogham sites are regarded suspiciously by most archeologists. One reason is that American archeologists are not trained to interpret ancient writing, mainly because there is no other evidence of any existing on this continent. Instead, these archeologists look for artifacts, and so far none have been found in the area that are not believed to be made by prehistoric Indians or by more recent settlers. True, a Roman coin once turned up when a septic tank was being dug in the nearby town of Springfield, Colorado, but skeptics point out that you can buy

Roman coins cheaply from any coin dealer, and therefore it could have been planted at a much later date than ancient times.

The situation is similar to what happened with the idea of a Norse settlement in America. For centuries, scholars had puzzled over the accounts in the sagas of Atlantic travel in the Viking Age, and they were skeptical over the ideas that famed Arctic explorer Fridtjof Nansen laid out in his book *In Northern Mists*. Yet only until indisputable Norse artifacts were found in the 1960s in Newfoundland, proving that a village had existed there, were the North American archeologists convinced.

At least those voyages had been described in a fairly reliable oral and then written tradition. Nothing similar exists describing voyages of Carthagian or Iberian Celtic explorers two thousand years ago—nothing except a series of rock inscriptions along the Arkansas River in Oklahoma and Texas, inscriptions which most archeologists prefer to attribute to ancestral American Indians.

In fact, if you suggest to many archeologists that explorers from ancient Libya (the ancient Carthagians) or the Iberian peninsula (some of whom spoke a Celtic language before it was replaced by Latin) came to America, you might be called a "racist." Many nineteenth-century scholars speculated that all evidence of civilization in this hemisphere, whether Mayan temples or the towns of the Mound Builders in North America, was derived from Old World models. These theories, that all civilizations derived from one or two places such as the Near East, were called "diffusionism." Now, modern researchers lean towards the independent invention of civilization in different places, and diffusionism is very much out of favor, its proponents often accused of pushing ideas of racial superiority. But this swing of the pendulum produces an attitude of scorn towards any evidence that ancient travelers might have come to North America.

Suppose that they had. Maverick American epigraphers, students of ancient inscriptions, make one powerful argument. At three particular sites in Oklahoma and Colorado, they claim, inscriptions can be deciphered to predict astronomical events such as a shadow falling inside a cave at a particular spot when the sun rises on the Spring and Fall Equinoxes. In addition, some controversial dating methods developed by archeologists at the University of Arizona produce dates of two to three thousand years before the present.

Another argument against these particular inscriptions being modern hoaxes is that in many cases the newer, sharper-looking inscriptions are dated and signed by a person from the late nineteenth and early twentieth centuries. That much I can attest to myself. A few years ago I sat in a small west-facing cave in the Oklahoma panhandle as the Sun sat at the Spring Equinox. As it disappeared, its horizontal light struck rock knobs that cast slow-moving shadows across the back of the shallow cave. Nearby were cut Libyan letters, which the late Barry Fell—an oceanographer and researcher on ancient seafaring at Harvard University—translated to read, "Enact at sunset the rites of Bell, assembling at that hour in worship." Nearby another inscription in Ogham letters has been translated to read, "The Sun six months north; sinks south for space of months equal number." Above the inscription is the "indicator," something like a marked-off ruler cut into the rock. On the Equinox, a pointed shadow passed the middle of the indicator. The marked-off increments corresponded to the days before or after the Equinox, showing where the shadow falls on each of the days.

At Crack Cave, located a little to the north in Colorado, a similar Ogham inscription reads, "Sun strikes [here] day of Bel." Nearby, again in Old Irish: "People of the Sun." And at a ranch not too far away, another cave inscription was translated to read "The ring along with the shoulder by means of sun and hill." However, nothing significant happened there on the Solstice or Equinoctal sunrises. Since another inscription nearby seemed to include the word "Lugnasa" (also called Lammas in English), the cross-quarter day between the Summer Solstice and the Fall Equinox, members of the ranch family visited the site several days running at Sunrise. On August 8, halfway between those two dates, the rising Sun shone perfectly through a square overhang before the cave.

If these inscriptions were made by ancient European and North African visitors—imagine for a moment that they might have been—then what kind of people were they? The "people of the Sun" inscription (if that's what it really says) suggests a sort of priesthood, something like the Druids of Gaul and Britain.

To be fair, we have to look at some good arguments against the epigraphers' case. Unlike with the Norse sites, no foreign artifacts have been found at any of the Ogham sites. But then no one has looked for them systematically. There might well have been none to find—for aside from bronze tools or weapons, or possibly iron ones, which rust away, their possessions might all have been biodegradable. The case for the Norse presence in Newfoundland was based at first only on a small stone weight used in spinning thread and weaving it into cloth. The local Indians did not use such a tool.

Next, the location is unlikely. This part of the United States is lightly populated now—and according to conventional archeology, it was even more lightly populated two thousand years ago. There are no large ruined villages such as those found on the other side of the Rockies at Mesa Verde National Park, only a few rock structures that might have been huts. Why would anyone want to come here? It was arid, rough country long ago even as it is now, and it was not on the way to another more-populated area. Why come all the way across the Atlantic to observe the sun's movements in a remote area inhabited by a handful of people?

Could the inscriptions have been made by Indians who learned the writing from visitors to these shores? This is a conceivable possibility, but that only replaces one mystery with a larger one.

In any event, some modern Pagans feel heartened by the presence of the inscriptions. The writings, if that is what they are, suggest a more peaceful interaction between visitors and natives. Conquering armies, after all, usually do not stop to make leisurely astronomical observations. Although the Norse sagas say that their colonists abandoned "Vinland" after a series of escalating conflicts with the Algonquin Indians, perhaps the "People of the Sun" maintained better relations with the people they met. When you consider that in 1999, the annual Columbus Day celebration in Pueblo, Colorado, the nearest city, turned into an angry confrontation between an Italian heritage group and American Indian Movement counterdemonstrators, it is tempting to think that history could have taken another, less violent turn than the history of European exploration that we all learned in school.

Lately, the study of "rock art," which includes both inscriptions and pictures made on rock, has become a new growth area in archeology. Scholars are beginning to move into territory that used to be considered too risky—such as the growing tendency to see some designs as depicting shamanic visions. What is more, younger British and European archeologists are beginning to take an interest in the possibility of ancient inscriptions in America. Having had different training—and not having the preconceived notion that "it can't be here" that is exhibited by many American archeologists, they could be positioned to evaluate these inscriptions more thoughtfully.

In the meantime, some of us continue to wonder: did the People of the Sun ever cross the High Plains, following the Arkansas and Cimarron rivers up out of Oklahoma to a country where the Rockies gleamed on the horizon? And if so, what were they looking for? Cities? Knowledge? Visions?

SUGGESTIONS FOR FURTHER READING

Farley, Gloria. *In Plain Sight: Old World Records in Ancient America.* Columbus, Georgia: ISAC Press, 1994.

McGlone, William, et al. *Ancient American Inscriptions: Plow Marks or History?* Sutton, Massachusetts: Early Sites Research Society, 1993.

McGlone, Bill, Ted Barker, and Phil Leonard. *Archaeastronomy of Southeast Colorado and the Oklahoma Panhandle.* Kamas, Utah: Mithras, 1999.

McGlone, Bill, Ted Barker, and Phil Leonard. *Petroglyphs of Southeast Colorado and the Oklahoma Panhandle.* Kamas, Utah: Mithras, 1994.

Kids' Crafts

By Breid Foxsong

Parents, these are several fun projects to do with your kids, perhaps on a rainy day when you're stuck indoors hour after hour with nothing but daytime TV to keep you occupied, or perhaps during the long dog days of summer vacation.

The first one is a simple window treatment, the second is a musical instrument, and the third is a wall hanging. Any of these can be done by children over three, as long as there is a little supervision and assistance by an adult.

Window Frosting

The first project is frosting windows. This is a perfect way to play winter in the summer! It's also excellent for creating privacy, such as in a bathroom, or for shielding an ugly view. Make sure you start by cleaning your windows completely.

Dissolve 4 heaping tablespoons of Epsom salts in 1 cup of beer. This mixture will foam, so be sure you do it in an area that you can easily clean up afterward. Let the beer mixture set for at least 30 minutes. The salt crystals will partially dissolve.

After the time has elapsed, apply the mixture to your window. This can be done with a cheap two-inch paint brush from any hardware store, but for a nicer effect, you can dip a facial tissue or terry cloth in the liquid and wipe over the window as if you were washing it. Smeary is better in this case, so let the child go to it!! Then while the window is still wet go back and dab and pat at the glass with the wet tissue to create patterns.

The mixture will dry to form beautiful crystals. It will look even better the next day, and lasts quite a long time. In time, the mixture can be washed off with water and a cloth, and it is easily reapplied. So you can do it over and over until you've got it just the way you want it.

Rain Sticks

The second project is to make your own rain stick. Many adults are possessive of their expensive musical instruments, but this project will allow everyone to have their own rainmaking instrument. It's also a neat way to recycle paper towel tubes.

You will need:

Paper towel rolls (one per rain stick)
Brown packing tape (or any kind of tape you can paint on)
Brown tempera paint
Toothpicks
White glue
Rice

For small children, you can pre-poke holes (a lot of holes) in the tube before the kids start to work on it. Bigger kids can poke their own holes though both sides of the tube. Either way, once the holes are done, cover one end of the roll with tape. Use tape you can paint on so it can be decorated later.

Paint the stick with brown tempera paint. Let the paint dry, then stick toothpicks so they go through one hole and out another. Glue both ends of the toothpick to the tube. The whole idea is to have the toothpicks going in at different angles to make the required sound. Have an adult cut off any protruding ends of the toothpicks.

Then fill the stick with rice. Let the child decide on their own how much to use; just have them put the rice in a little at a time and have them flip it back and forth so they can hear the "rain" sound until they have it just they way they want. It won't take a lot of rice.

Tape up the other end with paintable tape, and, there you have it, a rainstick!

WIND CHIMES

The third project is creating wind chimes. Wind chimes are very easy to make and calm any room they are hung in. And what parent doesn't appreciate a little calm?

For this project, you can experiment with materials a little bit, and see what makes the best sound. For outdoor chimes, you can go to hardware store and get hollow metal rods. Have the store cut the rod into different sizes for a beautiful array of notes. For indoor chimes, you can use metal trinkets, ceramic figurines, or anything your imagination can dream up. Terra cotta tiles are easy and sound great, but you can also use rods, pieces of porcelain tile, sea shells, bits of slate or stones, jewelry, glass, old toys, and so on.

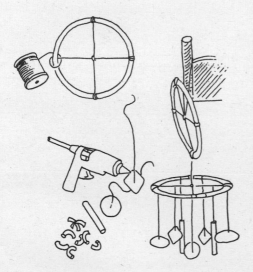

For starters, you will need an embroidery hoop, some fishing line and chimes to attach. Any sharp edges on any chimes need to be supervised for small children. You may simply want to get some sandpaper to deal with the sharp edges. Or for a safe and purely decorative chime for small children, try dipping macaroni into water color and using those.

To make the chimes, tie the fishing line across your embroidery hoop and then tie the other side to create a cross. From this you will attach your chimes. Tie a hanging loop on the hoop, and hang the hoop on the back of a chair. This will make it easier to attach your chimes and evenly distribute the weight.

Using the materials you have chosen, tie or hot glue the objects onto the fishing line, then tie around the hoop. Keep doing this at different lengths until you have chimes hanging from all around the hoop. Take care to spread the objects evenly, and to make them hang at lengths where they will come in contact with one another as they move in the wind or at the hands of your child.

Finally, attach some chimes in the center of the hoop where you first created a cross. Make sure your chimes are evenly balanced in weight and add a few more where necessary before hanging. Hang the chimes, and with your children, be sure to take time to enjoy the product of your own labor.

Stone Monuments of the Celtic Realms

By Kenneth Johnson

The landscape of the British Isles is dotted with monuments in stone—tombs, circles, rows, and monoliths. Some are world famous, others obscure. All of them resonate with powerful energies all their own.

We sometimes think of them as "Celtic," although in fact they are not. Most of them were already a thousand years old by the time the first Celtic tribes took up residence in the British Isles.

The monuments—called megaliths, meaning "great stones"—were constructed by the farming peoples who lived in northwestern Europe before the Celts. The first such monuments were gigantic tombs, erected on the shores of the Breton peninsula in France. They contained the remains of many people, perhaps entire villages, and the bodies of the dead were set with their faces to the west, the land of rebirth in later legend and lore.

Yet these collective tombs had other purposes as well. One such monument, New Grange in Ireland, has a window that captures the light of the rising Sun on the Winter Solstice. Then, on the shortest day of the year, a shaft of light pours into the tomb and illuminates its stone walls. Was it intended as a symbol of rebirth—that the spirits of the ancestors who were housed in the tomb would be reborn like the Sun on the Winter Solstice?

Or was it an attempt at scientific astronomy, measuring the year to establish a calendar? Or was it, perhaps, both of these things?

Some scientists have suggested that some megalithic monuments may have been intended as astronomical observatories. The most famous, of course, is Stonehenge, with its alignments to the Summer Solstice. But was Stonehenge a true observatory, or was it a temple, a place of worship?

There are other mysteries on the Celtic landscape, left there by those early farmers. What, for instance, was the purpose of Silbury Hill? A huge mound of earth, like a small mountain, it stands all alone in the middle of the fields. It took hundreds—perhaps thousands—of people countless hours to pile it up. But why? It has no obvious astronomical significance. Archeological excavations have uncovered no evidence that it was a tomb. Did it mark some tremendous place of power, a spot of magical significance? Was it a mythic world mountain, imitated here on Earth to serve as a focus of energy? We shall probably never know.

It has been suggested that many of the megaliths do, indeed, mark places of power. Some believe that lines of energy travel across the landscape, linking the old sacred sites in a kind of energetic network, with the megaliths themselves marking the nodal points of the energies involved. These lines, which are perceived as arrow-straight, are often called ley lines. Scientists scoff, rejecting the idea on the grounds that no such lines are visible. Yet sometimes there really are straight-line pathways from one monument to another. They appear as ditches on the ground. Such a ditch or pathway is called a cursus, and has no apparent practical purpose.

It is certainly true that many visitors to the old megalithic sites feel that these stone monuments are endowed with a presence and energy that can be felt quite easily—a presence and energy so powerful that it lifts one's spirit to heights of joy and contemplation. Perhaps the most powerful of such places is Avebury, a collection of stone circles, rows, and earthen ditches so vast that it dwarfs Stonehenge, or any other megalithic site. Here again, one wonders why they went to so much trouble. What did people do here?

At an obscure stone circle in Ireland, archeologists found the imprints of ancient feet buried deep in a stratum of mud. This suggests that the ancient people of the British Isles did in fact dance in the stone circles, much as romantic imagination would hope they did. Such a dance at a site the size of Avebury would probably have included thousands of people.

Whether observatories, places of rebirth, mythic landscapes, or centers of magical energy, the megaliths of the Celtic realm continue to delight and inspire, thousands of years after their makers have passed.

Practical Rocks

By Estelle Daniels

Many people find crystals and various rocks to be wonderful magical aids. Rocks run energy well, and they can aid psychic concentration. I will reveal a secret known to few people: rocks have other wonderful uses in magic beyond their energy qualities.

One of the original uses for rocks in ritual was for altars. It isn't practical to build a full stone altar, but a flat rock or stone flat surface—such as decorative tiling or a stone chessboard—makes a good altar. It also holds heat and is very waterproof.

One practical use for rocks is as quarter symbols. There are many beautiful rocks in many colors, and rocks with shades of yellow, red, blue or purple, or green or brown can make markers for the quarters of the Moon. If the rocks don't come in the correct colors, a bit of paint is always helpful.

Another use for rocks is for holding things, like papers and what not, down. It sounds weird to mention this, but people don't often think of this practical use for a good rock when they are looking for a good paperweight.

Rocks can also be ties to a distant place. If in your travels you find a rock from a special place, that rock can act as a tie to the place and a way of keeping connected. Be aware, however, that it is unlawful to take anything—including rocks—from a federal park. But in that case, there are access roads and areas near the park where you can usually find rocks or other such objects to carry home without violating the laws.

Rocks can also act as a tie to past times—even though the passage of time for a rock is usually measured in the many million of years. If you learn a bit about the geology of your area, however, a rock will be a portal to understanding where your area has been. And, if the rock has fossils in it—a fossil being a remnant of life, usually bone or shell, sometimes plants or bacteria—you have an automatic tie to an organism and a time and place far distant from your own. Or if you have a rock from an historical site, it can be a tie to that place in historic times.

If you live in an apartment or high-rise, a rock is a tie to the Earth, literally. People don't realize that most of us never actually touch the earth directly. There is usually at least a layer of asphalt or concrete between us and the soil or rock. If we want to get in contact with the Earth, why not use a plain old rock from the area. Use it for an altar or as a rest for your feet to keep in contact with Mother Earth.

I like to use a black and a white rock for my Goddess and God symbols. They are basic and generic, but still evoke much meaning to me. They are also portable and if they get lost, it is no big deal. I can easily go back to the source and find a couple of replacement rocks.

A rock with black and white together symbolizes the union of the Goddess and God. If you want to get more elaborate you can use special rocks for deity symbols. A stone with natural holes in it is considered a good luck charm and a Goddess symbol. An ammonite, or fossilized spiral shell, easily obtainable in rock shops, is another wonderful Goddess symbol. I have a piece of petrified coral I picked up at a rock shop for fifty cents. It is shaped like a phallus, and it makes a good God symbol. (So do pine cones, but they aren't rocks unless they are fossilized). Any rod-shaped stone can be used for a God symbol. Any round or oval stone with a cleft or depression can be used for a Goddess symbol. Keep your eyes open and your imagination engaged and you'll be surprised what you can find.

Where can you get good rocks? One very good source is in a stream or river bed, lake, or seashore. New rocks are uncovered especially after a storm when the water has been running. Combine a rock hunt with a stroll by your local water, and you can kill two birds with one stone (ha ha).

Another source is in gravel or decorative beds. Now I don't recommend raiding your neighbor's yard with a gunny sack, but many landscaping schemes, such as restaurants, shopping centers, parking lots, and other municipal structures include decorative rocks. I have kept my eyes open and through the years have found some wonderful rocks in my travels or just around town. Usually some rocks escape the beds, and taking one or two home in your pocket isn't a big thing in the grand scheme of things.

Driving along road cuts you can often find some neat rocks. Usually it isn't legal to stop along an interstate freeway, but the older state or federal highways have cuts in hills or cliffs for drainage. In past years, I have found many rocks washed up at the bottom of these areas.

If you garden, you will always find rocks buried in the soil. Examine them and maybe you will find a keeper or two.

Most sizable towns have rock shops. Know what you want, keep your eyes open for sales, and you can get some nice things at bargain prices.

Then there is my favorite place, the local yard sale. My belief is that everything is available at some yard sale or another. You just have to keep looking. If you keep rocks in mind, you may come across them more quickly. Since to most people rocks are just rocks, you can usually purchase them quite cheaply.

Rocks are sacred. In the myth of Deucalion they are called the bones of your mother, the bones of Mother Earth. They don't have to be fancy crystals or cut into elaborate figure and shape in order to be good, solid, practical magical tools. Blessed be, and good and happy rock hunting.

GLASTONBURY
THE COMMON GROUND OF AVALON

BY deTRACI REGULA

Pagan gathering place? Mystic refuge? Christian church? Goddess worshipper haven? Few places on Earth combine the many worlds between the worlds as effectively as Glastonbury, and in this small town of 8,000 inhabitants, you never know who you will meet. It's a place of quests, where everyone desires to find a touch of another world. And they may well receive it.

Glastonbury lies on the Salisbury Plain, facing the sea in the south of England. Once an island itself, the rhythms of water are still flowing through it. Chalice Well, with its entwined Vesica Piscis ponds, and the compelling White Spring which rises from the roots of Glastonbury Tor itself assure that the spiritual potency of water is never doubted here.

In the morning, before the crowds come, the destroyed remains of Glastonbury Abbey are curiously peaceful and without stain. The abbey was brutally suppressed by King Henry VIII, who had the then-abbot dragged to the Tor and hung; now, nature has reclaimed the gray stones and restored some peace. On one fragment, a dozen white birds nest; opposite, an equal number of black birds make the place home. At unlikely spots a bit of green clings to the wall itself.

Though Glastonbury has been troubled, it has purified itself. Walking through a Christian temple, ruined at the hands of other Christians, the visitor feels strangely at peace. "Henry has a lot to answer for," my companion, who had been completely uninterested in visiting Glastonbury, muttered as we wandered by the remains of the high arches.

It was hard to leave the Abbey, but the Tor beckoned, crowned with the tower of St. Michael, saint in charge of suppressing dragons. This is all that remains of a church which once covered most of the top of the Tor. The air was clear, sunny, and "filled with sparkles" as Dion Fortune described a particularly memorable day on the Tor where she lived at Chalice Orchard. Although the Abbey is near the Tor, iron gates keep the two separate, maybe a bit of magic keeping separate the  fairy and the more recent faith. We walked the long way around the grounds through the High Street and headed back toward the Tor, whose tower is strangely invisible even at close range, concealed by a subtle shift in ground level or a vigorous tree.

The other shift in ground quality was the incredible muddiness of the back way up the Tor, which we had been assured was shorter. And quicker. Rising up from a residential section of Glastonbury, the way looked easy enough, until, a dozen yards along, the mud was passing my ankles. We went around to the more commonly used way, and discovered the White Spring. Its sound caught our attention first, a gentle gurgling under iron gratings at the side of the street. Following the water, we entered a room out of another world—a cave filled with a coffee house. More of the spring ran in narrow channels through the floor at our feet, and a magical shop nearby offered ritual blades whose hilts were masterfully carved with divine forms. Roots from the Tor hung down from the ceiling, and the lighting was largely by candle-light. Beyond the public areas other chambers slipped away into shadow. Once again it was hard to tear ourselves away, but the top of the Tor was still calling.

The path up the Tor went by Chalice Orchard, where a sign reminded gawkers that it was private property. This side of the Tor, blessedly, was not muddy, and the way up looked reassuringly simple. We had only a few hours to spend in Glastonbury, so the remains of the maze path, which takes several hours, were beyond us. The ascent was dizzying, and though I was in reasonably good shape, my heart was pounding and the air seemed thin. I looked at the Tower in the distance and thought, with the body betraying the spirit for a moment, that perhaps this was close enough.

But now my companion had caught the glow of the Tor, and, thrilled with the ascent, thundered on, offering a hand to me at moments. In the last stretch, we passed a group of dun-colored Hathorian cows who lay unexpectedly along the path, lowing. Then we were at the Tower, whose height induced vertigo when we looked up inside it. As Dion had said, the air was full of sparkles outside, and around us, England stretched out like a tablecloth. Far away were the bell towers of Wells. Pastoral fields stretched in all directions, and, reminding us of the sea that once isolated this high hill, a flooded field shone glassy beneath the blue sky. The miraculously clear air changed as we watched, and a slight mist began emanating from the ground all around. As the sun descended, so did we. Someone began drumming in the tower, and the thrilling sound reverberated through the Tor.

Or was it in the Tower? Glastonbury has its legends as a hollow mound reaching into the Under—or Other—World as well. You can never be sure what world you're perceiving at magical Glastonbury.

The Origin of the Planets

By Kenneth Johnson

We all know the astrological planets—Mercury, Venus, Pluto, Jupiter, Saturn, and the rest. They're our good friends. But once, long ago, they went by different names.

Astrology as we know it was developed by the Babylonians, and in the beginning the planets bore the names of their deities. Behind the Babylonians lay the more ancient culture of the Sumerians, and many goddesses and gods whose names passed into the lore of astrology had more distant ancestors in that long ago era as well.

In Babylon, these were the names and attributes of the planets:

The Sun was Shamash, perceived as a kingly figure whose watchful eye in the sky kept track of the deeds of the human world here below. He was in some respects a judge, occasionally stern, but just as often benevolent, and he maintained the cosmic balance of right and wrong.

The planet Jupiter was known as Marduk, king of the Gods. It was he who slew the primal dragon Tiamat, using her body to fashion the Earth and sky, order the seasons and the paths of the stars, and establish the cosmic order over which Shamash was to keep careful watch.

Mercury was Nebo (also spelled Nabu), Marduk's most important minister and scribe. A record keeper by profession, he was the patron of the art of writing, and therefore of business and the civilized arts.

The planet we know as Mars was called Nergal, and he was a dangerous god. In charge of plagues as well as warfare, he scorched the Earth with his wrath. Having conquered many kingdoms in heaven and on Earth, he stormed his way into the underworld, displaced the ancient goddess who ruled there, and made himself king of the dead.

Saturn was known as Ninurta, or sometimes Ninib. In ancient Sumerian times, he was a dragon slayer like Marduk, part of an earlier generation of deities, now somewhat retired and retiring, moving slowly through the most distant reaches of the visible sky. He was regarded primarily as a god of agriculture.

Venus was the Goddess Ishtar, and perhaps the most important of the wandering planets. Wild and untamed, she was the patroness of free love and a lady of great passion. The lion and the bull were her totem animals, and she was just as often associated with the arts of war as with the arts of love. She was turbulent, tempestuous, untamed.

Finally, there was of course the Moon, who was the god Sin. (Mind you, the name is simply a Babylonian word and has nothing to do with the concept of wrongdoing.) Those with a background in Western astrology will be more than a little surprised to find the Moon manifesting as a god rather than a goddess, but there are many surprises in Babylonian astrology. This deity seems to have symbolized the "occult" side of the Moon, and to have been associated with lore and magic. He also functioned as a god of travel, and of trade—caravans moving through the desert under his light.

In the first few centuries before the Christian era, Babylonian teachers became popular in Greece and the surrounding regions. They brought with them the art of astrology, and the old names were translated into the Greek language. Therefore Marduk became Zeus, Nergal became Ares, and Ishtar became Aphrodite.

Finally, the Romans conquered the Greeks and changed the names to Latin. The Latin names for the planets are those that have survived—Mercury, Venus, Jupiter, Saturn, and the rest. Our good friends.

GEOMETRIES OF THE SWORD

BY JOHN MICHAEL GREER

A surprising number of people seem to think that the only martial arts in the world are those that came out of Asia. In fact, there have been fighting systems all over the world as long as people have been fighting.

In nearly every culture, thoughtful and perceptive warriors have drawn on their experience to create ways of combat that reach beyond the rough-and-tumble of sheer brute force. In many societies, too, these systems came into contact with traditions of spirituality, mysticism, and magic, creating esoteric martial arts—that is, martial arts in which combat training becomes a vehicle for the transformation of awareness and spiritual perspectives illuminate the difficult but sometimes necessary craft of the warrior.

At least once in the history of the Western magical tradition, this sort of fusion took place and gave rise to an extraordinary combat art. To trace the origins and history of that art, we'll need to make a journey in space and time to the Netherlands at the dawn of the seventeenth century.

This period was a troubled time all over Europe. Wars and rumors of wars were constant. The Netherlands were in the final stages of a successful revolt against Spain, concluded with a treaty in 1609. To the east, in Germany, tensions were rising between Protestant and Catholic factions, and would soon break out into the nightmarish Thirty Years War. Muskets and cannon had ended the reign of the armored knight, and new weapons and combat methods were under development. Into this dangerous world came a young man named Gerard Thibault.

Born in Antwerp in 1574, Thibault was the son of a wool merchant. Despite the poor health that dogged him all his life, he was devoted to the practice of swordsmanship from an early age and studied with Antwerp's famous fencing teacher Lambert van Someren. He also studied medicine, architecture, and painting in his early years.

Later, as a young man, he traveled to Spain and settled in the little town of Sanlucar de Barrameda, at the mouth of the Guadalquivir River. His family had connections there by way of the wool trade, though Gerard had his own reasons for going to the sleepy Andalusian town.

Sanlucar, in fact, was the nerve center of a revolution then under way in the art of swordsmanship. In 1582, Jeronimo Carranza, a native of Sanlucar, had published a book on fencing that set off shockwaves all over Europe. Like many of the new fencing masters of the time, Carranza used the rapier—a slender, elegant sword—in place of the heavy broadsword of the old knights. What made Carranza's approach unique, though, was his reliance on sacred geometry as the basis for his combat method.

To try to understand Carranza's discoveries, it's necessary to look at geometry through Renaissance eyes. Nowadays most people, when they think of geometry at all, remember dull math classes or useful tricks for measuring things at a distance. To learned people in the Renaissance, geometry was much more. Since the time of the ancient Greek philosopher Pythagoras, geometry had been a spiritual practice and tool expanding awareness. The scholars and magicians of the Renaissance remembered that heritage, and put it to constant use.

The same geometrical consciousness played a major part in the achievements in art and architecture that defined the Renaissance. Jeronimo Carranza was one of a handful of swordsmen who saw that this could be done with the art of the sword. He understood that the rapier was ultimately a geometrical line, moving through three-dimensional space to intersect another line or penetrate the complex planes of an opponent's body. Most fencers of the time already knew that a straight line was the shortest distance between two points in fencing as well as geometry, and they practiced quick, lethal thrusts instead of the ponderous cuts of the old swordsmanship; Carranza took the same realization much further, and created a wholly geometrical way of the sword, with techniques as exact as mathematical proofs.

The system that evolved from Carranza's insights didn't look much like modern sport fencing, and even less like the swashbuckling nonsense that passes for fencing in most movies. Fencers in what became known as the Spanish style stood straight, with feet a foot or so apart and sword-arm extended straight out toward the opponent like an antenna alert to any opening. They kept constantly on the move, following circular patterns of footwork that allowed them to evade the enemy's attacks while furthering their own. The key to survival was not strength or speed, but keen perception and a mastery of the geometries of the sword.

By the time Gerard Thibault came to Sanlucar, these insights had been developed into a complex and deadly fighting system. In the hands of Carranza's greatest pupil, the extraordinary Luis Pacheco de Narvaez, not only sacred geometry but many other parts of Renaissance lore had been made part of the system. In Narvaez' writings, for example, the fencer was taught to pay attention to the balance of the four elements in the opponent's actions. Were his movements quick and jerky like fire, flowing and responsive like water, nimble and light like air, or heavy and plodding like earth? Each of these helped the swordsman choose strategy and tactics.

In Spain, though, the Inquisition remained strong, and no one who valued his life dared be open about such investigations. Raised in the less-intolerant climate of the Netherlands, Thibault must have chafed at such restrictions. Still, he put his time in Sanlucar to good use. By the time he came home in 1610, he had mastered everything the Spanish fencers had to teach him, and begun to add elements of his own—including elements drawn from the occult revival of the time.

By 1611 he felt ready to demonstrate his new method publicly, and went to Rotterdam for a major fencing competition. Masters came from all over the Netherlands, but Thibault defeated them all, winning first prize. Prince Maurice of Nassau, the Dutch head of state, summoned Thibault to his court at once, and the young sword master was asked to demonstrate his methods. He did so with aplomb, beating all comers in an exhibition that lasted several days and gave him a continent-wide reputation.

Thibault became the most sought-after fencing teacher in the region, but his thoughts did not rest there. By 1615, if not before, he had already began drawing up plans for a book on swordsmanship, to be called *Academie de l'Espee* (Academy of the Sword). The book was finally published in 1630, a year after his death.

Academie de l'Espee is the longest and most elaborate treatise on swordsmanship ever published. In it, Thibault made clear the occult roots of his system. The first chapter, which presents the philosophy behind his fencing art, quotes such major Renaissance magicians as Cornelius

Agrippa and Pico di Mirandola, and the entire work is woven through with complex magical and mythological symbolism. It's impossible for anyone with a background in Renaissance magic who reads the book to avoid realizing that here, at last, the Western occult traditions had found a martial art of their own.

Like everything connected with the occult traditions, Thibault's work was consigned to the cultural fringes at the time of the scientific revolution of the late 1600s. In swordsmanship, as in nearly everything else, the Western world turned away from the entire realm of subtle awareness and inner experience toward a mechanical, rational approach to the world. Still, Thibault's art of the sword serves as a reminder of the potentials yet untapped within the magical traditions of the West, and his book—a time capsule of a forgotten martial path with magical undertones—remains a resource for those willing to seek it out.

Spell of the Witch's Ring

By Raven Grimassi

This is a simple spell designed to charge a ring that will serve as a protection. The Witch's ring is both a symbol and a tool of magic. As a symbol it identifies the wearer as a practitioner of the Old Ways, and declares one a user of magic. As a tool the ring connects the Witch to the meta-physical concepts whereby Witches weave their magic. The ring serves as a reminder to the Witch of the forces at hand, and acts as a conduit to and from those occult forces readily available to the Witch.

The preparation of the Witch's ring should begin two days before the first night of the Full Moon. Midnight is best but nine in the evening will do if necessary. The spell calls for a ring with a stone setting. Consult a table of occult correspon-dences for a stone that you wish to form an alignment with. Once you have the ring you desire to use, then perform the following ritual.

1. Consecrate the ring to the four elements. To do this, simply prepare four bowls. Pour salt into one bowl, and place smoking incense in another. In the third bowl set a lighted red votive candle. Pour clean water into the last bowl. Then touch the ring to each bowl saying: "I consecrate thee by earth (salt), air (incense), fire (votive candle), and water (water bowl)."

2. Pour a small amount of personal cologne in your burning dish. Light the fluid. Hold the ring over the flame, turning it, and chanting:

I dedicate and consecrate this ring with a stone of _____ and metal of _____ to be a ring of Witchery unto me with the powers of the Goddess three, the Lady of all Witchery, and as my word so mote it be.

3. Place an incense of the Moon in a bowl and light it. Set a bottle of Moon oil nearby. Hold the ring over the incense, passing it through the smoke three times. Then anoint the ring with the oil. Wrap the ring in a red cloth or tissue paper and leave it for three nights in a place where the Moon will shine on it each night, at the same hour (at least one hour after sundown on an odd-numbered hour.)

Chant the following over the ring (still in the red wrapping):

> *Any and all who perfect an image of me, with my likeness or as a crude consecrated image to be me, to do me bodily harm or to injure me spiritually and try to take my breath away, to cause me to dwindle or pine, pine away to nothing, to wish evil upon me, to badger me with their anger or bad thoughts, by picture, image, or name, the ring of my Lady protect me, metal and stone, flesh and bone, safe forever in your powers, free from evil, fear, or despair, on the sender of the evil will rebound by the law of the Lady thrice crowned, hearken all unto me, as I speak, so mote it be.*

At this point you are done. Wear the ring whenever you are in a ritual setting, or whenever you feel the need for protection. On the night of each Full Moon thereafter, anoint the ring again by rubbing a drop of oil on the stone. Then raise the ring up toward the Moon and ask for blessings in the name of the Goddess.

Ring Things

By Marguerite Elsbeth

Almost everyone wears some kind of ring or another. Rings come in all shapes and sizes, from decorative finger rings to the customary high school rings, from engagement rings to wedding bands, and from eyebrow rings, nose rings, and bellybutton rings to toe rings.

The perfectly closed circle of rings represents constancy, flow, unity, wholeness, and eternity. Sometimes the ring takes an animal form called ouroboros—the snake biting its tale. Other times it is a ring of fire, like the one surrounding Shiva as he performs the cosmic dance of life. The twelve fixed stars, known as the constellations or zodiac, also comprise a ring, and the planet Saturn has rings around it.

Rings are said to offer protection against demons, ghosts, and other evil spirits. People of certain cultures believe that the soul escapes through the natural round openings of the body, especially the mouth and nostrils, which is why it is a Hindu custom to snap the fingers whenever someone yawns or sneezes. Others believe that rings may be used to bind and hamper spiritual, mental, emotional, or physical activities. We have all heard the expression love knot—this once had a magical significance indicating a tie that was binding forever. The symbolism of rings, in other words, is very extensive.

Ring History and Lore

There are many fascinating stories regarding the magical and medicinal properties attributed to metal rings or those set with

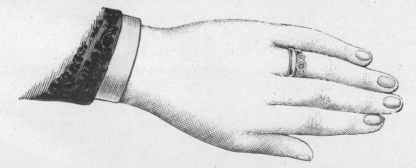

jewels and precious stones. This idea is based on sympathetic magic, which induces a physical reaction caused by vibrations we can instinctually sense from a neighboring vibrating object that is in natural harmony with our tastes, moods, and disposition. If we can absorb the properties of whatever it is we are attracted to, we can inherit its essential energy. Therefore, material objects such as a ring comprised of certain metals and set with particular stones, or a copper bracelet inset with magnets, will affect the person with whom it comes in contact, thus relieving the symptoms of illness.

Around the middle of the third century, massive rings which included stones wider than the finger were considered fashionable among Bedouin women, and the stone selected usually denoted personal power, wealth, or protection. Sometimes large rings of this nature were worn on each finger! This trend is back in style today, as Bedouin-style jewelry known as a kaff or glove—which consists of five rings, one for each finger connected by chain links to a decorative patch on the back of the hand and secured to a bracelet. Cache rings, the kind in which one can hide away talismans, perfume, or other secret things, were and are popular too.

The ancient Romans wore several slender rings, each set with a different stone which they united into one. The Pope annually blessed rings to ward off digestive and reproductive upsets up until the seventeenth century, a practice most likely based on the Greco-Roman myth of how Jupiter, the father of gods and men, bound Hercules to wear an iron ring set with a piece of rock from the Caucasus Mountains following his rescue of Prometheus, who stole fire from the gods.

The use of iron to comprise a ring was not relegated to the West; in the Orient, a mother would attempt to cure her sick child by attaching iron rings to the child's ankles and hanging an iron chain around the child's neck as a way of preventing an evil spirit from entering into the little one's body. The Philippine Bagobos placed rings of brass on the wrists or ankles of their sick for the same reason.

Meanwhile, the people of the Carpathus Islands in Greece were always careful to remove all the rings off the bodies of the deceased, for fear the fingers or toes of the one who had passed would trap the spirit inside, thus detaining its other-worldly travels. The pregnant women of Tyrol never took off their wedding rings, for they believed that to do so would give the spirits and Witches power over them. The Lapland person who was about to place a corpse in the coffin always received a brass ring from the husband, wife, or children of  the deceased, which was fastened around the right arm until the corpse was buried as a way of protecting the pallbearer from harm.

HOW TO WEAR YOUR RINGS

Chiromancy, or palmistry, is a divination system which ascribes the planets and fixed stars to various areas on the hand. We can use chiromancy to determine the appropriate fingers and toes upon which to wear our rings. When metals and stones are used together in this way, they induce a electromagnetic influence on the cells and organs of the body; for example, wearing a ring made of silver and tin, and set with lapis, may calm the nerves and settle digestive disturbances as well as heighten instinctual perception. Rings worn on other bodily parts may effect our phys-ical, emotional, mental, and spiritual health for the better through the meridians or ley lines, which channel life-giving energy to the vital organs.

Wear rings corresponding with the Sun sign, Moon sign, stars, and planets that relate to fingers or bodily areas you wish to heal or empower, as follows:

THUMB, BIG TOE, HEAD, GENITALS
Planets: Aries, Mars, Scorpio, Pluto
Metals: Iron, Sulphur

Stones: Carnelian, Garnet, Ruby
Effects: Muscles, Reproductive system
Keywords: Initiating, Energizing, Transforming

FIRST FINGER AND TOE, NAVEL, THIGHS

Planets: Sagittarius, Jupiter
Metal: Tin
Stones: Cat's-Eye, Aventurine
Effects: Liver, Pituitary Gland
Keywords: Enlivening, Expanding

SECOND (MIDDLE) FINGER AND TOE, SKIN

Planets: Capricorn, Saturn
Metal: Lead
Stones: Obsidian, Smoky Quartz
Effects: Gallbladder, Spleen, Teeth, Bones
Keywords: Evaluating, Concentrating

THIRD FINGER AND TOE, SPINAL COLUMN

Planets: Leo, Sun
Metals: Sun
Stones: Citrine Quartz, Topaz, Pyrite, Yellow Fluorite
Effects: Heart, Thymus Gland, Circulation
Keywords: Revitalizing, Loving

FOURTH (PINKY) FINGER AND TOE, CHEST, ARMS, HANDS, ANKLES

Planets: Gemini, Mercury, Virgo, Aquarius, Uranus
Metal: Silver or Platinum
Stones: Golden Beryl, Peridot, Clear Quartz
Effects: Brain, Lungs, Circulatory & Central Nervous System
Keywords: Communicating, Neutralizing, Discriminating, Inspiring, Electrifying

THROAT, LOWER BACK

Planets: Taurus, Venus, Libra, Venus
Metal: Copper
Stones: Malachite, Emerald, Opal
Effects: Kidneys, Lumbar Region, Parathyroid
Keywords: Enduring, Balancing, Creating

BREASTS, STOMACH

Planets: Cancer, Moon
Metal: Silver
Stones: Moon Stone, Moss Agate, White Coral, Abalone, Pearl
Effects: Female Reproductive System and its functions,
     Esophagus, Liver, Gallbladder, Bile Ducts, Pancreas
Keywords: Feeling, Remembering

FEET, EYES, EARS, NOSE, MOUTH

Planets: Pisces, Neptune
Metal: Platinum
Stones: Aquamarine, Chrysoprase
Effects: Thalamus Gland
Keywords: Imagining, Dreaming

THE RING OF LOVE

There is an old Hindu tradition which says you can attract the person you want to marry, or test your compatibility with the person you love, by wearing a ring attuned to his or her astrological Sun sign. The ring of love must be worn on the third, or ring, finger of your left hand, because this finger has a delicate nerve that connects directly to the heart. Do you want to get to the heart of the matter regarding your love interest? Try the ring of love spell on for size to know if your heart will be content:

First, you must acquire a particular stone. The stone you choose has to be from this particular list, which is quite different from any other:

Aries:	Bloodstone	Libra:	Peridot
Taurus:	Sapphire	Scorpio:	Aquamarine
Gemini:	Agate	Sagittarius:	Topaz
Cancer:	Emerald	Capricorn:	Ruby
Leo:	Onyx	Aquarius:	Garnet
Virgo:	Carnelian	Pisces:	Amethyst

Next, bring the stone to a jeweler and ask to have it set into a simple gold band. Note any changes that occur in your personal life as well as in the relationship from the moment you begin wearing the ring. The stone will seem to change the wearer into the kind of person who can attract and hold the Sun sign person.

One woman had a ring made to attract a man she was interested in, and the ring proved that the relationship would be impossible. Initially the stone fell out. She had the ring repaired. Then, the band hurt her finger, so she brought the ring back to the jeweler. He damaged the stone while mending the band! The ring was telling her that the relationship would be difficult.

Another woman tried the spell to see if her lover would remain with her on a more permanent basis. As soon as she placed the ring on her finger, he began to visit her more frequently. One day, her little boy pulled the stone from its setting. Shortly thereafter, the man called to say that while he cared for her deeply, he just wasn't ready to have a child in his life.

Finally, there is the story of a man who replaced the ring of love with a wedding band, when the woman of his choice asked him to marry her several weeks after he placed her Sun sign ring on his finger! See if you won't tie the knot with a little ring of love magic!

European Marriage Magic

By Marguerite Elsbeth

Who will you marry? When will you wed? How can you arrange your honeymoon and homecoming to ensure a happy marriage? If you have questions such as these burning in your mind's eye, try these traditional Old World wedding omens, charms.

Who Will You Marry?

To discover your intended, try a little apple peel magic. Pare an entire apple without breaking the spiral formed by the skin. Take the paring with your right hand and throw it over your left shoulder (reverse if you are left-handed). The shape the peel takes when it falls will resemble the first letter of your future mate's name.

Or try the "New Moon, new mate" spell. Your future companion may appear to you in your dreams if, on the first night of a New Moon, you go outside and gaze at the Moon without blinking, while softly whispering the following incantation to Selene, a lunar goddess:

All hail, Selene, all hail to thee.
I ask you, good Moon, reveal to me tonight,
the one to whom I'll wedded be.

Or, right before you go to bed, pass a crumb of wedding cake through a wedding ring three times, and place the crumb under your pillow. You should dream of your intended.

Or, place a borrowed wedding ring on the third finger of your left hand, a piece of wedding cake under your pillow, and the shoes you wore that day at the foot of your bed, arranged to form the letter "T." Sometime during the night, your future mate may be revealed in your dreams.

NEW RELATIONSHIP OMENS

Once you have an idea as to who might be The One, pay attention to what occurs when first you meet to ensure that all will be well between you in the future.

Avoid meeting each other, hugging or kissing, on stairways of any kind, or conflicts and arguments may
arise often in your mar-
riage. However, should you
fall while walking up stairs
while thinking of your
beloved, the relationship
may be blessed.

It is very lucky to meet
and kiss your sweetheart
out of doors under a New
Moon. Your relationship
will be one of endless love,
and it will continue to
flourish. Yet, problems may
develop if you both gaze at
the New Moon through a
window.

If you want your lover to be faithful and true, choose a hillside, or an area near a river, stream, or woods, as your meeting place. Avoid meeting on the banks of canals or ponds, on bridges, in valleys, or at a crossroads, for doing so may bring quarrels. Seeing a black cat or a white house while walking with your intended increases your chances for engagement. Be sure to wear turquoise jewelry and an article of blue clothing, as these may enhance your luck. Also, always use blue ink when writing a love note to your lover.

Speaking of love notes, try to complete your writing just as the clock strikes midnight. Use only three X's to symbolize kisses at the end of your note, and deliver the letter on the night of a Full Moon, though not on Christmas Day or on February 29 (leap day). Take care not to drop the note prior to delivery, or the relationship may end.

WHEN WILL YOU WED?

Timing is everything when you are ready to pop the big question, so use the following wedding charms to give you an inkling as to when it may happen.

The Moon Mirror. Perform this little ceremony on Christmas Eve. Ask a male friend or relation if you may borrow his scarf or bandanna. Find some alone time, on an evening between the New and Full Moon. Take the bandanna and a mirror to a stream, pond, or lake, and wait on the bank until moonrise. When the Moon has risen high enough, turn your back towards the water. Raise the mirror up until you can see both the Moon and its reflection in the water. Now, place the bandanna over your face and count the number of Moons you can see in the mirror. Two Moons indicate that more than a year may pass before you marry. If you see more than two Moons in the mirror, then you may be married in as many months as the Moons you see.

It's in the Cards. Call together a group of single friends. Have everyone sit in a circle. Take a deck of ordinary playing cards and deal the cards round the circle face up. Stop dealing to the women when one of them receives the King of Hearts. Continue dealing to the men until the Queen of Hearts shows up. The man and woman who receive these court cards may be the first to marry. Another method is to place a deck of thoroughly shuffled, ordinary playing cards in a box or bag. Each person must draw a card until there are no cards left. Whoever draws the Ace of Hearts will be first to marry. Pulling the Two of Clubs means will be last to marry. The one who draws the Ace of Spades may never wed at all.

Roses are red. Prior to seven o'clock on any June morning, pluck a perfect red rose in full bloom and place the flower in a white envelope. Lay the envelope on a table with the open end face up. Now, tilt a burning candle so that the wax drips onto the triangular fold, thus sealing the envelope closed. Impress the wax with the third finger of your left hand. Finally, place the envelope under your pillow just before you go to sleep, and ask for a wedding sign or omen to appear in your dreams. Symbols such as a silver Moon, colorful flowers, green fields, majestic mountains, laughing children, or people dancing indicate you may be married before the end of the year. If you dream of a golden Sun, critters of any kind, fairy creatures such as gnomes or giants, or paper-products, it may be five years before you wed. Visions of stormy weather, lizards or snakes, or the sound of ringing bells tell you that a wedding may not be in your future.

WEDDING DAY BLISS

Remember this little rhyme, based on the planetary energies of the days of the week, when planning your wedding:

> *Monday for health,*
> *Tuesday for wealth,*
> *Wednesday the best of all;*
> *Thursday for loss,*
> *Friday's a cross,*
> *Saturday causes a fall.*

MARRIAGE MAGIC FOR THE BRIDE

If your girlfriends are marriage-minded, have them sew hairs from their own heads into the hem and folds of your wedding gown to ensure they too will be soon be married. Wear a white gown for purity, with blue accents for luck. Green should never be worn by the bride or maids younger than she; however, bridesmaids who are older than the bride may wear something green if they desire to find a husband.

Try to awaken to the sound of singing birds on the morning of your wedding for a peaceful and constant marriage. Spiders symbolize the tapestry of life and bring prosperity to a marriage should you find one crawling on your gown or veil, or see one on the way to the wedding. Do not cry before the marriage takes place, and be sure to smile when you greet the groom at the altar, or unhappiness may follow.

MARRIAGE MAGIC FOR THE GROOM

Take care not to look upon the bride-to-be or her wedding attire before the marriage takes place, and no peeking when the bride walks up the aisle. Once you are en route to the ceremony, do not turn back. If you have forgotten something, send a friend to get it. When you place the ring on your bride's finger, push it as far down as possible or the marriage may not last long. If your bride assists in putting on the ring, she may be a strong force in the marriage.

THE HONEYMOON

Make like the Germanic peoples, and celebrate the wedding for thirty days following the event. Serve mead, an ale made from honey, to sweeten the marriage with fruitfulness and abundance. Also, remember not to break anything while on your honeymoon, especially a mirror. Lover's spats while honeymooning mean the marriage will endure hardship and have a happy future. The new bride may now wear the color green to honor Venus, the love goddess and increase the love in her marriage.

HOMECOMING

Once you have reached your goal of wedded bliss, and the gold band is wrapped tightly around your finger, have a friend or relation pour boiling water over the threshold before your husband carries you into your love nest. An oatmeal cookie broken over the bride's head while she is brought through the doorway brings the most magical marriage of all.

THE ART OF SENSUAL MASSAGE

BY EDAIN MCCOY

Massage, the therapeutic manipulating of someone else's outer body, has never been more popular. Overworked, underpaid, and stressed-out, more and more people are seeking massage therapies of all kinds to help them relax and feel healthier. The art of massage can also be used to help reconnect with your romantic partner—bring you closer emotionally to each other and reignite flames of romance that may be extinguished by the pressures of daily living.

This type of caressing massage is often referred to as "sensual massage," and it can be done by any couple. This isn't a massage for medical purposes; its sole purpose is to make you feel good about being with your lover and and enjoying the intimate touching of each other bodies. It doesn't requires a college degree or special training. It needs only your imagination, your willingness to carve out some quiet time together with your partner, and some basic guidelines and common sense.

It should go without saying that you and your partner should seek the proper atmosphere into which to share your sensual massage. Private, quiet space where you're not likely to be disturbed is a must. Unplug the phone and turn off pagers and other intrusions that aren't absolutely essential. If possible, seek soft lighting. Candles are a perfect antidote to the glare of workplace lighting and are inherently romantic.

Incense and relaxing music may also help set the mood. Red or pink are the colors most often magically associated with romance, and these can help bond you as lovers. Relaxing colors are blue and purple. Scents associated magically with romance are rose, lemon, lotus, rosemary, and vanilla. Scents associated with inducing relaxation include sandalwood, lavender, benzoin, gardenia, and peppermint.

Agree before you begin to keep your lines of communication open and positive. If something hurts or feels good, or if you require more or less pressure in the area being massaged, let your partner know. He or she should respond to your words and immediately adjust the touch accordingly. This must be an event of mutual pleasure, not one where one person feels uneasy or uncomfortable. This agreement will help improve your general communication skills as well.

Give at least a full fifteen minutes to each partner so that he or she can get fully relaxed. If you want to switch on and off, remember that professional masseuses believe that anything less than seven minutes is not enough to allow the body and spirit to relax fully. During your partner's massage time, don't complain if your hands are tired and refrain from talking about tense subjects like school, work, or bills that are past due.

Begin your sensual massage experimentation at your partner's feet. Press your knuckles into the arch of the foot, and rub the toes between your thumb and forefinger. Keep the pressure and movement steady. Talk soothingly to your partner, asking for feedback.

Work your way up the back of the legs, rubbing upward—always toward the heart—with the heel of your hand. Slowly knead tight muscles as you go, adjusting the pressure to suit your partner's taste. Do the same with the back, arms, hands, shoulders, and head until your partner is relaxed.

This relaxed state makes an ideal time to focus on a joint magical goal. This works best when the goal is connected with your relationship. For example, you might agree beforehand on a mutual wish, such as strengthening your relationship, finding a new home, having children, or overcoming impotence or frigidity. To do this, both partners should "tune in" to the rhythm of the massage and, either aloud or silently, say a simple present tense affirmation such as, "We find the perfect home for us," or "We are having a baby."

If you become too relaxed to focus on a goal, you can add a visual symbol that your subconscious minds can focus on during the sensual massage session. To make a symbol you need only agree with your partner on the precise outcome you desire; write it out, then decide on a nonverbal symbol which represents your goal. Don't worry that what you draw would make no sense to anyone else, as loving couples often develop their own subtle language and personal associations.

When the symbol is created, both of you need to spend some time looking at it before you try using it in your sensual massage. Don't stare, but keep your eyes steadily focused on your drawing while concentrating solely on your goal and how it is represented by your chosen symbol. You may do this together or alone. The important thing is that you let your subconscious mind know exactly what the meaning of the symbol is so that when it is used in sensual massage your subconscious can do most of the work while you concentrate on the physical pleasure of mutual touch.

Before you begin the next massage session, make several exact copies of your drawing and hang them where they can be seen from virtually any position in the area in which you will be working with sensual massage. As you relax, allow your eyes to gaze on the symbol you created. This time you don't have to focus too hard. Just connect with it and let your subconscious—which, in a relaxed state, is very receptive to suggestion—do most of the work for you.

Setting aside some time each week to touch each other will bring you closer emotionally and physically, allowing you each to get acquainted with each others' bodies in new ways, and helping you reconnect as a couple. If the routine becomes boring, try new and inventive ways of stroking. Use your tongue or your foot to caress your partner, or purchase a lotion or scented massage oil that you both like. Try massaging each other in the shower or bathtub, or use it as a prelude to sexual foreplay.

Sensual massage is an pleasurable event for established lovers. Just remember that it feels so good that it's virtually impossible to do it badly. Enjoy!

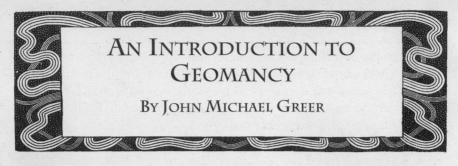

AN INTRODUCTION TO GEOMANCY

BY JOHN MICHAEL GREER

Geomancy is the forgotten oracle of the Western world. Few people know about it nowadays, but geomancy was among the most common methods of divination through the Middle Ages and Renaissance. It was imported to Europe from the Muslim world with the first wave of translations from Arabic in the early twelfth century, and spread quickly. Hundreds of geomantic manuals survive in manuscript collections, and these are only a small fraction of the total number that were once in circulation.

Like the Chinese *I Ching*, and other less widely known methods of divination, geomancy is based on binary processes—that is, processes that can give rise to one of two different answers. The "divination system" of flipping a coin is a very simple example of this. More complex methods combine some set number of binary events (even and odd numbers, for example) to produce a pattern that communicates meaning to the diviner.

In geomancy, four binary events were added together to produce patterns of meaning. There were sixteen of these patterns, or figures, and they made up the basic building blocks of geomancy. These, with their traditional meanings, are as follows:

THE GEOMANTIC FIGURES

NAME	FIGURE	QUALITIES
Puer (boy)	○ ○ ○ ○ ○	Rashness, violence, energy, destructiveness. Generally unfavorable except in matters of love and war.
Amissio (loss)	○ ○ ○ ○ ○ ○	Transience and loss. Favorable for love and for situations in which loss is desired, but unfavorable for material matters.

NAME	FIGURE	QUALITIES
Albus (white)	● ● ● ● ● ● ●	Peace, wisdom, purity; a favorable figure, but weak. Good for beginnings and business ventures.
Populus (people)	● ● ● ● ● ● ● ●	Multitude, a gathering or assembly of people. Good with good, evil with evil; a neutral figure, neither favorable nor unfavorable.
Fortuna Major (greater fortune)	● ● ● ● ● ●	Great good fortune, inner strength. A figure of power and success, favorable for any form of competition.
Conjunctio (conjunction)	● ● ● ● ● ●	Combination of forces or people; recovery of lost things. A neutral figure, neither favorable nor unfavorable.
Puella (girl)	● ● ● ● ●	Harmony and happiness; a favorable figure in nearly all questions.
Rubeus (red)	● ● ● ● ● ● ●	Passion, power, fierceness, and vice. Evil in all that is good and good in all that is evil.
Acquisitio (gain)	● ● ● ● ● ●	Success, profit and gain; things within one's grasp. Favorable in nearly all matters.
Carcer (prison)	● ● ● ● ● ●	Restriction, delay, limitation, imprisonment. An unfavorable figure.

Name	Figure	Qualities
Tristia (sorrow)	○ ○ ○ ○ ○ ○ ○	Sorrow, suffering, illness, and pain. An unfavorable figure except in questions relating to building and the earth.
Laetitia (joy)	○ ○ ○ ○ ○ ○ ○	Happiness and health. A favorable figure.
Cauda Draconis (tail of the dragon)	○ ○ ○ ○ ○	A doorway leading out. Favorable for losses and endings, but an unfavorable figure in most questions. Brings good with evil, evil with good.
Caput Draconis (head of the dragon)	○ ○ ○ ○ ○	A doorway leading in. Favorable for beginnings and gain, neutral in other questions. Good with good, evil with evil.
Fortuna Minor (lesser fortune)	○ ○ ○ ○ ○ ○	Outward strength, help from others. Good for any matter a person wishes to proceed quickly.
Via (way)	○ ○ ○ ○	Change, movement, alteration of fortune. Favorable for journeys and voyages.

In geomantic practice, these figures are produced by what amounts to a simple form of automatic writing. Traditionally, the geomancer would smooth out an area of sand or bare soft ground and take a pointed stick in one hand, then concentrate on the question the divination was intended to answer. The diviner would then seek a state of mental clarity in which no thoughts would rise up to disturb the process. Holding this state, he or she would let the stick move so that it made a line of marks across the ground.

It's important that the geomancer not count the marks while they are being made.

Once four lines of marks are traced on the ground, the diviner then counts up the number of marks in each line. An odd number of marks equal a single point; an even number, a double point. The result might look something like this:

First line: - - - - - - - - - - - - - -(12 marks)   O O
Second line: - - - - - - - - - - - -(14 marks)   O O
Third line: - - - - - - - - - - - - -(9 marks)   O
Fourth line: - - - - - - - - - - - -(13 marks)   O

The result, in this case, is the geomantic figure Fortuna Major, the Greater Fortune.

The same thing can be done using paper and a pen. Several other processes have also been put to use—for example, some geomancers take a random handful of pebbles from a small bag or bowl, and then count the pebbles to see whether they came to an even number or an odd one. Decks of geomantic cards have also been used at various times. There were even special dice made with either one or two points on each face; four of them would be rolled to make a figure.

There are various ways to use these figures in a reading. The standard method involves generating four of them—thus, making sixteen lines of points to start with—and then combining them in various ways to generate a total of sixteen figures, each of which makes its own contributions to the final reading. Done this way, a geomantic divination can be as detailed and informative as any form of divination in the world.

There's also a place, though, for a simpler approach. It can be useful simply to concentrate on a question, clear your mind, make four lines of dots, and interpret the figure that results as an answer to the question. Though this does have its limitations—in particular, the questions asked this way should be answerable with a "yes" or a "no"—it also provides a good introduction to the secrets of the "forgotten oracle."

ELEMENTAL EXERCISES

BY CLARE VAUGHN

D o you want to work with elementals, but you're not sure where to start? For most people the best place to start is with fire, water, air, and earth. As you make repeated contact with the elements, you are likely to make contact with elementals. These exercises are designed to help you do just that.

Do the exercises at a comfortable pace. Try each exercise at least ten times, at least once a week. You can do one element ten times and then go on to the next, or do a rotation—earth, water, air, fire once each and then back to earth for another cycle. All of these exercises can be done at any time of year, but all of them need to be done outdoors. Always, always, always write up your experiences in a journal! The record will be invaluable.

EARTH EXERCISE

Begin with earth. Pick a place where you can sit for a while without having to move. Sit on the ground if you can, or make sure some part of you touches the ground.

Settle down in a position you can hold without strain. Gather your energy and attention. Breathe slowly and evenly. Now turn your attention to the ground beneath you. Imagine yourself sinking into it. It is as comfortable to you as being above ground. What is the texture of the soil? How dense is it? Does it have color, taste, smell? Keep sinking. How does the soil change as you descend? If you pass through any rocks, examine their structure. Are there any beings? What are they like?

Go as far as you can comfortably go—all the way to the planet's core if you wish. Notice the changes from soil to rock to magma as you descend. Return as you came, drifting back up until you are once again on the surface.

WATER EXERCISE

Next go to water. This works best at the margin of a large body of water such as a lake, or if possible, the ocean. You can, however, do it by a river, stream, or pond. If you're in an inland city with no living water, a reservoir will do.

Sit or lie within a few feet of the water. Now imagine yourself leaping into the water. Feel it around you—the temperature, the texture, the liquid flow. Feel its energy. Notice its color, its wavelets. Dive in, and look again. Notice any changes. Are there beings in the water? What are they like? Return to the shore when you are ready, and imagine yourself sitting back in the spot where you started.

AIR EXERCISE

Now move to air. A windy and cloudy day is best. Go outside and face the wind. Feel it on your skin. Watch the clouds and their movement patterns. What does this tell you about the winds? Imagine yourself leaping upward and flying in the wind. What do you see and feel? Motions, moods, energies? Beings? Rise up into the clouds, riding the air currents. If any of the clouds are changing shape, enter into them and feel the changes taking place. When you are ready, imagine yourself floating back down to the Earth again.

271

FIRE EXERCISE

Now, finally, experience fire. Sit in the Sun, facing into its light but not looking directly at the orb. Don't wear sunglasses, they interfere with energy flow. Sunscreen, on the other hand, is okay. Close your eyes. Feel the heat and light of the sun pressing on you, as a physical presence all around you. Be aware of the heat and light, absorb it, open up to it like a flower. Become aware of the fire within you. Imagine yourself merging with the fire around you, becoming a part of it. Remember this is fire that warms but does not burn. It cannot harm you.

When you have merged with the fire, open your perceptions as fully as possible. What are you experiencing? What color is the fire? Are there beings present? When you are ready, or when you feel you are nearing your sun exposure limit, slowly become aware of yourself as a separate being again. Look away from the sun to close the contact. It's normal to feel an extra inner warmth at this point, so don't worry if you experience this.

Chances are good that if you complete these exercises, you will encounter elementals. They appreciate our desires to understand the elements. If you approach the exercises, and the elements, with joy and desire, you are likely to be welcome in their kingdoms. Keep in mind on your travels that elementals can appear to human beings in a variety of shapes and sizes. Do not assume you know what form they will take, or you may miss something. Elementals manifest entirely within their elements. Occasionally you may encounter more than one type of elemental because more than one element is present: during a storm, for example, you may meet both sylphs and undines. However you won't meet either a sylph or an undine in a hunk of granite unless air or water are somehow present in the stone.

With practice, you are likely to notice elementals in all kinds of places, at all kinds of times. This is normal. This can be enjoyable, and can add to your understanding of the aliveness of the world. It can also deepen the possibilities for natural magic. Elementals are likely to participate in, certain types of natural magic. They appreciate blessings, healings, and invocations of divine energy aimed at helping the natural world. If you work toward such goals, you may find elementals working with you.

CINNAMON WILD RICE PUDDING

BY STEVEN POSCH

The Anishinabe (Ojibwe) elders tell that the People once lived in the east until the Great Mysterious told them, "Follow the Sun until you come to a land where food grows on waters. This will be your home forever." And so they came to a land of wild rice-filled lakes: Minnesota, the promised land.

The elders also tell that the Great Mysterious gave the People two harvests to sustain them forever: wild rice and maple sugar, a harvest of autumn and a harvest of spring. The following recipe combines the two sacred harvests of the Anishinabe—truly a sacrament of the Minnesota land.

CINNAMON WILD RICE PUDDING

⅔ cup uncooked wild rice (2 cups cooked)

1⅓ cups water

2 cups half-and-half

½ cup maple syrup

2 eggs

1 teaspoon vanilla

½ teaspoon cinnamon

¼ teaspoon nutmeg

Combine uncooked wild rice and water in a heavy saucepan. Heat to boiling. Reduce heat, cover, and simmer for 30 minutes. Check for doneness. Continue simmering until rice is tender and all water is absorbed. Add more water, a tablespoon at a time, if needed. Preheat oven to 350°F. Combine half-and-half, maple syrup, eggs, vanilla, cinnamon, nutmeg, and wild rice. Turn into a buttered 1½ quart casserole. Sprinkle with additional cinnamon. Bake for 1 hour or until pudding is set. Best served warm, with milk or cream. Serves 8–12; it's very rich.

THE GIFTS OF ATHENA

BY JIM WEAVER

Almost every Greek child is raised knowing the legend of how the Greek capital, Athens, received its name.

When the ancient Greeks of Attica wanted to name their most important city, a contest was held between Athena and Poseidon. They were each asked to create something that would be useful to the human race. Poseidon created the horse, but. Athena caused the first olive tree to grow. The gods decided the olive tree would be the greatest benefit to human-kind and named the great city Athens in Athena's honor.

Today the products of the olive tree are still very important to the Greek economy. No part of the tree goes to waste. Greek olives and olive oil are exported around the world. The pits are crushed and used as fertilizer; residue left from olive oil press-ing is used for soap. On chilly winter days, the fires glowing in hearths are frequently fueled by the wood of the tree.

In the realm of folk magic, precious olive oil is perhaps the most important product of the olive tree. This amber-colored oil is Athena's greatest magical gift to the world.

Here are a few ways to use olive oil in everyday magic. To bless a new appliance in your home, apply a drop of olive oil to your finger and trace a holy symbol according to your spiri-tual path—perhaps a cross or a pentagram—on the appliance while saying a prayer asking that the new appliance will serve you for a long time. For candle magic, olive oil is a good substitute for other annointing oils to "dress" the candle before a ritual. One of the most unique magical uses for olive oil is scrying. Here is what you'll need:

1 cup water

1 tablespoon olive oil

1 dark colored bowl, soup-bowl sized

1 white candle

Select a time when you won't be disturbed. Pour the water into the bowl, then add the olive oil. Wait a moment for the separate drops of oil to float together and form a circle about three inches across. Place the bowl containing the water-oil mixture directly in front of you on a table. Set the candle about a foot beyond the bowl. Light the candle and darken the room. If you see flame reflected directly in the water, it's too close. Move the candle so it casts a soft glow. Relax. Visualize yourself surrounded by a protective white light. Say words of power if you wish. Concentrate on your question and gaze directly into the circle of oil. Does it seem to move? Do you see a shape that might have some meaning to you? Don't stare, just blink naturally. For your first few attempts keep the scrying to ten minutes or so. If you see nothing, don't worry. You will some other time. Extinguish the candle. Dispose of the water in a respectful manner.

In certain areas of the Mediterranean, scrying in this way was thought to reveal the face of a person who may have cast the evil eye. Some people who have scryed with olive oil will stir the mixture with their fingers and then "read" the shapes of the oil droplets as they move—similar to reading tea leaves.

Finally, for a little beauty "magic" take a few drops of this sacred oil and do what women in Greece have done for years—rub it on your hands to keep them smooth and soft. I'm sure you can think of other magical uses for Athena's prized oil. But, it's nice to know one of the most versatile and ancient magical aids is as close as your kitchen cupboard.

The Enchantment of Sourdough

By Nuala Drago

About five thousand years ago, in Egypt, a wild spirit of nature invaded a bowl of gruel or flatbread batter and started to foam. The Egyptians believed that a divine entity had breathed life into it. Perhaps they were right, for that wild spirit transformed their lives, as the tombs of ancient Egypt attest in drawings depicting the use of sourdough in their daily and ritual life.

Often seen is the image of Pharaoh bearing enormous loaves of sourdough bread as offerings to the gods. After all, Osiris, god of the Egyptian Otherworld, was resurrected after each harvest as the seed of grain. The tomb drawings also illustrate the distribution of giant sourdough-leavened loaves to the masses of workers, the thousands who toiled in building the pyramids at Giza, one of the seven wonders of the world.

Since sourdough bread was already considered to be touched by the divine, and grain was the embodiment of Osiris, bread was a useful medium to all the social classes in their religious rituals. They practiced imitative magic and believed in the potency of symbols. Bread could easily be molded into any shape and be ritually transformed into the essence of whatever it represented. It was even accepted as a substitute for human sacrifice.

Sourdough remained a staple of the human diet and ritual for thousands of years. Under Roman occupation, Egypt was dubbed the breadbasket of the Roman Empire. In time, religious pilgrims and traders had carried sourdough cultures to all corners of the globe. Although beer yeast was also used in breadmaking in later times, it was not available to many, and so, through the course of

the centuries, a good sourdough culture was coveted, protected, and passed on from generation to generation.

Throughout medieval times in Europe, before plates were fashionable, food was placed on large rounds of sourdough bread, called trenchers. Often, the trenchers were kaleidoscoped with herbs and flowers, and diners would use them to sop up every drop of juice from their comestibles. In the last century, a tribe of Alaskan Indians shared a long-lost Egyptian secret with the forty-niners of the gold rush. Not only does sourdough make good breadstuffs, it also produces a beverage with an alcohol content similar to wine. That is, the clear liquid that separates to the top of your starter is crude alcohol.

Today, there are websites devoted to sourdough, and science has discovered many practical things about it—such the fact that a natural antibiotic is produced in the sourdough culture. Sourdough is a living, breathing, and quite irresistible force, which nourishes the senses as well as the body. There is a symbiosis between a sourdough culture and one who nurtures it, so if you would like to experience the potency of sourdough and raise your energy, you should start your own sourdough culture.

SOURDOUGH STARTER

For this, you can purchase a culture, or you can culture wild yeast as the ancients did. However, because harmful bacteria often come with it, I don't recommend capturing wild yeast until after you have begun a starter from commercial dried yeast. One must learn how a starter should look, taste, and smell. Besides, your starter will probably be taken over by wild yeast in time.

2   cups flour
3   tablespoons sugar
1   packet active dry yeast
2½ cups warm water

To begin your own sourdough starter, or culture, place dry ingredients in a glass or plastic pitcher with a ventable lid. Add water, enough to produce a pancake batter consistency. Make sure the water does not exceed 105°F. It is a good idea to use bottled water if your tap water contains many chemicals.

Stir only with wooden or plastic spoons. No metals should come into contact with your starter. Be sure to vent the lid because the vessel could rupture due to the carbon dioxide gas that is formed during fermentation. Cover the container with a dry towel and set in a warm place for about 3 to 5 days, stirring twice each day. Note that at cool temperatures the process could take a few more days.

Your sourdough should now be foamy and aromatic, almost like beer. It should be creamy in color and the liquid, which rises to the top, should be clear to pale amber. (If it is not, discard it and start over.) You can use some right away, or you can stir it down and refrigerate it, stirring every couple of days, and keeping the lid vented.

Once each week to ten days you must remove a portion to use, or discard some and feed the rest with equal parts of flour and water, three quarters to one cup of each. Let it stand overnight, stir down, and refrigerate. Remember to clean the pitcher each time you feed it. Either by pouring the starter into a nonmetal bowl while you wash it or keep another pitcher for it.

The following recipe is healthful and easily free-formed. Sheila-na-gig, Celtic knot, egg-shape, or wheels are just a few of many useful shapes in this bread. It is also well suited for trenchers, and by hollowing a large round loaf or individual small ones, it can serve nicely as a symbolic cauldron from which to serve your ceremonial stews.

1½ cups milk

1 stick butter

¼ cup sugar

½ teaspoon salt (optional)

2 cups each: barley, whole wheat, oat, and brown rice flour

1 envelope active dry yeast

3 eggs

1 cup sourdough starter, at room temperature

Heat milk and butter in a saucepan, without boiling, until the butter melts; remove from the heat. Stir in sugar and salt. Set this mixture aside to cool to lukewarm while you mix the flours together in a large bowl. Next, sprinkle dry yeast over a quarter cup warm water. Allow to proof for five minutes. Meanwhile, beat eggs in a large bowl, add the cooled milk mixture and one cup room temperature sourdough starter. Stir in the proofed yeast and 3 cups of the flour mixture, beating well. Add enough flour mixture to make a stiff dough, shape into a ball, and place it in a large greased bowl, cover, and let rise until it is doubled. Punch it down and shape as you wish.

Place the shapes on a greased or parchment-lined baking sheet, cover and allow to rise until doubled. Bake at 400°F until dark brown on the outside and it sounds hollow when tapped. Baking times will vary with the size of your creations.

Invoke the spirits of nature as you care for your sourdough culture. It will improve with age. Use it often, and don't forget to share the magic so that it will keep coming back to you. That is part of the enchantment of sourdough.

Fondue: The Divine Food

By ShadowCat

I n the winter of 1998, a friend of mine visited one cold evening and brought some food to share. She heated up a cheese mixture and we dipped bread in it. It was so creamy and delicious, I couldn't help but ask her what it was. Imagine my surprise when I learned it was fondue, a food popular in the 50s, 60s, and 70s.

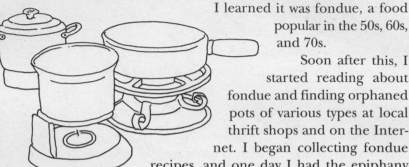

Soon after this, I started reading about fondue and finding orphaned pots of various types at local thrift shops and on the Internet. I began collecting fondue recipes, and one day I had the epiphany that fondue is the perfect food to serve after ritual or sabbat. Look at the symbolism. The pot with the flame under it is the cauldron, symbol of divine female. The fondue forks or swords are symbols of the divine male. The cheese and bread are foods of the earth as is the wine. Heck, with fondue you can honor the Goddess and God, while entertaining everyone.

Fondue has been around for centuries and is the national dish of Switzerland. Recipes exist in many cultures around the world, and while there are various folk tales of how the first fondue recipe originated, in fact is no one knows for sure. In Switzerland, many small villages and farms are cut off from larger cities in the winter months. Traditionally, the farmers and villagers made cheese in spring when the cream was the richest, and baked bread in late summer when grains were harvested. The cheese and bread would carry the people through the winter, hardening with every day. At some point, someone put some wine in a pot, heated it, added some cheese to melt and dipped their dry bread in the mixture to soften it. And so, fondue was born. Peasant food at its finest.

Fondue was first introduced in the United States at the 1939 World's Fair. During the 50s, fondue became a popular supper among the alpine skiers. It was a communal meal and a relaxing social time to share the adventures of the day. Fondue pots of various types spread through the world as it became a favorite party trend. The earthenware pots were used for cheese and chocolate. The metal pots were used for hot oil and meats. The enamel served both purposes, but tended to burn the cheese if the flame was too high. Electric pots revolutionized fondue because the settings could be changed for the type of fondue on the menu. Sadly, fondue died out in the 80s as people were less interested in informal socializing, focusing more on career and their busy family lives. For a while, fondue became a lost art in this country, if not in Europe, though it is now making a comeback.

This is a call to all Pagans to bring people to the cauldron for a little bread and cheese and wine, if you please, especially on cold winter nights. As we enter the new millennium, many of us are feeling alienated from our neighbors, friends, and even family—so busy we have forgotten how to have a good time. So, for your next ritual gathering think of serving fondue. Not only does it have centuries of history and is a communal meal for sharing, it is easy to make. I have tested all of the recipes in my kitchen.

TRADITIONAL SWISS CHEESE FONDUE

1   pound grated Swiss cheese grated, or ½ pound each of Gruyere and Emmenthaler grated

3   tablespoons flour or cornstarch

1   clove garlic

2   cups dry white wine (or apple juice if you prefer)

3   tablespoons Kirsch (cherry brandy), or brandy

   A dash of pepper, nutmeg, or paprika

Mix flour or cornstarch with grated cheese in a separate bowl. Rub the fondue pot with garlic, or crush garlic and add to wine. Heat wine in fondue pot until it bubbles, but do not bring to a boil. Add cheese and flour mixture a handful at a time, stirring to melt. Add Kirsch or brandy halfway through this process and stir and add the cheese mixture. Stir in a figure-eight pattern until the cheese is melted and ready to serve. Add a bit of pepper, nutmeg, or paprika to bring out the flavor of the fondue. Serve with a green leafy salad and hot French bread. The bread should be cut in 1-inch cubes. Boiled potatoes and cubes of ham may also be served for dipping. I also like to serve a nice plate of green olives and dill pickles. Serves 4.

CHEDDAR FAMILY FONDUE

2 cups shredded cheddar cheese (about ½ lb.)

¼ cup butter or margarine

¼ cup flour

A dash of pepper and salt, if desired

¼ teaspoon dry mustard

¼ teaspoon Worcestershire sauce

1½ cups milk

Melt butter in a pan over low heat. Add flour, salt, pepper, dry mustard, and Worcestershire sauce. Stir until blended and smooth. Turn off the heat and stir in milk, then heat until boiling while continually stirring. After a minute, add cheese and turn down to low heat, stirring in a figure-eight pattern until cheese melts. Pour in fondue pot and transfer to heating unit. Stir occasionally. Serve with hot pieces of English muffin or French bread out of the oven, ham cubes, breakfast sausages, or boiled potatoes.

MEAT FONDUE WITH HOT OIL

At first, I thought fondue with hot oil would be horrible. But, I decided, if I was going to learn everything I could about this method of entertaining, I knew I had to try it.

In time, I discovered a blend of canola oil and vegetable oil was the perfect medium for fondue. Canola makes it lighter, and heats it faster—thus searing the meat immediately, keeping it very juicy and tender without a heavy coat of oil. I like to cook beef and chicken together. I buy filet mignon and skinless, deboned chicken breasts. I partially freeze the meat by putting it in the freezer for about 45 minutes to an hour. It is firm, but not frozen and much easier to cut into pieces. I like a little bigger chunk of about 1½ inches cubed. Here is what is needed:

1   pound lean red meat

1   pound skinless and boneless chicken breasts

32 ounces canola/vegetable oil blend

1   teaspoon salt

Choice of sauces for dipping all can be found commercially prepared or in any fondue cookbook: creamy horseradish, steak sauce, teriyaki sauce, mushroom gravy, creamy curry sauce. In a metal fondue pot, add oil until about half full. Heat the stove until it reaches between 375°F and 400°F. Place it on the table cooking unit. If you are using an electric fondue, follow the directions that come with your set. You can test when your oil is ready for fondue by dipping a piece of bread on a fondue fork into the hot oil. If it comes out golden brown in about one minute, the oil is ready. Place meat on fondue fork and dip in hot oil. The nice thing about this type of cooking is that each participant can determine how well done they want to cook their food. A chunk of beef will be medium well and juicy after about 2 minutes in the hot oil. Remove from oil and drain on a paper towel, if desired. Dip into the prepared sauce and enjoy! I usually give my guests 4 forks of the same colored tip so they can continue to cook while they are dining. I also serve sliced, hot French bread and a green leafy salad with this fondue. If you want to really impress your guests, make your first course fresh homemade French onion soup. It serves 4 hearty appetites.

If after reading this you are interested in fondue, I suggest you shop used bookstores for fondue cookbooks, check with thrift stores for used retro fondue sets and cookbooks, or ask you parents or grandparents if they have some fondueware they would like to pass on to you. There are also a number of new fondue sets on the market and a few fondue cookbooks still in print. This is a fun, easy way of entertaining, and it is so participatory that everyone is assured a good time.

Blessed be!

Pesto Delle Streghe

The Pesto of the Witches

By Steven Posch

Pesto… It's the essence of summer, the edible soul of the Green God, the most seductive drug I know. Pesto. Take all the most delicious flavors in the world and combine them. Pesto, the ultimate aphrodesiac, never, ever, to be eaten alone.

In Hindu India, many plants are assocated with deities, but only basil has its own goddess. One bite of pesto and you'll know forever why.

What you see below is my own personal recipe, carefully refined through many steamy summers. I got this recipe from another American Witch, who learned it from an Italian Witch, or strega, from Genoa. Another great gift from the land of Aradia: the pesto of the Witches.

Pesto Delle Streghe

½   cup pine nuts, almonds, or sunflower seeds

½   cup freshly grated Parmesan cheese

¼   cup butter at room temperature (optional)

3   large cloves of garlic, peeled

½   teaspoon salt

    Scant ½ cup olive oil (¾ cup if not using butter)

1   pinch cayenne

2   pinches fresh marjoram (or 1 pinch dried)

1   overflowing cup fresh basil leaves, washed, stripped
    from stems, and firmly packed

Lightly dry-roast the nuts in a frying pan until golden. (Use almonds or sunflower seeds if you're on a budget. They'll do the job, but they're not really as good.) Chop lightly. In a bowl, hand-mix nuts, cheese, and butter. In a blender or food processor, place garlic, salt, cayenne, marjoram, and blend thoroughly. Introduce the basil a bit at a time, and blend to a smooth, green, aromatic paste. Pour this into the bowl and mix well with the nut-cheese-butter mixture. Toss with hot pasta—rotini (spirals are traditional, but any kind will do)—pour a glass of hearty wine and prepare to be seduced.

I should add that this pesto freezes nicely, for wintertime consumption. Make it without the parmesan in this case and add the cheese just before serving, otherwise it will lose its nice texture.

ISIS IN ALEXANDRIA

BY deTRACI REGULA

Alexandria was born out of the testosterone-laden energy of Alexander the Great, the Macedonian miracle-worker who led a crafty conquering army through the ancient world, then died before he saw his accomplishments crumble. In building Alexandria, he created a city that would also be a world-changer and world-conqueror, but in a much more feminine, brain-above-brawn way.

Originally a tiny Egyptian fishing village on the edge of the Mediterranean called Rhacotis, Alexander saw in the natural harbor the possibility of greatness. And so he arranged for the city to be built on Egyptian lines yet mingled with Greek qualities. After his death, when his empire was parceled out among his generals, one named Ptolemy successfully seized Egypt, and another dynasty was born.

Pre-Alexandrian remains of Rhacotis are rare, and there is little to speak of why this new city became so much the special province of Isis. Perhaps Alexander was familiar with her worship back in Greece, where her shrines began to be erected around the sixth century B.C. The Queens of the Ptolemies took to her worship, taking on her attributes long before Cleopatra did so in such inimitable, tragic style.

While imposing Greek attitudes and elevating Greek speakers in all areas of government, the Ptolemies nonetheless revivified traditional Egyptian religion, which had experienced a period of decline under the Persian rulers Alexander had ousted. Scholars debate what exactly happened with the sudden ascendancy of Serapis, originally an aspect of Osiris represented by the Apis bull. Instead of the shadowy, Lord of the Dead Osiris, Isis found herself with a revivified husband very concerned with the world, and the pair were adopted to be the special patrons of the Ptolemies. Older research suggested that Serapis was nothing more than a political convenience, a somewhat Egyptian god under the control of the Greek Ptolemies, but current scholars see less political maneuvering and more genuine religious fervor to explain the vigor of the cult of Serapis. One reason for this reinterpretation is that Serapian temples and shrines are often found in insignificant towns and cities, while major centers where the Ptolemies might well have wished to exert additional political and religious control had none. The details of Hellenic practice were probably put together by Timotheus, Manetho, and Demetrius of Phaleron.

Hailed again as a dynamic Queen, less as an eternally mourning wife, Isis stepped forward into the limelight happily. She turned her hand to protecting seafaring for the ship-building Greeks, calming storms and guarding trade. She was not too haughty to provide favorable winds, and would stoop to put her own hands on the sails when necessary. Beside this, she provided food, nurtured children, healed, and developed useful technologies when she was not serving as a muse to scholars at the Museum. Personal shrines to her were common, and public shrines and temples were erected throughout Alexandria.

On the islands of Antirhodes, so named because it resembled the splendor of the much larger Greek island of Rhodes, a shrine to Isis has been found next to the palace of Cleopatra. A single statue of one of her tonsured priests still stood guard underwater, holding a vase representing the cool water of Osiris.

Isis was revered under many titles in Alexandria. Though some records may have referred to a single temple by more than one name, she was obviously well worshipped in the seaside town. There were temples to her in the names of Isis-Fortuna (Tyche), Isis-Demeter, Isis-Pharia, and Isis-Aphrodite. Other temples included those to Isis-Lochia, the temple of Isis at Ras el Soda, which in modern times has been moved closer to Alexandria for the convenience of tourists, and the Temple of Isis on the promontory of Silsileh, where the palace of the Ptolemies was long believed to stand. Another supposed temple was in a sea-cave on the island of the Pharos lighthouse.

The Temple of Serapis was built about 286–280 B.C. to plans designed by Parmeniscus, boasting a statue by the renowned sculptor Bryaxis. Now located on Amoud al Sawari Street, this is a likely location for the famed Library of Alexandria. There are three subterranean galleries where the Apis bulls were buried, which can be visited, along with the remains of the Nilometer, the sacred structure used to measure the rise of the life-giving Nile flood. Pompey's pillar is nearby. A large temple of Isis was adjacent, contained by a rectangular enclosure wall of 173.7 by 77 meters. Ionic capitals of white marble decorated her colonnade. Nineteen subterranean chambers along the south wall were cut into two groups by the colonnade; some have counted twenty-two, leading to attempts to link these chambers with the twenty-two trumps of the Tarot.

The Graeco-Roman museum at Alexandria is a treasure trove of Isian objects, including a pair of unfortunately headless black basalt statues and a statue of an Apis bull, many coins, and a marble statue of Isis reclining against a sphinx. This image portrays Isis in her role as goddess of the Nile—eight children climb over her, each representing the fertility brought by a perfect Nile flood of eight cubits at Alexandria.

Even today, Isis still is acquiring new titles—one source reports that when a colossal bust of Isis was drawn up from the waters, a workman dubbed it "Megamammia" after he saw her nourishing breasts reemerging from their watery tomb. As in Philae, her jewel-like temple once submerged in the waters of the Nile, Isis is emerging once again, in forms both old and new.

SCARECROW MAGIC

BY LYNNE STUTEVANT

They have been known by many different names through the centuries. Scarebirds. Jacks-of-straw. Tattybogles. Watchers of the Corn Sprouts. Terrifiers. Although we call them scarecrows, these eerie human effigies frighten more than the birds. Countless legends describe scarecrows who come to life under the Full Moon or serve as hosts for dangerous, disembodied spirits. Though friendly, clownlike scarecrows dominate today, the jack-of-straw's traditional, more sinister nature lurks just beneath his tattered cloak.

Scarecrows are as ancient as agriculture, and many different types developed around the world. The Zuni and Navaho hung dead crows from poles in their corn fields. They hoped the sight of rotting carcasses would serve as a warning to other birds. The ancient Greeks placed wooden statues of the ugly god Priapus in their vineyards, and the Germans took Witch figures to the fields in early spring. After the Witches drew the evil forces of winter from the ground, they remained as scarecrows until the fall harvest. During the years of the Black Death, British farmers began making "modern" scarecrows by stuffing old clothes with straw.

The Pennsylvania Dutch erected scarecrows in pairs. A male figure, called the *bootzamon* or bogeyman, stood at one end of the field. The *bootzafraw* or bogeywife stood at the other. The two worked together and kept each other company. This custom may be the source of the folk belief that scarecrows travel in groups. As soon as one is placed in a field, others are sure to follow, mysteriously springing up overnight.

Japanese farmers invited the god of agriculture to leave his home in the mountains each spring and enter their scarecrows, called kakashi. The kakashi could see everything, and the birds who landed on them whispered secrets to the god. When the autumn harvest was completed, the kakashi were taken down and stacked in a pile. The farmers prepared rice cakes to thank the god for his service and to provide food for his long journey back to the mountains. After the rice cakes were placed around the *kakashi*, the pile was set ablaze and the god was released. The ceremony was known as "The Ascent of the Scarecrow."

Even in this day of farming as big business, the scarecrow still performs his ancient duties. Agricultural supply companies sell inflatable scarecrows with moving arms and legs. A glow-in-the-dark version is even available. But why not honor the ancient traditions and make your own frightening tattybogle?

The goal is to create a figure that suggests a human being. The simpler the form, the more menacing its appearance will be. Before you begin construction, decide where you will put your scarecrow. If he is going to be outdoors for an extended period, he will get wet. Keep that in mind as you select your materials.

1. Construct a wooden cross to serve as the scarecrow's skeleton. If you don't have appropriate pieces of wood, tomato stakes, broomsticks, or mop handles will work. Nail or attach the horizontal piece about one third of the way down from the top of the vertical pole. The horizontal will be the scarecrow's arms. The vertical will be his spine. Stick the vertical pole into the ground or anchor it in a flower pot or bucket filled with dirt and rocks.

2. The scarecrow's head can be made from a variety of items: a pumpkin, bucket, milk jug, stuffed pillow case, old mop or broom top, plastic jack-o'-lantern. Mount the head on the vertical pole, then cover the neck with a scarf. Add a hat or clothe your scarecrow in a hooded sweatshirt. Attach ivy, hay, weeds or leaves for hair. It's not necessary to add facial features, but if you do, make them large and simple—just eyes or leering mouth with a red rag dangling like a flapping tongue.

3. Finish dressing your creation. To use pants and shirt, the pole can be one leg while the other pant leg hangs free. Bales of hay for stuffing are available in the fall at nurseries, garden shops, craft stores, and farmers' markets. You can also drape an old sheet, bedspread, or blanket over the form and tie a rope around the scarecrow's waist. Fray the hem or tear into strips so the tatters will fly in the wind.

4. Add the scarecrow's hands. Old gloves are traditional, but twigs that resemble skeleton fingers also work. You can suspend tinfoil pie pans from the ends of the horizontal pole or give your scarecrow a walking stick. Tie rags, streamers, or strips of foil to the stick. As they flutter, the movement and reflection will frighten the birds and other animals that invade the garden at night.

Situate your scarecrow comfortably in the garden, then give him a small offering: a flower, some kernels of corn, a handful of seeds, or a green tomato. Don't neglect him. Check on him from time to time, especially after storms. When the growing season ends, be sure to thank him for his hard work. You can store your scarecrow and bring him out again in the spring. But if you believe the old legends, that won't be necessary. Scarecrows despise the cold. As soon as the first frost touches the fields, they will vanish on their own.

MAGIC IN THE WORKPLACE

BY ESTELLE DANIELS

Some people think that the workplace is not an appropriate place for magic. And for some types of magic, this is true. Most bosses would frown on taking time out to set up an altar or create a circle for clearing the mind. But we all encounter stresses in the workplace, and magic can be one effective means for deflecting stress so we can be more effective workers.

The most basic magic for the workplace is creating a shield around your workspace to filter out noise and distractions. This can be a simple spell—such as visualizing yourself in a golden bubble of energy, or placing precharged wards around your desk. You can use postcards that remind you of each element, placed in orientation to the cardinal directions. A rock or ordinary object charged at home works too. If you contain the proper energies, your space can be made an island of calm.

To siphon off excess frustration, use a grounding object such as a meditation stone disguised as a plain paperweight. Rinse it in water every so often, or place it in the sun, to drain off excess or negative energy. If you have coworkers who you have trouble dealing with, a simple mirror can help deflect their negative vibes away from you. Just face the mirror outward toward the person, and any negative energy will be deflected. The trick is to have the mirror facing the person, and it's better if they can't see it.

Having a cubicle goddess or god can help protect your space. Postcards, greeting cards—whatever has a pleasant image that reminds you of your favorite deity—can be used. Some people have small figurines that do the trick. If you have a sit-down job, charging your chair to be a shield can work, provided it is your chair and you don't have to share it.

Simple meditations and visualizations or mantras that you can do in your head go a long way in a tense situation. The most basic, taking three cleansing breaths, eliminates negativity and calms the mind and emotions in just seconds. While you are doing it you look like you are just pausing to think. In doing this, consciously breathe out the negative energy, and breathe in calm and peace while feeling yourself in your body. Another good visualization is a grounding and centering meditation. Visualize your feet growing roots and connecting to the earth. Use that connection to ground and center, and thereby calm and shield yourself from nasty outside influences.

If you like mantras, try something simple that is either a statement of purpose or evokes some thoughts or emotions that are calming and peaceful. The Goddess or God is with me always. Relax and center. Say, "I am calm as a still pool. I will bend like the willow. All this is transitory. In a hundred years, nobody will remember what happened here today."

Laughter is very therapeutic and cleansing, especially humor that brings perspective, or that highlights the absurdities of life. Many people clip cartoons and have them in their workspace. Keeping a list of inspirational sayings can also help. These can be whatever makes you pause and think. Some workplaces have restrictions on religious materials, but there are many sayings that can invoke sacred feelings which are not specifically religious. If you cannot display them, having them on a card in your desk or wallet to be reviewed in times of stress works well. Greeting cards have many wonderful sentiments, and there is no rule that you cannot purchase them for yourself.

Another technique is to take a break and look out a window. In other words, reconnect with nature. Washing your hands with the intent of washing off the negativity and bad energies helps reset your brain. Going to the bathroom and consciously eliminating negativity is another idea. You have to go anyway, why not make it a magical act? Drinking water (especially good pure water) can also help wash away negativity. Do it with intent.

If you get a meal break, get out of the work area, preferably out of the building. Taking a walk can relieve stress. Breathing fresh (or different) air helps. Wipe the negativity off your feet as you leave your workplace. Try not to eat lunch at your desk, especially if you have a stressful job. You may end up ingesting all the negativity and bad vibes, and your food won't taste as good or be digested as well.

These are simple yet effective techniques to keep you calm, centered, and as free from stress as possible. See which work best for you in your work environment.

Disarming the Bad Boss

Magic for a "Dilbertized" Workplace

By Edain McCoy

Scott Adams' popular comic strip *Dilbert* has given us many good laughs over the vagaries of management decision-making in the corporate world. Unfortunately, those day to day realities don't seem so funny when we endure them. While Adams' laughter therapy can go a long way to making us feel better about a bad boss, when all avenues of arbitration and common sense have been exhausted and your boss is still impossible to work with, magic may be your last resort.

The Egg of Mirrors

If you suspect your boss is the sadistic kind who enjoys upsetting his subordinates, block his efforts with an impenetrable egg of mirrors. Before you report to work, mentally surround yourself in a large egg made up of thousands of small mirrors. Visualize them shining around you, reflecting unwanted energies back to their source. Mentally boost the egg's reflective power several times each day before your boss targets you as his next victim. When he mounts an effort to annoy you, simply listen politely while visualizing your mirrored egg reflecting back his negative intentions. Eventually he will learn that trying to make you feel bad only makes him feel bad, and the taunting will cease.

Some Personal Space Mace

Place an item on your desk or work area—or even in your pocket—that you have mentally programmed to invoke feelings of peace and calm. This is your personal zone, a private space extending about five feet in each direction from the object. Anyone entering this zone will be affected by your talisman's influence and act accordingly. Think of it as mace for the atmosphere. A special stone, crystal, or piece of jewelry will work.

FOOD TO SOOTHE

Food is a popular pacifier and makes a good centerpiece around which to socialize casually with coworkers. Bake a treat to share in your workplace containing as much vanilla as possible. Vanilla imparts peace and feelings of compatibility that can help defuse tense situations. Magically charge your vanilla to this goal before baking the item. Make sure your boss gets an extra large helping!

PEPPERING TO PURIFY

Sprinkle a little ground black pepper around your workplace to neutralize the negative vibrations caused by clashes with your boss.

CONFIDENCE CREATES CONFIDENCE

If your boss seems not to trust you or your judgment in spite of all evidence to the contrary, construct an aura of self-assurance around yourself by mentally surrounding yourself with blue or yellow light. Blue is the color of fidelity and calmness, and yellow projects an intellectual image. Wear these colors to work, visualizing beforehand what you want them to say to your boss.

VISIBILITY AND INVISIBILITY

There are times we really want the boss to notice how hard we're working, especially if we're in a new position or handling an exceptionally critical item. There are also times we wish the boss would look the other way, if just for a moment, as we fumble with something difficult. Naturally, the reverse is always true—the boss watches when you don't want her to, and isn't looking you want her to. But you can make yourself fade in and out of the boss's visual range by using magic. When you want to be unseen for a while, visualize yourself and your work area fading, becoming more transparent. Work diligently but silently, making as little verbal or eye contact with others as possible. When you want your boss's attention, visualize yourself in vivid color. Imagine a ray of light shining down on you and your work. Where appropriate, chat companionably with coworkers; smile and make eye contact with all who come near you, especially your boss.

GIVE YOUR BOSS A PROMOTION

Sometimes the only way to rid yourself of a problem personality in a position of authority is simply to wait until that person is moved on to yet another position of authority. If you hear even the slightest suggestion that your boss might be up for a promotion, help him along with a "banished-be bag." This is a charm or magical object designed to make someone go away, but this is not negative magic. You're not willing harm on anyone; you're just helping them go where they might be happier. Someplace on your work property, place a small bag holding raw meat soaked in vinegar. Visualize it making your boss go away and let the energies of the land decide in a positive way where that is to be.

NICE STROKES FOR NASTY FOLKS

Often, a boss is unpleasant to subordinates simply because he or she lacks confidence in her own abilities and is desperately trying to juggle a fearful load of items she feels inadequate to handle. Without lying or resorting to flattery, let your boss know when you think she has made a good decision, guided a project well, or handled a difficult personnel situation with grace. Knowing that someone beneath her in the chain of command thinks she handled the situation well is just as soothing as knowing someone above on the chain feels that way.

DON'T TAKE IT HOME

Sometimes we have no choice but to take work and its problems home with us, but we don't have to take the stress and bad feelings that have grown in us during the workday. Before you get in your car, bus, cab, or on your bike, take a moment to shake off the bad vibrations. Breathe deeply as you leave work, inhaling the heady aroma of private time. With each beat of your feet repeat a simple mantra such as, "This time is mine," or "I'm my own boss now," and feel the stress ease out of you. Then touch the ground with your hands if you can and visualize the jitters and worries of the day pouring safely into to mother earth, to be grounded far away from you.

MARTINMAS

CELEBRATE YOUR CHARITY ON NOVEMBER 11

BY LILY GARDNER

Martinmas follows Samhain as a continuance of the harvest season. At Lughnasah, we celebrate the fruits of our labor; at Mabon, we settle our debts and strive for balance; and at Samhain, we remember and honor our dead. At Martinmas, we share our bounty with the less fortunate.

Martinmas, otherwise known as Hollantide or Old November, was the original Samhain festival before the Gregorian calendar reform in 1752. The Christians renamed the festival Martinmas after their Saint Martin of Tours: a man famous for his charity. Legend has it that as a young soldier, Martin encountered a beggar by the side of the road. Because Martin had no money to share with the man, he cut his coat in two and gave half to the beggar. The French claim St. Martin as the patron saint of winegrowers and use Martinmas as the day to break out their new Beaujolais. They've circulated the story that St. Martin's beggar was drunk. St. Martin's emblem is the goose, an ancient messenger between the underworld and earth. Goose is traditionally served on this day.

As the Wheel of the Year turns, so Martinmas has been a traditional weather marker through the centuries. An old rhyme says:

> *If ducks do slide at Hollantide*
> *At Christmas they will swim*
> *If ducks do swim at Hollantide*
> *At Christmas they will slide.*

In agricultural communities, Martinmas was the traditional day to butcher animals that could not be wintered over because of lack of feed. The butchered animals were salted down to store over the winter. Some people themselves or their thresholds with the blood of the slaughtered beasts for prosperity through the winter. November's Full Moon is still known as the Blood Moon.

It seems fitting as we look towards winter that we share our prosperity with neighbors, knowing that what you send returns three times over. Martinmas celebrations begin at midday with a sacred circle. Place a portion of the charity on the altar, burning cedar incense for prosperity. Cast the circle, and say:

As Above, so Below
As I Take, so I Return.

Call in the directions and light an orange candle for Spirit. Thank the Mother for the year's blessings, and say:

May every living thing
Be filled with bliss
Hear my prayer
This Martinmas!

Thank the directions, close the circle, and go into the world, distributing what you collected for the needy. Serve a traditional goose dinner and feast with family or coven, remembering to look for the crone goddess, Carlin, who rides the winds this night. Her presence is known to mortals by the call of wild geese.

ROASTED GOOSE

1 goose
1 lemon
5 tart apples
  Beaujolais
  Salt and pepper

Wash the goose and pat dry. Rub the skin and the cavity with salt and lemon. Stuff the bird with wedges of apple and sew the cavity closed. Place the goose in a greased roasting pan and add an inch of water. Bake uncovered in a 400°F oven for 30 minutes, then cover and bake at 325°F for 1½ hours. Skim the fat and baste the bird with Beaujolais twice during the baking time. Turn the bird over and bake additional 1½ hours. Skim fat and baste with wine twice more.

Remove the roasted bird from oven and let rest as you prepare gravy from pan drippings mixed with a little flour and water.

Serve goose with mashed potatoes and sauerkraut.

Remember as you enjoy your dinner that for centuries people have eaten this same meal on this same day.

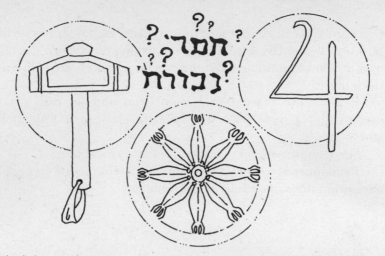

The Gods and the Tree of Life

By John Michael Greer

The Tree of Life is the great symbolic pattern of the Cabala, central to nearly all traditions of high magic in the Western world. Most ceremonial magicians, and a good many Wiccans and other Pagans, study it intensively at one point, and with good reason. Not only does the Tree comprise a powerful language of magical symbolism, but many old texts, traditions, and rituals make use of it.

Still, for many people in today's magical revival, there is at least one major problem with the Tree. The Cabala has its roots in Judaism, and so the spiritual powers assigned to the Spheres and Paths of the Tree are those found in Jewish lore and belief—archangels, angels, spirits of various kinds, and the Names of God found in Jewish tradition. For those who are comfortable relating to the Divine by way of these Names and their symbolism, this is fine, but those who aren't do end up with problems.

The result has been a great many attempts to relate the gods and goddesses of other pantheons to the Tree of Life, putting these powers in place of the Divine Names of Jewish tradition. Projects of this sort have a long history, and from the point of view of the Western magical tradition there's a definite place for them. Still, if they're going to be useful, such reorientations of the Tree need to be done competently.

This has unfortunately not always happened. There are at least three pitfalls that many systems have struggled with. The first pitfall is the idea that the Spheres of the Tree of Life are separate beings, personalities, or entities. In the Cabala, the Tree is a pattern of energy flow, and the Spheres and Paths are stages and interactions in that flow. The Tree is dynamic, not static, and should be treated as such.

The implication here is that one god or goddess may relate to more than one Sphere, and more than one deity may be present in a single Sphere. There has been quarreling about where the Norse god Odin should go on the Tree. Some claim that, as Allfather, he belongs at Chokmah, the Second Sphere—the Supernal Father in Cabalistic thought; others insist that as Lord of Magic, he belongs in the Eighth Sphere, Hod; still others point out that as a sacrificed god, he belongs to the Sixth Sphere, Tiphareth. In fact, he belongs to all of these, and possibly to others.

Similarly, there have been disputes about which Norse deity ought to correspond to Yesod, the Ninth Sphere. Some point to Frey, whose fertility-god aspects fit; others call on Heimdall, the guardian of the rainbow bridge, who was born of nine mothers. Again, both answers are right, and so are several others. This may suggest that simple, cut-and-dried answers are not very useful in this, and that is true. The second pitfall, then, is the tendency to rely too much on the rigid use of astrological correspondences.

Each Sphere of the Tree corresponds to a planet, among many other things, and most gods also correspond to planets. It can be very seductive to use these correspondences in a simplistic way to connect gods to Spheres. Unfortunately, as often as not, the result isn't very effective. For example, many cultures have a goddess who corresponds to the Moon. Since Yesod, the Ninth Sphere of the Tree, also corresponds to the Moon, many pagan Trees assign a Moon goddess to Yesod. But in the Cabala—as in Norse, Japanese, and many Native American mythologies—the Moon-sphere Yesod is decidedly male. Most Moon goddesses, meanwhile, relate more closely to the Third Sphere, Binah, which belongs to the Triple Goddess, or to the Tenth Sphere, Malkuth, which relates to the Maiden Goddess of the cycles of nature.

The third pitfall is the idea that because a deity in pantheon A corresponds to a given Sphere, and a deity in pantheon B is similar to the deity in pantheon A, then the one from pantheon B belongs to the same Sphere. Unless the connections between the two divinities are very close, however, this is likely to land you in a great deal of confusion. For example, Jupiter—the god and the planet—corresponds to the Fourth Sphere, Chesed. Meanwhile, Jupiter is a thunder god, so it has been assumed that all thunder gods relate to Chesed. The problem is that the Roman god Jupiter is not just a thunder god; he is lord of treaties, contracts, justice, and fair dealing, and all strangers and travelers are under his protection. Since these are Chesed factors, Jupiter's position on the Tree is based on much more than his role as hurler of thunderbolts. Other thunder gods, such as Indra and Taranis, are warriors which belong to Geburah, not Chesed.

The lesson in all of these confusions is simple enough: if you want to work out the relation between the Tree of Life and a pantheon, you need to know both of them thoroughly before you start. It's important to remember that none of the symbols or traditions of the ancient Pagan pantheons were arbitrary or random. Like all living spiritual traditions, they were created and developed out of personal encounter with the divine powers of the cosmos. They offer the same kind of experience to us today, but only if we take the time to learn them, understand them, and use them in an intelligent and sensitive way.

DARK POWER HERBS

BY ANN MOURA

Most herbs can be adapted to any type of magical activity, but there are also herbs specifically related to dark power magics, offering attunement to death, transitions, rebirth, the Underworld and Otherworld, and to the aspects and divinities identified with the Crone and the Hunter. Some of these herbs can be used as teas to aid the practitioner from within, but most are best utilized in spellwork with candle magics, incense, charms, oils, washes, dressings for ritual objects, and sachets.

In magical practice, besides attunement, dark power herbs have the energy to return harmful intent and negativity back to a sender of such things. These herbs may be used in protection spells. Other herbs, on the other hand, are deflection-oriented, able to diffuse general malevolence or ill will when you are not certain where the negativity is coming from. Still other herbs have the effect of retribution, returning energy to the generator with the additional power to seal it there. These would be used in spells where you not only return the negative energy to the sender, but bind it with the generator.

Some herbs assist in curses, but these should never be used in stress-related dark magics because what is sent comes back. Intent is what matters, so caution is required in such a working—for instance you might perhaps curse a vicious criminal with capture and justice, but you should not curse just anyone with bad things. Herbs can be used in exorcisms to disperse negative energies and allow positive energies to enter a space. By censing a new home before moving in, or after unpleasant guests have left, you can clear out doubts, frustrations, and usher in a fresh start. Samhain sabbats sometimes contain a call to troubled or confused spirits so that they may find help in moving on to Shadowland. This type of ritual is powerful and requires the practitioner have sufficient experience to deal with the upswelling of psychic energy.

Dark power herbs can also be used in purging and releasing spells, which are lesser exorcisms invoking the herbal energies to cleanse and turn away negativity or absorb it for removal. Garlic and onions are braided and hung in a house for this purpose, then disposed of at the end of the year and replaced. You can also use this type of spellwork to turn away from bad habits, release obstacles to development, and clear out impediments to success.

Nonpoisonous herbs can be added to the candle flame during a ritual or spellwork, but always use caution that the fumes are not overpowering. The herbs may be used simply to honor the divine, the sidhe, and the elementals at rituals dedicated to them or soliciting their help. These types of herbs are good for the cleansing and dedication of dark power-oriented tools. Poisonous herbs have traditionally been used to strengthen the power of charms and spells, but even handling some can be dangerous with the toxins absorbed through the skin.

Herbs that relate to the Crone and the Hunter, dark Moon, lunar eclipse, solar eclipse, Underworld, Otherworld, protection, death, passages, transitions, and rebirth include: absinthe, acacia, amaranth, anise, apple, ash bark and leaves, artemesia, balsam, bay, bayberry, blackberry, black currant, briar, burdock, cypress, damiana, dandelion root, dianthus, dittany of Crete, elder, elecampane, fennel, garlic, ginger root, hawthorn, hazel, jasmine, lavender, lilac, linden, mace, marigold, mugwort, mullein, myrrh, oak, orris root, paprika, patchouli, pomegranate seeds, purple heather, rosemary, rowan wood, sage, sandalwood, skullcap, St. John's wort, tansy, thistle, thyme, valerian, vervain (verbena), willow, and woodruff.

Herbs for return-to-sender spells include: agrimony, ginger root, lady's slipper, mullein, nettle, rue, tamarisk, thistle, and unicorn root.

Herbs for deflection: anise, blackthorn, boneset, elder, ginger root, lady's slipper, mullein, nettle, orris root, paprika, pennyroyal, peppercorn, rue, tamarisk, vetiver, and willow.

Herbs for retribution include: blackthorn, elder, rue, vetiver, and willow.

Herbs for curses include: cypress, dragon's blood, wormwood, rowan wood, yarrow (arrowroot).

Herbs for exorcisms include: agrimony, asafetida, avens, boneset, clove, cypress, dragon's blood, fern, frankincense, garlic, ginger root, juniper berry, lavender, lilac, mullein, nettle, peppercorn, rosemary, rue, sage, sandalwood, tamarisk, thistle, unicorn root, vervain (verbena), and yarrow (arrowroot).

Herbs for purgings and releasings include: elder, fern, garlic, hyssop, lavender, lilac, mugwort, onion, sage, skullcap, St. Johns wort, thistle, valerian, willow, and woodruff.

The use of herbs adds potency to spellwork because they encompass all of the elementals. Earth is represented in the roots, leaves, flowers, nuts, and berries; air with the aroma and fragrance; fire with growth from sunlight and the astringent or internally affecting qualities; and water in the juices flowing as nourishment through the plants.

Select herbs for the changes they are perceived to produce, or for the qualities they possess, represent, or relate to. When you add herbs to your Craft work, you are not only increasing the connection between the elementals and the spell, but also between the elementals and yourself. The four qualities vibrate within you and the herbs, and are focused to work in the spell by your invoking of those powers through the characteristic of the herb, directed to a specific goal as described within the framework of the spell.

CHRISTIAN WARRIOR

BY BERNYCE BARLOW

As a Christian with a close associations with the Native American, Wiccan, and Pagan communities, I often feel overwhelmed on all sides. Everyone's hackles seem up so often, I no longer want to hear how my ancestors put small pox in the blankets of Native Americans and how they burned Witches. There is too much divisiveness between spiritual groups. The way I see it, you are be part of the problem or part of the solution.

Guilt is a spiritual power weapon that is used by all sorts of people, but it can cause major damage if allowed to. Intolerance, also utilized by certain groups, breeds active prejudice. Guilt and intolerance needs to be replaced with respect, compassion, and wisdom if we are together going to overcome our differences.

Then there is the ego—ordinarily a sweet little package, it can also carry a destructive emotional bomb. Our egos define our self-importance, for better or worse. As such, it is the weapon of choice for many individuals. In fact, the teachings of all the great masters warn us about the power of our egos. From the ego, personal fear and anger can manifest. But on the flip side, active healing and empowerment can issue from the ego. It all depends on whether or not a person can walk their talk, not if they are Christian or Pagan. Although there is such a thing as righteous anger, when we are very honest about it, most of our fear and anger comes from self-importance and ego. While we need our egos as a significant part of our conscious psyche, we must take care not to use its power in the wrong way and let it become objectively destructive.

When John the Baptist was beheaded, Jesus went to a mountain to grieve, do ceremony, and pray. When Jesus's followers wanted to come with him he asked them to leave him alone in his grief. The Baptist and Jesus were best friends, their mothers best friends. They grew up together and loved each other, so when the Baptist's head rolled, Jesus was righteously angry and hurt. Under the circumstances he no doubt could have done some major damage on a magical scale, but he made another choice. The folks at the bottom of the mountain were waiting around to see what Jesus would do to those who had just murdered his best friend. When he came down off that mountain righteously pissed off, he looked at the crowd that had gathered, read their intentions, and rather than striking them down, he healed them all.

This story, of course, shows that Christ-consciousness is a part of the solution when it isn't all tangled up in the guilt and intolerance possible in Christianity. Knowing the difference between Christ-consciousness and the bad sides of organized religion helps one keep the ego and judgment in check. We all get hurt feelings at times. One group calls another names, makes fun of its doctrines, or accuses them of being dark or evil. Eventually a wall between the two groups is formed. One way to take the wall down is by understanding where the ego ends and where tolerance begins. This is a higher law that can and does bring results in a spiritual circle. The beauty of this is that when practiced honorably, we belong in the same circle.

So I bring this challenge to Pagans, Wiccans, Buddhists, Native Americans, Christians, and all others. Walk in the light. When Christ said, "My burden is light," he didn't mean its weight. He meant it as an active principle that will push away guilt, intolerance, ego, and judgment among us, whether we end our prayers in aho, blessed be, harm none, or amen. As for the other guys, you can really mess with their heads them up by coming down off the mountain and sending them love and light. Heal them instead of hating them.

KHEPERA

BY deTRACI REGULA

The world's first "Beetlema-
nia" may have occurred
thousands of years ago when
the Egyptians took delight in
carving stone scarabs.

At once amulet, seal, and
decoration, thousands of scarabs
were produced in ancient Egypt.
At first, the mummified bodies of
beetles themselves were revered and
placed in predynastic burials. Before Ra
grew in power, Khepera was an original creator god, tied to both
earthly clay and the heavenly Sun. Flying in the heat of the day,
when few other creatures would stir, the beetle seemed doubly
divine. Its metallic carapace glittered like precious metal as it flew.

Scarabs carved in stone served as seal stones, with the owners
name, rank, and titles carved into the flat base of the stone. The
stone was pressed into the clay or wax seals used to protect docu-
ments, gateways, and storage jars. Big stone scarabs were issued
in multiple copies by Amenhotep III to announce important
events in his reign. A stone "heart scarab," often with wings, was
laid over the chest of mummies, to protect the heart below.

Yves Cambefort believes that Egyptians patterned their mum-
mification process after the life processes of the beetle. Certainly,
the bandage-wrapped mummy resembles the pupa of the beetle,
which has light indentations which resemble wrappings. From a
dung-fed worm, the bright powerful beetles sprang, after a time
of burial which transformed and revivified them. They were said
to be all males and entirely self-generating, growing out of the
"mud" of the life-giving Nile.

The mystical processes of the beetle is revealed in the word
itself. The word was written with a beetle determinative, a small
image of the sacred insect. To the Egyptians, *kheper* meant to create, to become, to manifest, to change.

TO PROWL THE SHADOWED HOURS

BY ELIZABETH BARRETTE

soft summer twilight
bejeweled with fireflies

a velveteen breeze
eases the sun's passage

moist kisses of wind
coax the night awake

a yawn, a stretch—
dark Goddess rises

while crickets sing
hosannas to her grace

then with a languid shake
she sets off

to prowl the shadowed hours
until dawn

COLCANNON

BY STEVEN POSCH

Samhain eve, sunset. The gates of the new year swing wide, spirits throng to their ancestral hearths for the once-a-year feasting, and you are wondering what to serve the hungry dead. The voices of Irish tradition speak unanimously: colcannon.

Colcannon, or "northern bubble-and-squeek," as Jane Grigson calls it—one could hardly ask for simpler, more homey fare: fried onions, potatoes, cabbage, salt, and pepper. Still, what a synergy of flavors, and substantial enough to stick to the ribs of the hungriest ghost.

But enough rhapsodizing. The name is, of course, Gaelic: *cal ceannan,* meaning white headed-cabbage (as in kale or cole slaw). Though the dish does not predate Raleigh's mid-Renaissance introduction of the spud into Britain, in the intervening centuries it has become the signature food of the Irish (and Scottish) Samhain celebration. Because Samhain is a time of divination, it's traditional to hide tokens in the colcannon: a coin for money, a ring for handfasting, a thimble for spinster-hood or creativity, a tiny doll for a baby. In Scotland they add a wishbone and a—presumably miniature—horseshoe as well.

Colcannon is hearty fare, served throughout the winter. In Minnesota, it's customary to serve colcannon only during the dark half of the year, from Samhain to Beltane. Eating the winter's last colcannon is my invariable pre-Beltane custom.

There's no set recipe for colcannon. Any Irish or Scottish cookbook will list at least one variant, as will many vegetarian collections. Here's my own favorite, given, in true folkloric fashion, without specific measurements.

1 part onions, chopped

2 parts potatoes, cubed (leave skins on)

2 parts cabbage

Vegetable oil or butter

Too much salt

Too much ground black pepper

Fry the onions in oil to cover the bottom of the pan. Stir periodically until the onions carmelize (the darker, the more flavorful—though I usually draw the line at black and crispy). Meanwhile, in a large pot, steam, or boil the cabbage and potatoes until the cabbage is cooked through and you can pierce the potatoes with a fork. Drain and mash them together, with enough of the cooking water to produce the consistency of mashed potatoes. When the onions have caramelized, add the potato-cabbage mash, and season with salt and pepper (be generous). Fry, stirring continuously, for half an hour or so, until the entire mass sticks to itself. Turn out into your finest serving dish and add the divinatory tokens, or place in a buttered, covered casserole dish and keep warm in the oven.

Colcannon is a lot of work to make, so you might as well make a lot of it. Believe, me, people will eat seconds and thirds. Be sure to set aside a healthy portion for the honored ancestors, and maybe someone will do the same for you someday.

In the words of an old Scots Samhain blessing, *Gum fosgladh dorus na gliadhna uibhe chum sith, sonas, is samchair.* May the door of the coming year open for you to peace, happiness, and quiet contentment.

CREATING AN ANCESTRAL SHRINE

BY LILITH DORSEY

One of the most important concepts in Voodoo and other African-based traditions is the reverence for ancestor spirits. Voodoo practitioners, like followers of many Eastern spiritual traditions, believe that all of those who have come before are important spirits and are worthy of tribute. Central to this principal is the creation of an ancestor shrine. It is an ideal way to begin exploring your own spirituality.

The process is simple. It does not require any special knowledge, except what is already known about your ancestors and your heritage. To begin creating the ancestor shrine, sit down and make a list of all of the relatives who have passed on who you can remember. Then begin collecting photos of them and any items of theirs—these are to go on the shrine. Also to be placed on the shine are the things that they enjoyed in life, including food, jewelry, books, money, and the like. At our ancestor shrine here at *Oshun African Magickal Quarterly,* in addition to the items described above, we have cowrie shells, crystals, the family bible, war medals, mass cards, prayers, cosmetics, coffee, beer, wine, cigarettes, flowers, and candy.

One of the most important things you can do for your ancestors is provide them with food offerings. Many modern Pagans have chosen to dispense with food offerings as part of ritual, but they are central to all the African diasporan traditions. Several times through the year you may feel the need for an ancestor feast. A feast provides the ancestors with special tribute. The traditional

times for this feast are November 1 and 2, known for the days of the dead celebrations that take place throughout Central and South America, and January 2, known as Ancestors' Day in Haiti. This feast can be held as a solitary practice by one person making many different dishes to honor their heritage. A much more enjoyable practice, however, can be gathering with your family and friends. Everyone brings an item to honor their own heritage and culture. Each person leaves a portion of the food on the shrine, and then shares the rest while exchanging stories about their family history. The food items placed on the shrine are not to be consumed by the living. Once they have been on the shrine for a few days (customarily one week) they are removed, placed on the open earth, and replaced with fresh items.

The importance of the ancestor shrine is based on the belief that these were the people who cared for you in life. Therefore, these are the people who are still most concerned and responsible for you in the afterlife. The ancestor shrine should be seen as a place to meditate on your own life and the lives of those that have come before you. Ancestor spirits can be helpful in all life situations, giving their children energy, courage, and knowledge that they accumulated during their time on earth.

Samhain Ancestral Cakes

By Mario Furtado

Jack-o'-lanterns glowing on the windowsills, spicy incense wafting to the heavens, and figures dancing around blazing bonfires; it must be that most magical of nights—Samhain night. Wouldn't it be great if you served your Samhain celebrants and ancestors a truly magical treat? These cakes are sure to please even the most finicky of spirits.

These cakes have been a sweet addition to the Samhain feast at my house for as long as I can remember, and I truly hope that you'll add them to your Samhain table this year. Remember that while baking for a magical or ritual purpose you should visualize your intent. In this case, it's honoring your ancestors.

Cookies

1½ cups unbleached flour

¾ cups brown sugar

¼ teaspoon salt

1 teaspoon baking powder

½ teaspoon baking soda

1 pinch each: sage, cinnamon, cloves, and all-spice

1 egg, at room temperature

½ cup unsalted butter

1 teaspoon vanilla

1 teaspoon almond extract

½ cup hazelnuts, finely chopped

GLAZE

¼ cup warm water

1 cup confectioner's sugar

2 drops orange food coloring

Few drops apple essence

Begin by sifting the dry ingredients in a medium-sized bowl. In a large bowl, beat the sugar and butter together until fluffy. Add the egg, vanilla, almond, and milk to the butter mixture. Stir the dry ingredients in portions into the butter and egg mixture, taking care not to overstir the batter. Finally, fold in the hazelnuts and drop by spoonfuls onto a greased cookie sheet. You can drop them into muffin tins instead; this will give you a more uniformly shaped cake. Bake in a preheated 375°F oven for 12–14 minutes. While baking, combine ingredients for glaze. To make apple essence, steep apple peels in vodka in a sterile, tightly sealed jar for a week or two. When cakes are done, cool and glaze.

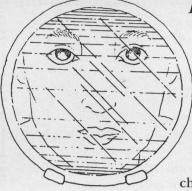

MOTHERS OF TIME: A BLACK MIRROR MEDITATION

BY ANN MOURA

For this meditation, you will need a table and chair, black mirror, black candle, mugwort incense, libation bowl, and a chalice containing a dark beverage such as blackberry wine, grape juice, or cranberry juice. Arrange the table with the mirror at the center, the black candle in front of it, the libation bowl in front of the candle, the incense to the right, and the chalice to the left. Cast your circle around the table and chair. With the room dark, light the candle and the incense, then sit so you can look comfortably into the mirror.

> *Mothers of eternity, passing thy light through me; mother love through time, mother love from past to future generations flows; our genetic bonds tie our love through the ages. Mothers of my ancestry, mothers of my heritage, we are connected. All the mothers of my line, pass our love through all time. Past, present, future family, mother love is blessed be, blessed be, blessed be, now as then to eternity. So mote it be.*

Let the incense smolder, adding more of the mugwort herb as needed. Gaze into the mirror and see your own reflection. Keep watching your reflection, and now see how it changes first into that of your mother, then your grandmother, and then in more rapid progression, the images of your maternal ancestresses will appear. Notice how they differ. Sometimes the features show similarities to yourself or other family members, other times the face will seem strange. But all are your mothers in time. Greet them with love and remembrance.

> *Mothers of mine in time, I honor thee. You who have passed the gift of life unto me, I honor thee. Mothers of my line and my blood, I honor thee.*

Take your chalice of dark beverage, lift it up before the mirror in a salute, then pour a libation from the cup into the bowl. Now take a sip from the chalice. You may want to reflect on the many faces that pass into view in the mirror, perhaps asking one or two to pause and show you something of their lives. Remember that these are the faces of your own family, and you should feel at ease and comfortable with them. They live in your blood. Offer more of the mugwort herb to smolder, and waft the incense to the faces in the mirror.

Mirror of time and love, I offer the scent of remembrance unto my mother heritage. Blessed be the mothers of my family now and through all time. Without them, without their sacrifices and love, I would not be. Blessed be the wombs that have carried the children of my line. Blessed be the hearts that love the children of my line. Blessed be the eyes that see, the hands that heal. Blessed be my family.

This meditation can also be used as part of a spell for fertility simply by adding a request to your mothers in time to help you to pass on the blood of your line:

Mothers of mine, mothers in time, you who have passed the blood of my line: hear me in my call to thee, aid me now to emulate thee. You have had your child and now I seek mine. Help me to carry on our family line. Give unto me thy support for our family, guide new life into me, that I as thee may blessed be. This is my call unto thee maternally, that as I will so mote it be.

When you have completed your visit with your ancestry, snuff out the candle. Waft the incense to your mirror:

Mirror mine I clear thee now. Images gone, memories linger, thy purpose has been fulfilled and you are sent to your rest.

Cover the mirror with a black cloth, open your circle, and put away your tools.

Reincarnation: We Shall Live Again

By Marguerite Elsbeth

We all know that someday we will experience death of the physical body. This destiny is part of the human condition, and for most there is no escape. For those who believe in reincarnation, however, a return from death into a new body marks an adventurous beginning after a period of rest.

The Return Home

Many religions teach us that when we die, we are returning to our spiritual home—the Otherworld or the land of the ancestors. The return home is symbolic of death, yet it does not indicate total destruction of the self. Rather, it implies a reintegration of the human spirit with the Great Spirit; the soul and spirit have simply relinquished their human form to return to their true essence for a time.

Tibetan Buddhists perceive an afterlife wherein the soul is said to travel through three states of transition. First, there is light and bliss. Next, the soul has a series of visions, some good and some bad. The soul is then judged according to the actions and responses it demonstrated in life. Finally, the soul is called to a new incarnation and proceeds to follow a path leading back into rebirth.

The belief in reincarnation does not solely originate from Eastern religions; many leading Christian and Jewish

religious scholars support the idea, and it is taught among our European, African, and Native American ancestors. For instance, when death calls to the Nordic and Germanic peoples to return to their ancestral home, it is common to hear the old ones say: "We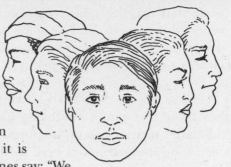
shall come again." Among the Lapp, a deceased relation is said to appear in the dreams of a woman who is near to giving birth, informing her which ancestor will be born again in the body of her infant. Reincarnation was also a dominant theme among the Celts in Druidic times; they believed that the spirit rested after death, until it was time for the soul to return again to earth. Some West African tribes refer to reincarnation as "the shooting forth of a branch." The Yoruba consult a Santero, or priest of Ifa, god of divination, soon after a child is born, in order to determine what ancestral soul has come back into life.

The Paiute Indians of North America perform the Ghost Dance, a ceremony wherein the dancers enter into a trance-state in order to commune with their ancestors. Spiraling round and round, they sing, "We shall live again," in hopes the ancestors will return to repopulate the earth. The Lenape Indians of Delaware and New Jersey say that the pure of heart can recall their former lives. These days, anyone who has had an out-of-body or near-death experience knows they will survive death to live again.

THE SPIRAL DANCE

While feelings of grief and sorrow accompany the loss of a loved one, most contemporary indigenous cultures do not view death as something to be feared. This is because they see the demise of the physical body as one aspect of the synchronistic cycle of life.

The Earth spins on its axis as part of the cycle of life. The life-cycle is a never-ending spiral wherein we are each objects in motion. The spiral symbolizes the evolutionary process, animating breath and vivifying spirit comprising the progressive development of the dance of life. This spiral dance can impel our motion up or down, towards constructive or destructive action, yet death remains a part of the synchronicity of the life cycle.

Cosmic Memory

Everything that comes into being has its origin in the cosmos. Visionaries such as Joan of Arc, Edgar Cayce, and Black Elk were able to tap into memories held by the cosmic ether. However, most of us cannot perceive the spiritual realms with the ordinary senses; we need to develop supersensory perception in order to see past events. Many adults and children are known to have past life recall, although true memories pertaining to another existence are far more prevalent in the young. Children between the ages of two and four frequently often offer spontaneous remarks alluding to previous lives. While a limited vocabulary makes it difficult to reveal all that is remembered, it is not uncommon to hear children naming former relatives, the towns in which they lived, or the possessions they once owned.

Once we enter into adulthood, the subconscious mind has been exposed to an abundance of extraneous information; therefore, even if we do catch a glimpse of a former life, we tend to confuse our memories. It is because of this jumble that past life memories are likely to be dismissed as dreams and fancies, hallucinations, or simple educated guesses.

Who You Were Now

We have all experienced déjà vu, the vaguely familiar recognition of a person, place, or thing never before seen. When this sensation occurs, the soul is remembering. The soul has an emotional quality; it reveals itself through our instincts and feelings, and through it we are connected to all our ancestral memories.

The soul is interwoven with the subconscious mind, the place from which our dreams emerge. Dreams can be a potent venue for past life recall. The spirits of the past take many forms in our dreams. Also, dreams are how the elements, demons, gods, and spirits talk to us about ourselves and the situations and conditions that surround us. Sometimes, dreams can lead us astray with fanciful imaginings based on every thought, word, deed, picture, feeling, and situation we've ever experienced. This is why, when seeking to reconstruct our past lives, we may be led to reinvent ourselves in startling and erroneous ways. We cannot all have been Cleopatra, Dion Fortune, Crazy Horse, or the King of Atlantis.

Archetypal memories are inherited from a particular cultural group of people. These spirits may influence our perceptions, function as energy forms, be activated by inner or outer situations and problems, express themselves through our daily actions and in dream sequences. However, while archetypes grant us insight to emotional wants and needs, we cannot be them for they are greater than us. In past lives, we were likely ordinary people leading ordinary lives.

Past Life Recall

All spiritual traditions say that life is eternal, without beginning or end. Just as there are seasonal cycles in nature, human beings are born, expand to fullness, die, and are born again, thus continuing the natural order of creation. Seeking knowledge of our personal process of continuous return to physical existence can be beneficial, helping us to remember some unfinished business, or providing us with understanding regarding difficulties in this life.

Yet, keep in mind that we all experience many incarnations in one lifetime. Going back in time only stands to reveal one stopping point among the many crossroads of life. No matter who you once were, what remains is the emotional essence of all your old personalities combined. Now, these memories, feelings, and shadowy images are merged within a new personality. Your parents, relations, and friends, along with all the circumstances comprising your life-experience, are bound together to indicate who you were and what you may potentially become.

This means that everything you need to deepen and grow is currently at your disposal. Whether you can remember your past lives or not, you are living in the quintessential moment of your past, present, and future self right now.

WIDDERSHINS

By Sedwin

Dictionaries describe widdershins as "going against" or "to move in a wrong or contrary direction." The word *widdershins* is German and has a first recorded use in 1513. Widdershins is movement in a counterclockwise direction, the opposite of deosil, or clockwise—sunwise—motion.

Doing something with a widdershins motion has been called the "Witch's way." In ancient Scotland it was believed to be unlucky or evil to walk around a churchyard in a counterclockwise direction. Even today there is a general perception that moving widdershins represents an undoing, regressive, and backward energy. On the one hand, it is used for negative magical purposes; however, it is also said to be used for dispersing negative energies or diseases.

The idea that clockwise is the "right" way to move may have its roots with sundials. Our early ancestors were aware of and celebrated the movements of the Sun and Moon. Because they were keen observers, they must have been aware of shadows moving from left to right as the Sun moved through the sky each day. Because the Sun angles shadows toward the north (in the Northern Hemisphere), early Europeans would have faced north to see their own shadows. It was natural that the design of the earliest sundials required people to face north in order to read them. Taking their cue from the Sun, movement in sacred ritual also followed the deosil (clockwise) direction.

According to Starhawk in *The Spiral Dance*, widdershins "is used for decrease and banishings." While widdershins movement in ritual seems to have been avoided by many Wiccans (except for occasional use in dispersing the circle), people are beginning to reevaluate its merits.

Movement in both directions helps to stir the cauldron of ritual and raise a balanced energy. Using widdershins-only direction in ritual during winter months can be beneficial for quiet self-work.

When working deosil with the cardinal directions, we build energy that moves outward. Starting in the east, the place of the mind, we begin with knowledge. In the south, the place of spirit, we build heat an energy. The place of emotions, the west, gives us love and intuition to shape our intentions. Finally, north, the place of the body, nature, sustenance, and creativity, helps us move the energy of ritual out into the universe.

Working widdershins begins in the west where we call on courage for the inward journey. The heat of south burns away false masks to allow us to see who we really are. As we approach our inner selves, we begin to heal the wounds that life can inflict on us. Moving to the east we begin to learn about our true selves and who we are. Then we are able to move to the north, place of death, birth, and growth. Here we come to our center, home of spirit. In discovering our true spirit, we find the divine. By moving within we can discover the spark that links us with the web of all things in the universe.

In ritual and self-work, the act of moving inward ultimately brings us back out. In essence, we are dancers moving through the spiral dance that is our lives. It has its cycles of inward motion where we nurture our souls, which, in turn, prepares us to continue our dance and sweep outward with beauty and energy to enrich the world around us. We are but a mirror of Mother Earth going through our own seasons.

May your self work of the winter season be richly rewarding.

Ministering to the Grieving
Pagan Funeral Rites

By M. Macha NightMare

The number of people now following Pagan paths in this country has grown considerably in recent years. Unfortunately, practitioners are still too few to meet the demand of training newcomers. To assist in the effort to train, I offer the following information about working with the dying and their loved ones and creating effective funerals and memorials for Pagans.

Paganism draws from many sources. In general, Pagans have many notions about what death means, and where we go after we die. Some feel strongly about being cremated, while others are passionate about green burials. It is important to keep in mind, though, that I know of no law in any state that requires embalming. Since most Pagans view the decay of the body as a matrix for new life, preserving the body is not in keeping with Pagan notions. In my experience, most clergy and funeral professionals are open to collaboration on creating an effective ceremony that meets the needs of all mourners. However, if that is not the case, you can always create a different rite for Pagan survivors in addition to the more conventional one for the family. Our country today is multicultural and multifaith. Our loved ones who are dying and those who are grieving their loss are often not Pagan. Now is not the time to advance your own spiritual agenda; keep in mind that everyone suffers the pain of loss, not just you. It is important to respect the feelings and faith traditions of everyone involved in a dying.

While Pagans may have many beliefs about death and dying, many of us have great talent in employing intuition in our work—that is, true intuitive knowledge that comes from a direct perception. If a loved one is undergoing a prolonged transition from life to death, perhaps wasting from a disease, you have the opportunity to sit vigil with the dying. Since each death, like each birth, is unique, and has its own sequence, process and pace, sitting vigil is very similar to midwifing a birth. This is a time to use your intuition in order to do what is best for your dying loved one. Therefore, take your cues about what you should do from the dying person. If she is responsive to being lead through a guided meditation, then do a meditation.

Death is often a time when old, unresolved interpersonal conflicts resurface. But death offers a blessed opportunity for healing rifts. Be aware that those who are going through the passage will be on an emotional roller coaster, from anger to acceptance. Allow for behavior that may be deemed peculiar or unacceptable under normal circumstances. Whether a death is expected or sudden, I recommend that if at all possible all family and loved ones be involved in washing and preparing the body for disposal. This way, the absolute truth of the loss can be understood by all on a more kinesthetic, gut level. To do this, you should respectfully and lovingly, using clear spring water, wash and bless each part of the body, from the toes to the top of the head. Or you may wish to use water mixed with salt and bay instead of plain water. Speak aloud a blessings in the presence of each other and your deceased.

After you have washed the body, you may wish to anoint it with a pleasant-smelling oil that retards the growth of bacteria. A citrus oil base combined with rosemary works well for this. You can also add rose for love, lavender for peace, frankincense, honey, myrrh, or cypress. Some Pagans also rub red ochre pigment all over the body.

At this point, if the death occurred in the home, call the local coroner or funeral director to pick up the body. Have the necessary garments, perhaps ritual robes, ready to give to the funeral professionals. Instead of clothing, you may wish your beloved to be laid out under a sheet, blanket, or other cloth. Or you may wish to wrap the body in silk, scented with the herbs mentioned above or others of your preference.

Though we may be rigid in our attitudes about what is the right method of disposal or the right service, always keep in mind the wishes of everyone involved—particularly the wishes of the newly deceased. In most states, the wishes of a dying person can be ensured by her having executed a durable power of attorney naming the person or persons she most trusts to carry out her wishes. These wishes must be kept in mind when planning a funeral or memorial.

One area in which Pagan and non-Pagan survivors can usually collaborate is in building an altar in memory of the deceased. Use your collective creativity to encorporate photographs, jewelry, and other belongings of the loved one in an altar that will honor and celebrate the person whose loss you both mourn.

Also, at the funeral you can provide the opportunity for everyone to share personal stories about the beloved. I recommend using a "talking stick" method. For this, you may wish to use an object that belonged to the deceased, such as a trowel if she had been a gardener, a glove if she played baseball, or a wooden spoon if she loved to cook. To ensure that everyone will have an opportunity to speak, explain the process and suggest a time limit. Have plenty of tissue on hand too, as these stories often elicit tears.

You may wish the conclude the ceremony with everyone singing this simple round: "When we are gone, they will remain, wind and rock, fire and rain. They will remain when we return. The wind will blow and the fire will burn."

If you're like most people, you probably feel at a loss as to what to say to a friend who has recently lost someone to death. Remember that grief has no timetable. It is unkind to say to someone in mourning, "It's been a year now; it's time for you to stop crying and get on with your life." Unfortunately, our mundane culture expects us to soldier on in spite of the profound emotional shock that death engenders. Grief should be respected, and we should be patient.

Pagans celebrate our beloved dead in community once a year at Samhain, the night when the veil that divides the worlds is thinnest. This offers us an opportunity to mourn our dead, this time collectively rather than individually.

May these suggestions help you and your loved ones to share the sacred time of crossing over. Remind yourself, when you are overcome with grief and find no way to openly express it, that what is remembered, lives. We keep our loved ones alive in our memories.

Dark Moon Banishing Ritual

By Maria Kay Simms

This ritual is intended for use during the final phase of the Moon, at or just past the time when only a sliver of waning crescent can be seen before dawn. Consult your astrological calendar to make sure that you are working before the time of the actual conjunction of Moon with Sun which marks the New Moon. It is this phase of the Moon that is best for rites of banishing. It is a time when you can most easily release what is no longer needed in your life. You can bring closure to whatever has caused you negative feelings or grief. You can break habits that are injurious to your health and spirit.

Preparation

Drape your altar in black cloth, and arrange on it a black candle in a metal holder. Also, prepare a spool of black thread, a banishing oil (frankincense, myrrh, lemon, pine, rosemary, or rue), a bowl of water, salt, incense stick in a burner, and matches. Your athame or wand may also be used, but are not essential. Place candles at the four quarters of your circle area: yellow in the east, red in the south, blue in the west, and green in the north. Soft music may be played in the background, if desired. Turn off the phone so you won't be interrupted during the ritual.

Centering—Kneel before your altar, close your eyes, and breathe deeply while you relax. When you feel ready, anoint your forehead with a drop of oil, and say: "Dark Queen, before your altar, at dark of Moon this night, I kneel to ask your blessing and your magic in this rite."

Cleansing and Consecration of the Elements—Light the incense. Draw a pentagram in the air over the bowl of water, saying: "In the name of the Dark Goddess I do banish and cast from thee all that is impure and unclean." Motion with your hand as if casting off, and raise your hand to the sky to gather energy. Touch the water with your finger and visualize energy flowing into it as you say: "I do charge thee to my magical purpose." Use the same procedure to cleanse and charge the salt and the lighted incense.

Calling of the Quarters and Casting the Circle—Go to the north, and light the green candle, saying: "By the Earth that is Her body." Go to the east, and light the yellow candle, saying: "By the air that is Her breath." Go to the south; light the red candle, saying: "By the fire that is Her spirit." Go to the west; light the blue candle, saying: "By the water that is Her womb and blood." Walk once more clockwise around the circle, saying: "In the name of the eternal Goddess, and of Her dark aspect, Crone, who stands at the portal of death, sees beyond and is midwife to new birth—I bless and consecrate this sacred circle of power."

The Rite of Banishing—Return to your altar. Anoint the black candle with oil. Cleanse it with water, saying: "With the power of water I do cleanse this tool." Sprinkle it with salt, saying: "With the power of earth, I do cleanse this tool." Pass it through the incense smoke, saying: "With the powers of fire and air, I do cleanse this tool." Replace the candle in its holder.

Break off a three-foot length of black thread. Holding it in your hands, think about what has bound you in the past. As you think of each negative emotion you wish to banish, tie a knot in the thread and feel how much you have allowed that binding to restrict you. Then focus not upon things or people, but rather on your own negative emotions. Know that nobody or nothing can force you feel bad unless you give it power over you. Take back your power! When you change inside, the outer world will respond to you. You will find that what you thought prevented your sense of serenity, success, or happiness has become insignificant. You have now released it and moved on in new strength.

When you are ready, take up the candle and wind the knotted thread tightly around it. Sprinkle the bound candle with water, saying: "With the power of water, I do charge this tool and arm it to my will." Sprinkle with salt, saying: "With the power of earth, I charge this tool and arm it to my will." Pass the candle through the incense smoke, saying: "With powers of fire and air, I charge this tool and arm it to my will." Replace the candle.

Invocation of the Dark Goddess—Say, "O, Dark Lady, Queen of Wisdom, I invoke and call thee. Let thy power flow in my soul. Let this magic set me free." Light the black candle, and continue: "Burn, O flame of dark Spirit, that I may clearly see. What shall no longer bind shall no longer harm me, so mote it be!" As the candle burns, sit in mediation before it. Let the candle burn down, meditating until it is finished. Then, close your circle formally.

Closing of the Circle—Say to the Dark Goddess: "Dark Queen, as now we bid farewell I see the endings that I now accept. I give my thanks to thee." Go the north, and say: "By the earth that is thy body, I thank thee for strength and healing. Farewell, and blessed be." Extinguish the green candle. Go the east, and say: "By the air that is thy breath, I thank thee for clarity and new winds of change in my life." Extinguish the yellow candle. Go to the south, and say: "By the fire that is thy spirit, I thank thee for the courage and the will to change." Extinguish the red candle. Go to the west, and say: "By the water that is thy womb and blood, I thank thee for the release of negative emotion, and for the serenity in my soul." Extinguish the blue candle. At this point, say: "May all beings and elementals attracted to this rite now go on their way in peace. This circle is open, but never broken. Merry meet, merry part, and merry meet again. Blessed be."

Concluding the Spell—If any wax or thread residue remains of the black candle after it has burned, bury it in the ground, walking away from the spot without looking back. Know now that as this spell ends, as with all endings, something else will begin to fill the void. When one door closes, another opens.

The Dark Goddess within you has now released that which has ended; now may she cut the cord as midwife to release a new birth of creativity into your life. Perhaps you will begin to dream, now, as the dark Moon turns to New, of what will soon begin. And remember: when the Spirit moves you, work magic at the New Moon to open yourself to new possibilities.

WORKING WITH THE SIDHE

BY ANN MOURA

The second dark Moon to occur in a Solar month is a reflection of the Full Moon in the Otherworld, and provides a glimpse into it. As such, it is called the Other Moon, Fairy Moon, or Sidhe Moon, and is thought to enhance craft work that calls on the fairy powers and seeks the aid of the sidhe in fairy magics, familiar magics, and companion magics.

During the Sidhe Moon, a sidhe companion may be honored or may be sought to participate in a companion quest. The Sidhe Moon may also be used as a time for your companion to visit home, or perhaps take you along to his.

Cultural viewpoints on the sidhe vary, but in earlier times the fairy folk were not considered diminutive, but taller and more slender than the average human. The image of fairies today, formulated over the past century, is similar to the older concept of devas—the energies of plants, stones, trees, rivers, and other nonanimal entities of nature. The sidhe are sometimes called elves and fairies, and are often subdivided into separate manifestations such as pixies, leprechauns, brownies, and other little people.

A thorough research into how the sidhe are perceived was conducted by W. Y. Evans-Wentz in 1911. Testimony, traditions, theories, religious significance, and his own conclusions were published in his book, *The Fairy Faith In Celtic Countries,* offering a number of associations for who the sidhe are and how they contact and interact with humans. Over time, the other people have been seen as a separate race, as deities, as the spirits of the dead, and as a psychological remnant derived from a tradition of nature reverence found in cults focused on tree, well, fountain, and stone veneration. If you consider the Celtic tradition of rebirth, it makes it likely that the spirit interpretation derives from the death process of entering into Underworld, passing to Summerland for a time of recuperation from the psychological, physical, and emotional rigors of the life just exited, and then chosing to remain unreborn but close to humanity by dwelling for a time in Otherworld rather than moving back into mortal life through the cauldron of rebirth.

With sidhe magic, then, your focus is very important. You could end up calling on another guiding spirit as easily as the sidhe, so always be aware of the distinct differences between the two. After the quest, you may want to find a crystal—flourites and labradorites are excellent—to act as a focal point and gateway for your companion. When calling upon the sidhe for aid in magical workings, prepare the atmosphere by setting out the gateway crystal and burning some lavender or rosemary incense. Candles should be light gray, lavender, or mauve, and your circle casting starts at the west, with your altar positioned so you face west.

Growing herbs, particularly rosemary shrubs, and planting your yard with elder, birch, willow, elm, or rowan trees will help attract the presence of the other people to your home. Milk and flowers, grain, or bread are traditionally left outside for the fair folk, especially on nights of the Full Moon. Depending on the season and location, wine, whiskey, beer, blackberry, currant, raspberry, or cranberry juices, or coconut milk may be an appropriate gift. Find a secluded spot or enticing niche where you can set up a space dedicated to the Other People. Show your desire to work with them by making your home agreeable. They like a clean home, green plants, flowers, trees, an occasional remembrance with food, flowers, and beverage, as well as the scent of rosemary and lavender. These two herbs are used in spellwork for protection, cleansing, purification, and opening the psychic centers, so their energies are attuned to the sidhe. Be sure not to grow broom around your house as this plant, with its heavy musty odor, is offensive to the Other People. When creating or purchasing your besom (ritual broom), one made of straw, palm fronds, or other such material is better than  broom plant. Fairies can be called into a blade of straw, which is then laid at the door to dissuade intruders during ritual. Because fairies often inhabit straw, never burn any without giving them warning and providing an alternate dwelling.

In working sidhe magic, any divine aspects you address should be associated with Otherworld—the Lady and the Lord of Greenwood or the Wildwood, Titania or Mab, and Oberon or Fearn. There are other names you can associate with the rulers of Otherworld, or you may simply use a generic title such as Lady and Lord of the Sidhe, Queen and King of Otherworld. When setting up your altar for circle casting, use dandelion root or burdock root instead of salt for the consecrating elements of earth, and water in the preparation of blessed water.

Salt is both a purifier and a preservative, which is appropriate for both light and dark power magics, but not for the already pure and undying realms of Otherworld. Almagamated metals, ceramics, pottery, and tools of copper, tin, gold, and silver are also better than anything made of iron. Natural objects such as shells, gourds, and seed pods are excellent for use on the altar for bowls and cups.

Manners are also important with fairy magics. One basic rule is that you have to give a gift to receive a gift, which is a typical witchcraft practice in using objects from nature. Another basic rule is that you should not thank the Other People, for this can come across as dismissive—"you've done what I wanted, so run along now"—and terminates a relationship. Instead, express your appreciation by praising the meaningfulness of what you have gained, and you will leave the lines of communication open.

Part of the reason for leaving offerings to the sidhe is so they are aware of your desire to express kinship and to remain in a relationship with them. Along with giving and receiving gifts comes the rule of never rejecting a fairy gift. These little tokens and items that appear out of nowhere always have a sensation about them that lets you know what they are. The gifts could be simple things like seed pods that make perfect altar bowls, a shiny pebble that sparkles at you, or a feather dropped at your doorstep.

By retaining your childlike sense of wonder in nature you can open the gateways between the worlds with greater ease. Visiting with the sidhe can be accomplished through astral travel, meditation, and by melting the barriers between the worlds—as occurs during Samhain and by invitation. When you enter, do not look back, as this can be interpreted as fear or hesitancy, and it will propel you out the way you came in. To leave Otherworld, you then turn around and see your entry point as a dark spot in the scenery, which as you approach grows in size until you pass through it and are back at your place of origin.

Ancient Norse Oracles in the Neo-Pagan World

By Diana L. Paxson

You've met her in a thousand tales—about the Gypsy fortune-teller, or the Witch in the wood, or the pythonee perched on her tripod at Delphi. And behind them sit the shadowy figures of the holy Three who spin our fates. These tales are telling us one thing—that ways of foreseeing the future are found the world over. Every culture has its soothsayer—whether on a street corner or a psychic hot-line—whose pronouncements are sought by those in need.

In general, the gift of truth-seeing is a mixed blessing, descending without warning on the seer—who has no choice but to pour out prophecies to disbelieving ears—and often flickering in and out of perception in frustrating glimpses which disturb without enlightening.

It is assumed by most people that these talents must be inborn, and can neither be fostered nor controlled. But what if there were another way—a disciplined, workmanlike craft of seership which could unlock a potential for prophecy in all of us without any harm? Many ancient cultures did indeed have such traditions, and trained seers had an honored place in their societies. In the Mediterranean world, for instance, the people came one by one to the oracle, who resided at a location where the earth power was strong and the gates between the worlds opened easily. In northern Europe, the seers travelled from place to place, gathering the people and answering their questions.

In today's more secular society, channelers and psychic readers are common. Openly or in secret, people seek their services, but there is, for the most part, no community environment to support either the seer or the seeker. In the Pagan community, meanwhile, the tradition of divining for ourselves and others is fostered through the use of Tarot, I-Ching, pendulum, and several other means. But in the past ten years, a new tradition of oracle-work based on the practices of ancient Scandinavia has developed. Beginning with the work of Hrafnar, an Asatru group in northern California, this practice has spread not only to the rest of North Ameria but to Europe as well.

In 1989, I began an attempt to recover the techniques of oracular seidh and develop a process that would enable me to serve the Pagan community just as the seers of the north served their people long ago. The work was based on the ancient lore, as studied as the basis of our experience in ritual and shamanic and other types of trance-work.

The best description we have for any Viking religious ritual is the account of Thorbjorg, called "the Little Voelva." The story is in *The Saga of Eric the Red,* and it tells how Voelva came to a farmstead, and, after she had had time to rest and make contact with the spirits of the place, sat upon a raised platform to answer questions from the people. In order for her to go into trance, a young woman was found who knew the sacred song. Voelva was able not only to tell the farm folk when the famine would end, but foretold the future of the girl and many others. In the *Elder Edda,* a collection of Viking Age mythological poems, there are several accounts in which Odin visits the Underworld and calls upon the archetypal Voelva for information about the past, the present, and things to come. Their interchanges have a formulaic quality which suggests they were modeled on actual dialogue.

With this information, I was able to create a basic ritual format, consisting of an an introductory section, a journey to the Underworld, and an answering of questions.

The first part, in which we establish sacred space and invoke Freyja and Odin, the two deities traditionally associated with seidh craft, serves to help people who are often coming from a variety of Pagan traditions move into the Germanic sector of the collective unconscious. In addition to the gods, we call on the three Norne, or weavers of fate, to help us speak and hear clearly, as well as on the ancestors to whose realm we are travelling and on one or more "power animals" who assist the seers.

By the time we have finished the first part, everyone will be involved in the ritual experience and ready to settle down for the pathworking. Our standard route takes us inward to the plain of Midgard that lies within the mind with the Worldtree as its central axis. From here we can journey to any of the nine worlds, but we have found that Hellate kingdom, where most of the ancestors wait, is the most useful place from which to answer questions.

Together, the group makes the journey to the gate. And here everyone stops. The seer then ascends the *seidhjhallr*, an elevated chair also known as the "high seat," and gives formal consent to go further. Of necessity, the process must be interactive, as the people raise energy which the seer will use to seek wisdom for the people. The group, for instance, may sing a song which the seer has been conditioned to respond to by sinking into a much deeper trance in which all bodily functions, except the ability to speak, are curtailed. From this point on, the guide who has been leading the ritual becomes the "ground control" who connects the seer with the outside world. The guide uses formulaic expressions to focus the seers' attention and facilitate his or her interaction with the people who have questions. When all questions have been asked, the guide brings the seer back through the gate and leads everyone back to the Upper World.

In general, answers may come in a variety of ways from seers. Sometimes the seer simply has a sense of certainty, or is given words. Often, the question acts as a stimulus which causes a vision to form. Sometimes it is enough to simply describe what is seen; at other times, the seer will offer an interpretation of meaning. The imagery is often extremely symbolic. Responses generally make sense only to the person who asked the question. I have found that questions about life choices, relationships, and spiritual direction generate the most useful answers.

For example, at one session when I was in the high seat, a woman asked whether she should change jobs. She had been working on a project for several years, she said, and didn't seem to be getting anywhere. The image that came to me in response was of a mouse in a wheatfield, scurrying about and making tunnels between the stalks, gathering up fallen grains, one by one. My interpretation was that she should keep at it, and eventually she would achieve her goal. Later I learned that the woman was a biologist who had been waitressing every winter in order to earn money to continue her summer fieldwork, a study of rodents in grassland!

Admittedly, the people who receive good answers are the ones most likely to tell us about it afterward. Not all answers will be on target, and some do not make sense until much later. Some answers may simply be generally sound advice, but because the questioner is psychically open, he or she is often able to hear the response in a way impossible when one is in an ordinary state of consciousness.

When the crowd is large, or the seers are new, only a few questions may be answered at a time. An experienced seer, however, can answer up to forty questions in a single session. Perhaps because everyone is in a state of rapport at the sessions I have attended, answers can also cause an unexpectedly emotional reaction among the seekers. My groups often stations "wardens" around the circle to help anyone who needs comfort or grounding. We also try to provide for follow-up counselling if needed.

Seidh sessions have taken place in a wide variety of settings— underground or on rooftops, in a redwood circle or an open hillside, in hotel rooms and living rooms, and in a tent in the rain. Audiences have ranged from dedicated followers of the Norse tradition to the general Pagan community to people with no background at all. Our group has appeared at festivals where people save up their questions all year, and come back to ask them. We have found that when the procedure is properly conducted, both seers and questioners remain psychically and psychologically safe.

Although by the Viking period, seidh seems to have been practiced mostly by women or gay men, we have found that with discipline, practice, and the support of a trained group, almost anyone can open up sufficiently to get useful answers, and neither gender nor gender preference determines skill.

In the course of conducting workshops in oracular seidh over the past few years, I have begun to understand not only how the process works, but why. The seidh-rite of the North is only one example of an oracular tradition whose essential elements can be identified in a variety of cultures—an intuitive skill which is native to the human psyche, though in most modern societies repressed. The larger society is gradually coming to understand the validity of intuition and the need for contact with the Divine, but we will not recover the full potential of our ancestors' religion until our spiritual practice takes place within the context of a supportive and educated community.

Holda: The Goddess of Yule

By Lily Gardner

At Yule, the Wheel of the Year seems to halt and darkness reigns. At this time we honor the Teutonic goddess, Holda, who ruled for centuries as a kindly sky goddess until Christianity gained influence and turned her from saint to temptress and hag. Though nearly unknown in the United States, she is still burned in effigy in some rural areas of Germany.

As a sky goddess, Holda combed her golden hair to make the sunshine; when she washed her linens, it rained; smoke from her fire made fog; and when she shook her feather quilts, it snowed. As the divine mother goddess, Holda taught her people to spin and weave cloth.

It was the worship of Holda that inspired the Saint Ursula legend of the Middle Ages. Saint Ursula, a virgin princess sailing the Rhine with her eleven thousand maiden attendants, was struck down by a band of marauding Huns. She was said to have been martyred on October 21, A.D. 237—this despite the fact that the Huns who killed her weren't in force for another two hundred years. Nevertheless, because of her great modesty and piety, the Church made Ursula a saint, and at the same time it encouraged a celebratory custom of rolling a decorated ship mounted on wheels through the German villages on her feast day. In times past, Holda was known to sail a silver boat (the Moon) through the night skies and disappear into the mountains at dawn. By inventing Saint Ursula, the Catholic clergy transformed Pagan Moon worship into a religious practice honoring their new saint.

Even today, Mt. Horselberg is still called "Dame Holda's Court" by locals in Eisenach, Germany. This is the site where Holda was said to have seduced Tannhauser in the thirteenth-century legend of "Venus and Tannhauser," a tale later made famous by Swinburne, the poet, and Richard Wagner, the composer. Legend has it that the poet knight, Tannhauser, caught a glimpse of the magnificent goddess as he rode past the mountain. She beckoned to him and he followed her into the caverns of Horselberg, where they lived for seven years. Eventually, Tannhauser left Holda and asked for forgiveness from his local priest, who passed him to another priest, and so on, from priest to priest to bishop till eventually he sat before Pope Urban. The pope declared that his own scepter would sprout green leaves before Tannhauser could hope to be forgiven for such debauchery. In despair, Tannhauser returned to Holda and was never seen again by mortals. Three days later, Pope Urban's scepter sprouted leaves, and Tannhauser was summoned but never found.

Tannhauser's manservant, Trusty Eckhart, figures in another Holda legend. It is said that Trusty Eckhart sits by the side of the road during the season of Yule to warn travelers to find shelter from the Wild Hunt. The Wild Hunt is a train of demons and hellhounds that scream and howl through stormy weather. In this legend, the train is led by Holda, who, along with her train of demons, kidnaps Eckhart and forces him to ride the storms in the Wild Hunt until the end of time. Any person found outdoors during a storm can be swept up into the train. Holda's reputation for kidnapping travelers, and also unbaptized babies, according to another legend, is the reason why she is burnt in effigy in Eisfeld, Germany.

Hans Christian Andersen used Holda as the basis for the Snow Queen, from the tale of the same name. The Snow Queen, the personification of the frozen, dangerous, Danish winter, was very beautiful but her kisses were freezing. Her soldiers, her servants, and her clothing was made of snowflakes, and her throne rested on a frozen lake. The Snow Queen was neither good nor evil, but she was as deadly.

Holda became the crone figure in the Grimm's nineteenth-century fairy tale, "Mother Holle." In the story, a virtuous young woman fell down a well trying to retrieve her spinning reel. Instead of treading water at the bottom of the well, the girl found herself in a rural landscape much like her home. There she encountered Mother Holle, an old woman with matted gray hair and large, ugly teeth. The girl worked diligently for the old woman and was rewarded. When the hard-working girl returned home, she was covered with gold. Her lazy sister tried her luck with Frau Holle, but because she was lazy and selfish, she was punished and returned home covered with pitch that would not wash off.

These legends contain two common threads: Holda's influence over the weather and her interest in domestic arts. The spinning wheel is Holda's symbol, and spinning and weaving her special province. To honor Holda during the season of Yule, no wheels were used. Or as the old saying put it: "From Yule till New Year's Day, neither wheel nor windlass must go round." The idea being, too, that as the Sun seems to stand still at Yule, so we cease the movement of our wheels. Once the Wheel of the Year turns anew on New Year's Day, so we begin again. Yule is Holda's feast day. Honor her by quieting the motion of your life for this one day when the "Sun stands still."

MOTHER BERHTA'S COMING TO TOWN

BY STEVEN POSCH

You've heard of Mother Berhta, right? Every year, during the season of Yule, there she is, leering from every billboard and greeting card, riding her goat Gnasher Skeggi with greasy old sack slung over her shoulder, brimming with wonderful presents. But it could be filled instead with squirming, cauldron-bound children. With Mother Berhta, you can never tell for sure.

Oh, I've heard about the old days, before Berhta made it big. Pagan households were few and far between in those times. Berhta was not a baby-napper back then.

Back in the old days, too, the days would grow cold and the nights would grow long, and suddenly it would be Mother Night, the night that gives birth to the rest of the year—also known as Midwinter's Eve, the longest night of all. From out of the darkness, you would hear the sound of bells, which meant You Know Who was coming. And sure enough, soon there'd be a pounding on the door to make the windows rattle, the door would fly open, and in would stride Mother Berhta, like an indoor blizzard.

"Good Yule, you Yule-time fools!" she hollers, dropping the goatskin sack on the floor, and dragging out the feast. And oh, what a feast! Roast goose stuffed with chestnuts, turkey with wild rice dressing, plum puddings, cranberries, pizza—whatever it is that you most like to eat. Berhta brings more food than anyone can eat in all thirteen nights of Yule, much less one sitting.

Then, with an ear-to-ear grin, old Mother B hollers, "Come 'ere ya old goat!" and Gnasher Skeggi prances innocently. Berhta then grabs him by the forelock and pulls his head back, and pht! The athame flashes and the goat's throat is cut, neat as you please! Mother Berhta is not a goddess for the faint-hearted. In a jiffy, she guts him and skins him and chops him into little pieces to throw in the cauldron with some onion, a little garlic, some sage, a pinch of rosemary. Et voila! Goat stew!

And just as everyone sits down to eat, Mother Berhta tosses her old goatskin sack down on the floor right next to the table, yelling: "Throw the bones in here, and don't break any!"

Of course as we eat we are careful to do just as she asked. When the feast is over, Berhta grabs the sack and gives it a shake, and in a voice to wake the dead she bellows, "Come on out, you old goat!" and sure enough, out capers Gnasher Skeggi, just as raunchy and as randy as ever. Mother Berhta slings the sack over her shoulder, hops up onto Skeggi's back, and off she goes.

And don't forget the presents. Along with the feast out of her sack come presents like you've never seen before, in all shapes, colors, sizes, and styles.

Of course, it went this way for I don't know how many years, until one day everything changed. A little boy, whose name I'm afraid nobody remembers anymore, broke one of the bones when throwing it back into Berhta's sack. So when Berhta gave the sack a big shake and hollered, "Come on out, you old goat!" Out hobbled poor old Gnasher Skeggi on three legs, looking not at all happy.

346

Well! In all those years of Berhta, nobody had ever seen her quite as angry as this. "You imbeciles!" she yelled. "Now I'll have to carry my goat instead of riding him!"—which, of course, is where that expression comes from, if you've ever heard it before.

Before anybody realized what was happening, Berhta had grabbed the little bone-breaker by the scruff of his neck and stuffed him into her sack just like that. Then, slinging the sack over one shoulder and Skeggi over the other, she tromped out into the dark. I'm sure I don't need to tell you that nobody ever saw that little boy again. And now, on Midwinter's Eve, when the door flies open and Mother Berhta comes storming into your living room, you never know for sure whether she's going to dump gifts out of her sack—or stuff little kids in!

THE HISTORY OF MOTHER BERHTA

I first heard of Berhta maybe thirteen or fourteen years ago. My coven was living together at the time, and Yule was coming up. We'd been doing a lot of research, and one interesting thing we discovered was that—contrary to what you might think, with Santa Claus's Yule monopoly in this culture—in most places in Europe, the one who brings gifts around Solstice is usually an old woman, a crone. In Russia, they called her Babushka, "little granny." Italians have Befana, and they admit she's a Witch—in fact she even rides in on a broom. Germany is filled with different Yule crones, all with funny names: Budelfrau, Buzebergt, and Holle. But of all the winter hags of Germany, the meanest and the nastiest, was Frau Berhta, who was also called Percht. Her special day was Old Yule, the last of the thirteen days of Yule.

In Minnesota, where I live, the climate is rather cold. So it was obvious that only the oldest and meanest of all Yule hags would do for us. That year we had a visit from Mother Berhta, and she has been a regular during every Yule since then. She embodies the truth about what winter is like in Minnesota—it is dark and frightening and deathly, but it brings you all sort of gifts. She is also an interesting character. Her name means "bright," and she's a washed-up old goddess of Sun or Moon or hearth fire. Martin Luther, of all people, mentions her in writing you shouldn't leave offerings for "Frau Percht with the iron nose" because that's what Pagans do. (You've got to figure if old Martin Luther didn't like her, she must be okay.) I might add that even Martin Luther could not stop people from leaving things for Berhta.

Somewhere along the line, Gnasher Skeggi got attached to her—as her goat, her son, her boyfriend (oh those incestuous gods!). There are plenty of Scandinavians in Minneapolis, and in their tradition it's a goat, the Julebok, that brings the gifts at Solstice. *Skeggi* is a Scandanavian word which basically mean shaggy, or bearded. And since one of the goats that drew Thor's chariot was named "Tooth-Gnasher," maybe that's where the rest of the name comes from. Skeggi's teeth are made from flint, and when he gnashes them like goats do, they strike sparks.

Goats are great animals—smelly, dirty, with a mind of their own—and all over the world, they are sacred to Pagans. Those of us who have managed to hold on to the old ways, often were forced onto lands that nobody else wanted in the mountains and hills. Such living is sparse living, with room enough only to pasture a goat—and not a cow. So it's been goats for us for years now.

As for the sack, it's Berhta's special attribute. Obviously, if you think about it, the sack represents a womb of sorts. All food and all gifts come from there. Skeggi goes in dead, and comes back out alive. The little kids go in alive, and come back—well...

There's a song the little Witch kids in Covenston sing.

Berhta loves the little children,
all the children of the world:
boiled or roasted, baked or fried,
with some french fries on the side:
Berhta loves the little children of the world.

348

Some adults I know—even some Pagan ones—think Berhta's too scary for kids. But they've obviously forgotten what being a kid is like. Kids love to be scared. They know intuitively that when we face up to things that frighten us the most, what we get in return are the gifts we never dreamed of. The world is filled with scary things, and pretending that they're not there doesn't make them go away at all. In fact, it just gives them more power. The best way to deal with the scary things is to face them eye to eye. In a symbolic way, Berhta makes it easier to face real life.

Not long ago I had a realization. Remember that little boy nobody ever saw again? What do you think happened to him? Into the cauldron, probably, right? Then she ate him up, right? That's what we're all afraid of. What do you think happened then? Well, we already know, because the story tells us: into the sack go the bones, and with a big shake, it's, "Come out little kid." That's downright shamanic—the death and dismemberment that comes before a rebirth. The little boy became Berhta's apprentice, I'm sure of it. Her little kid. You'll notice something important: it's not the rule-followers, the ones that do just what they're told and don't break and bones, that Berhta takes. No, the ones she wants for herself are the rule-breakers, the ones who don't always do what people say they're supposed to. Breaking taboos can be a creative thing, in fact a sacred act. So chew over that a bit. Berhta wants the ones that don't follow the rules; and there's a little bit of rule-breaker in all of us, isn't there?

Lately Mother Berhta has been showing up at namings around my part of the country—child-blessing ceremonies.

"This one's mine," she says.

The parents, of course, try to talk her out of it. "Hey, Berhta, I hear they're baptizing a nice chubby one over at First Presbyterian today," they say.

"Christians don't taste as good!" says Berhta. "I want this one!"

So relatives and friends of the parents make vows to buy Berhta off: "Let us have this one and I promise I'll plant three trees in her name." "I'll take ten dollars worth of food to the food shelf," they say, and so on. And you know, when enough people have vowed on the kid's behalf, Berhta relinquishes her claim and goes away. The community has proved that the newborn is welcome, and that a support system is willing to act on her behalf.

The truth is that the little ones belong to Berhta. After all, life is a fragile thing. Back in the old days newborns often didn't survive, especially if they were born during winter. Obviously, this was because Berhta took her. In today's world, it's scary to think the child you love so much might die. Berhta helps us face that fear, and makes us promise that we'll do what we can to keep it from happening. Face your fears, and they may just give you gifts.

Much of what's wonderful about Berhta is clearly evident in contrast with Santa Claus. I know a lot of Pagans who think that Santa's basically okay. To them it doesn't really matter that he's the direct lineal descendant of that icky old heresy-hunter, Archbishop Nicholas of Myra. (That bit about Santa having originally been Odin was made up by the same nineteenth-century folklorists who managed to find a Pagan under every rock. In fact, there's no real historical connection. Besides, if a mythological figure were going to pay a visit to your children, would you really want it to be Odin?)

In the old days, Santa Claus used to have a dark side. He'd carry presents in one arm, and a sheaf of birch rods in the other. One hand dealt with the good kids, the other beat the bad ones.

Or he'd come accompanied by a dark, hairy guy—Pelznickle, Black Peter, and the like—who'd play Dark Twin to Santa's Bright. That kind of Santa I have no objection to. But the sweetness-and-light-goody-goody that Santa Claus has become in American culture is bogus, imbalanced, and, above all, what my covensib Tom called "Yahweh Claus"—just another version of the all-loving One God. This kind of perfection is just not how things are in the world, as well we should remember at Yule.

With all the lights and the parties, it can be easy to forget the most important things of all. Yule is really for us to remember that this is the darkest time of the year. Yule isn't so much a festival of light as it is a festival of darkness. If it's a festival of light at all, it's about one teeny-tiny spark of light all wrapped up in tons and tons of darkness; and that's what Mother Berhta's all about.

The truth of Mother Berhta is plain to see in the way she's spread through the Pagan community. In a mere thirteen years, she's spread from coast to coast. This is because she's real, because what she tells us and shows us is true. She's earthy, she's tangible, and she reveals the truth about ourselves that we're scared to admit. She's ugly, she's mean, and people love her. She's Old Witch Winter, and every year she comes to remind us that sweetness, light, and summertime are only half the story.

There's a little thing that Berhta says every year after the Yule meal before she stomps out into the darkness. It goes like this:

"Don't give me any of that Santy-Claus crap about naughty and nice. Mother Berhta doesn't care if you're good. Mother Berhta doesn't care if you're bad! What does Mother Berhta care about? Mother Berhta cares only if you care about Mother Berhta! You care about Mother Berhta, don't you?"

And you know, no one ever says they don't.

DIRECTORY

OF

PRODUCTS

AND

SERVICES

Save $$ on Llewellyn Annuals

Llewellyn has two ways for you to save money on our annuals. With a four-year subscription, you receive your books as soon as they are published—and your price stays the same every year, even if there's an increase in the cover price! Llewellyn pays postage and handling for subscriptions. Buy 2 subscriptions and take $2 off; buy 3 and take $3 off; buy 4 subscriptions and take an additional $5 off the cost!

***Please check boxes below and send this form
along with the order form on the next page.***

Subscriptions (4 years, 2002–2005):

☐ Astrological Calendar.................\$51.80
☐ Witches' Calendar......................\$51.80
☐ Tarot Calendar \$51.80
☐ Goddess Calendar.....................\$51.80
☐ Spell-A-Day Calendar..................\$43.80
☐ Daily Planetary Guide \$39.80

☐ Witches' Datebook.....................\$39.80
☐ Astrological Pocket Planner........\$27.80
☐ Sun Sign Book...........................\$31.80
☐ Moon Sign Book.........................\$31.80
☐ Herbal Almanac.........................\$31.80
☐ Magical Almanac.......................\$31.80

Order a Dozen and Save 40%: Sell them to your friends or give them as gifts. Llewellyn pays all postage and handling when you order annuals by the dozen.

2001	2002		
☐	☐	Astrological Calendar.........................	\$93.24
☐	☐	Witches' Calendar............................	\$93.24
☐	☐	Tarot Calendar	\$93.24
☐	☐	Goddess Calendar............................	\$93.24
☐	☐	Spell-A-Day Calendar	\$78.84
☐	☐	Daily Planetary Guide........................	\$71.64
☐	☐	Witches' Datebook	\$71.64
☐	☐	Astrological Pocket Planner...................	\$50.04
☐	☐	Sun Sign Book	\$57.24
☐	☐	Moon Sign Book	\$57.24
☐	☐	Herbal Almanac............................	\$57.24
☐	☐	Magical Almanac............................	\$57.24

Individual Copies of Annuals: Include $4 postage for orders $15 and under and $5 for orders over $15. Llewellyn pays postage for all orders over $100.

2001	2002		
☐	☐	Astrological Calendar.........................	\$12.95
☐	☐	Witches' Calendar............................	\$12.95
☐	☐	Tarot Calendar	\$12.95
☐	☐	Goddess Calendar............................	\$12.95
☐	☐	Spell-A-Day Calendar	\$10.95
☐	☐	Daily Planetary Guide........................	\$9.95
☐	☐	Witches' Datebook	\$9.95
☐	☐	Astrological Pocket Planner...................	\$6.95
☐	☐	Sun Sign Book	\$7.95
☐	☐	Moon Sign Book	\$7.95
☐	☐	Herbal Almanac............................	\$7.95
☐	☐	Magical Almanac............................	\$7.95

Llewellyn Order Form

Call 1-877-NEW-WRLD or use this form to order any of the
Llewellyn books or services listed in this publication.

SEND TO: **Llewellyn Publications, P.O. Box 64383,
Dept. K-963-6, St. Paul, MN 55164-0383**

Qty	Order #	Title/Author	Total Price

Postage/handling:
ORDERS $15 AND UNDER: **$4.00**
ORDERS OVER $15: **$5.00**
Subscription orders, dozen orders,
  or orders over $100: **FREE SHIPPING**
2ND DAY AIR: **$8.00 for one book**
(add $1 for each additional book)
*We cannot deliver to P.O. Boxes; please supply a
street address. Please allow 4-6 weeks for delivery.*

Total price	
MN residents add 7% sales tax	
Postage/handling (see left)	
Total enclosed	

☐ VISA   ☐ MasterCard   ☐ American Express
☐ Check or money order – U.S. funds, payable to Llewellyn Publications

Account # _____   Expiration Date _____

Cardholder Signature _____

Name _____   Phone (____) _____

Address _____

City _____ State _____ Zip/PC _____

Questions? Call Customer Service at 1-877-NEW-WRLD

MA01

SEE YOUR WORK IN PRINT!

We invite you to submit material for our 2002 annuals—the *2002 Moon Sign Book, 2002 Herbal Almanac,* and *2002 Magical Almanac.* If you're not a writer but have questions you would like answered or topics you would like to see covered, we would like to hear from you, too. Writers who request *and adhere to* writers' guidelines will get first consideration for publication. Enclose a self-addressed stamped envelope (SASE) when requesting writers' guidelines. Llewellyn reserves the right to select and edit materials submitted for publication. Please include an additional SASE with your submission if you would like your materials returned.

2002 Moon Sign Book (Deadline 12/01/00)

This is a yearly planning guide that teaches you to use Moon cycles for optimum timing. We are looking for articles on lunar astrology, gardening, medical astrology, moonlore, and anything to do with using the energies of the Moon. We are interested in articles about gardening, health, and business.

2002 Herbal Almanac (Deadline 12/01/00)

This is a yearly compendium of all things herbal, with sections on growing and gathering herbs, culinary herbs, herbs for health, herbs for beauty, herb crafts, and herb myth and magic.

2002 Magical Almanac (Deadline 12/01/00)

This is a compendium of magical tidbits and practical guidance on magic, earth religions, and folklore. We are looking for articles, factoids, *very short* fiction, spells, crafts, rituals, meditations, and recipes of interest to those magically inclined.

To Get Writers' Guidelines

Write to Michael Fallon, Annuals Department Manager, Llewellyn Publications, P.O. Box 64383, St. Paul, MN 55164-0383.

Touch the Magic
of the Goddess

R evel in the many manifestations of the goddess—from Greece, Egypt, China, India, Scandanavia, Africa, to the Aztecs, Celts, and the Bible—with the 12 original soft yet powerful paintings by Hrana Janto.

Patricia Monaghan, author of the award-winning *The New Book of Goddesses & Heroines,* provides the introductory essay, "The Significance of the Goddess in Our Lives," as well as twelve monthly invocations. Llewellyn's *Goddess Calendar* is a fascinating look at religious/mythological histories from around the world that's perfect for anyone who wants to make a conscious connection with their inner goddess energy.

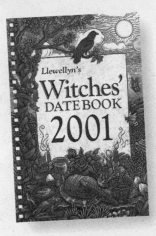

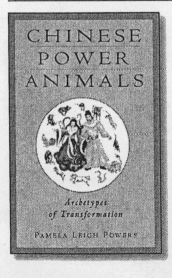

THE WITCHES' QUARTERLY

This quarterly newsletter appears at each change of season: the Vernal Equinox (March 21st,) Summer Solstice (June 21st,) the Autumnal Equinox (September 21st,) and Winter Solstice (December 21st.) Each issue boasts a myriad of special features including an astrological forecast for each day, myths, useful information about plants and animals, and rituals and lore to help celebrate the passing seasons. Available by subscription. 12 pages. Mailed in a discreet envelope.

To order: Send your name and address along with a check or money order payable in U.S. funds to: Witchery Company, PO Box 4067, Dept. L, Middletown, RI, 02842

Subscription rates:
1/2 year (two seasons) $16.00
1 year (four seasons) $28.00

A CATALOG

A collection of hard-to-find, quality items sure to be of interest to the serious practitioner. To obtain your copy of this full-color catalog, send $2 along with your name and address to: *Witchery Company,* Post Office Box 4067, Department L, Middletown, Rhode Island, 02842

THE WITCHES' ALMANAC

Established in 1971 and published in the spring of each year, *The Witches' Almanac* is an indispensible guide and companion for adept, occultist, witch and mortal alike. An annual that offers insight and inspiration through the passage of seasons with herbal secrets, mystic incantations and many a curious tale of good and evil. 96 pages. To order send your name and address along with $7.95 plus $2.50 s&h in U.S. funds.

For information on our other titles send us your name and address and we'll send you our brochure.

The Witches' Almanac, Post Office Box 4067, Dept. L, Middletown, RI 02842